Good fishing

Steu Tinney

STU TINNEY

Life's No Fun Until You Get Your Feet Wet

Wading Through the Mainstream of Life With the Famous and Infamous

BUTLER BOOKS

To Mom and Dad, still watching I know, who lit the flames of my burning passion to live life to its fullest. To Lindsay, my wife and best friend, who continues to fan that flame on a daily basis. For Susan and Mitch, who constantly stoke the embers and keep me young at heart. And my siblings, Jeanne, Myra and Michael, constant reminders of how very important the word "family" is to all of us.

And finally to you. You who have touched my life and you who have yet to do so, but are within my destiny. It is you who are the keepers of the flame, and for this I am eternally grateful.

CONTENTS

PREFACE

I don't think that fishing would hold much interest for me if it were simply tossing a lure into the water and waiting for a fish to bite. No, fishing would have to be a heckuva lot more than that.

Everyone fishes, even if they don't realize what they are doing. We are all born fisher-persons, and from our first breaths continue to learn the art of angling.

As babies, we fish for attention, our lures loud, protesting cries. As grown up children we have already learned how to lure our parents into giving us much of what we want: "Gee dad, my best friends are wearing designer jeans and Nikes."

As teens we perfect the art of throwing lines at the opposite sex, some of us more successfully than others. Still, we never give up casting.

We angle for the best grades, the best jobs, the best spouses. We constantly search for better fishing holes. In crowds, we fish for attention. In life, we fish for the best bargains. There are those who fish for souls.

In truth, most of us go through life as anglers and die without realizing what the true fishing experience has meant to us.

The dictionary explains fishing as simply "the act or practice of one that fishes." Now, Mr. Webster, that sure as hell explains a lot, doesn't it? NOT!

The greatest majority of the human population goes through life day after day, year after year, generation after generation, fishing for a better life, a better world. Trouble is, in their searches, they have made the catching considerably more important than the fishing.

I'm not sure that those few of us who have been

fortunate enough to latch on to what fishing really means could ever explain it. My son Mitch knows, as does my dear friend, Vic. Lee Wulff knew, and Homer Circle knows. Bill Dance knows. Grits Grisham and Glen Lau know.

Tom Mann knew. Matt and Mongo had a firm grasp on it, before Mongo left us. Ron Whitehead came closest of all to being able to explain it. Even guys like Ray Scott and Earl Bentz, who make tons of bucks off of fishing, knew what it was all about long before they began their respective business ventures.

My life has been connected to people in other states and other countries who are fully aware, yet none, including me, are capable of explaining fully the meaning, the impact.

Opinions are like rear ends, everybody has one. I don't feel the least bit hesitant about adding mine to the mix– after all, it's only an opinion, and perhaps not the total answer but simply a clue.

The true fishing experience revolves around expectation. If you set yourself up for failure, you immediately disqualify yourself. The experience will be exactly what you want it to be, if you simply surrender yourself to it. If you wish it to be spiritual, it will be. Calming, exciting, you name it, and it's yours for the taking as long as you leave expectations behind and completely surrender yourself to the moments at hand.

Think of the original Garden, and its two lone inhabitants. Surrounded by unspoiled beauty, untroubled by any intrusion, they simply had an opportunity to enjoy what was their birthright – the gifts that had been created just for them.

That's where you must be in your mind when you begin your fishing experience. Surrendering to your total surrounding, expecting nothing, yet being prepared for everything, is the only way to start.

On my tenth birthday, I awoke early enough to see my

very first sunrise. It was mostly blocked by tall buildings, yet it so inspired me that I made myself a promise to never miss a sunrise again. I have kept that promise. On my seventy- first birthday, I witnessed my twenty two thousand, two hundred and eightieth such event. In all that time, in all those places, alone or in company with others, there have never been two alike. Each has its own beginning, each its own wonder. I know the last day of my life will happen when I recognize a sunrise that I have witnessed before.

Everything that has happened in my life has somehow been part of surrendering myself completely to fishing. The stories, the people, the places, all have the same beginning. It's all about fishing.

Fishing has been my life, and will continue to be so until I am no more. I'm a traveler who has come far but still has many more roads to travel. There are places, people and experiences yet undreamed of, and still so unknown. There are wonders I have yet to see. I will continue on, with no expectations.

The stories I have related here are true; the people are real. I have changed a name or two, simply to avoid embarrassment – please allow me that. Those few involved will know and hopefully appreciate it.

And now I invite you to come along with me as we get our feet wet angling in the mainstream of life.

— *Stu Tinney*

1

WHY WRITE A BOOK

Herb Blackwell was an outdoor writer from New Jersey. If memory doesn't fail me, he wrote an outdoor column for a newspaper in Trenton. This was back in the 1970s and 1980s. I can't recall ever reading anything Herb wrote, other than what he sent to us at *Striper* Magazine. We never published anything he ever sent us. Writing for a magazine just didn't seem to be Herb's forte. He did, however, have another amazing talent. Herb was the greatest story teller I have ever known.

Striper Magazine put on 35 tournaments annually, all leading up to qualification for the championship event. Anglers would then compete for both individual and state team honors. Since the winning teams would vie for sizeable cash awards to donate to their home state's fisheries departments, media interest was always high. We were the only tournament organization, at that time, doing anything like that.

Being a member of O.W.A.A. (Outdoor Writers Association of America) I had easy access to the names of outdoor scribes from across the country. It was our habit to invite at least two press representatives from each state that had qualified entrants in the championship event. Normally, that meant 80 to 100 press folks.

We offered food, booze and lodging, leaving travel expenses to the individual invited writer, or his or her newspaper or magazine. In Herb's own words, in answer to his many invitations to attend these annual events, "free booze would make me drive to Hell and back, so count me in."

The actual event took place over a long weekend, but pre fishing and press meetings made it last a whole week. Press folks would be out in boats interviewing and photographing competitors from their respective states. They also could take advantage of getting in a bit of fishing themselves, before the actual start of competition.

Lindsay, our event coordinator, would have pre-planned activities for fisher-folks, spouses and kids. She created a fun, almost carnival-like atmosphere. There were day trips for non-competitors, organized activities for kids, and loads of melt down ideas designed to relieve the tension among tourney entrants. Two of our major sponsors, Coors and Makers Mark, made it virtually impossible for any red-blooded member of the press corps to miss an evening's meeting. It was at these meetings, where food and drink were abundant, that Herb Blackwell shone like the sky's brightest star.

Imagine a room full of professional story tellers, each vying for attention, each playing the one-upsmanship game, and every one of them better at it than your average Joe. Add to that the warmth of beer and bourbon, friends re-visiting with folks not seen in awhile, and the general good feeling always apparent when outdoor folks get together. A magician, waving his magic wand, could not find a better scenario to set the stage for a virtuoso.

Enter Herb Blackwell. With the simple words, "Have you folks ever heard..." Herb would make the room stand still. He would softly spin yarns about "the way it used to be." His stories were nostalgic, happy, sad, gut-wrenching. One minute there would be laughter, the next minute would be sobs, or gasps, or looks of quiet reverence.

Herb Blackwell was like a giant clothes wringer, who could make the most stoic of us realize every emotion known to man, and then some. And he would make us not be embarrassed to show them. His stories were almost like narcotics – once we were hooked, we never seemed to be able to get enough.

For years I had been threatening Herb. I threatened to bring him to one of our events a week earlier than anyone else. I would then lock him in a room with a tape recorder, a port-a-potty, and serve him anything he wanted to eat and drink until his voice gave out. I'd then let him rest, regain his voice, and repeat the whole procedure again and again until all his stories were recorded. I deem one of the most serious failures of my life to be not having done just that.

Herb passed away before I could accomplish that task. Sadly, there are none among us capable of re-telling those stories. It would dishonor the man for me, or anyone else, to even attempt to repeat them; they just would not be the same. It is sad for us that Herb took his stories with him. Those of us that knew him hope that he is entertaining the angels. I've always looked at that episode of my life as if it were a hole that could never be filled.

I recall relating this to my younger brother Michael who, though not showing much interest at the time, later enlarged on my idea, and did a marvelous thing with the information. Our dad, a brilliant linguist suffering from serious macular degeneration, was still devouring a book a day via ear-phones. Mike took it upon himself, unknown to the rest of his siblings, the task of visiting dad each day, for days on end, to tape record the story of his life.

I had always thought I had my father pretty well figured out, but the revelations in that recording added not only to my pride in the man, but also to a much deeper and sweeter understanding. Dad's gone now, but I need only to pop that recording in the tape player to bring him to my side. I've shared his recordings with my children with the hope that the story of their grandfather's life would enrich their own. It seems to have worked its magic. If anyone reading this book gets nothing more from it than this idea, it certainly will have been worth the effort.

On several occasions I've been approached by various publishers wanting me to write a "how to" book on catching striped bass. I never thought I was up to the task, and satisfied myself with doing teaching seminars all over the country. It seemed a whole lot easier to show and tell than to think of how to properly put it on paper. Well, I'm no longer the only expert in the field, and lots of good books have been written on the subject. I'm not sorry that I never gave it a shot, though, since every "how to" book I've ever read seems to speak with great authority but with little or no heart. I'm afraid I've been infected with Blackwell-itis, and demand that stories have souls. Information changes, but souls live forever.

And perhaps that's why I've written this book.

I happened to be talking on the phone one day with my son, Mitch, getting his "daily fishing report." Mitch is a fishing guide and an outdoor writer. He knows I get a great deal of enjoyment out of listening to the tales of his daily exploits. They are rich, full of fun, and exhibit the joy of life I've tried to instill in my kids. During that conversation, I told him he was bringing back memories of my old friend Herb Blackwell.

"Explain," he said.

And I did.

He responded, "You know, dad, you've been entertaining me and Susan all of our lives with fun stories of your adventures; recording them sounds like a great idea to me. I think you need to get started right away."

He's a tough customer and refused to let me off the

hook. My refusals based on inability or memory loss rolled off his back like water from a duck. No manner of what he kept calling weak excuses seemed to make a dent in his resolve. The whole thing was pretty unnerving, since I almost always used to be able to out-fox him.

When I had exhausted every sly, sneaky, clever ploy, I finally came up with the one I just knew would work. I gently placed the nail, held it firmly in place, raised the hammer, and struck a mighty blow. "Okay, son, I'll agree to this journey into nostalgia if you'll accompany me on the trail." I suggested that we simply swap tales, one for one, until we exhausted our inventory of stories.

I just knew he'd opt out because of a busy schedule, a headache, stomach cramps or some such nonsense. I was willing to be a great dad and let him slide out of this gently.

"Sure, Dad," was his reply. Where in hell can a guy go after that?

Together, we have penned tons of stories, certainly too many for one book. During the process, I have seen the truth in the old adage, "what goes around, comes around."

Mitch has the same story-telling skills I once enjoyed in my old friend Herb Blackwell, but I'll let you judge that for yourself. I've convinced my publisher that he needs to include a few of his tales, along with mine.

And though Mitch still has more than 30 years to catch up to the old man, I'm going to threaten to lock him in a room with a port-a-potty, a tape recorder, and the spirit of Herb Blackwell. Keep your fingers crossed that his own book will follow this one.

2

THE FAT LADY'S DANCE

It was the late 1940s and the war was over! Cheap Japanese products hadn't yet hit the marketplace and American manufacturers were once again making goods that had once been scarce. That was easy for a bunch of twelve- and thirteen-year-olds to figure out; all we had to do was eyeball the clothes lines full of things hung out to dry. Women didn't hang out their real personal stuff, but stockings fluttered everywhere and almost every line had the prize we sought...a girdle. As far as the eye could see, there were girdles everywhere. Ours for the taking (oops, borrowing).

One might wonder why such an obsession with a plump woman's undergarment. One might even suggest psychiatric attention, or at least a visit to a priest, minister or rabbi, whichever was closest at hand. Perhaps any of the above might have saved our endangered souls, but we were bent on destruction and way beyond help. We desperately needed those girdles! And, whatever it took, the prizes would be ours!

Planning on girdle forays had to be done in secret. There were four of us in on the plot, and we knew all too well what the penalty of capture would be...it was scary. We had formed a bicycle brigade, so transportation was not a problem. We were mobile enough to not only case our own neighborhood, but others as well. The reports were encouraging. There were as many girdles on the next block as there were on ours. We could do the deed in places where, if seen, we wouldn't be recognized. But we had to practice in our own backyards, to get the timing down to the second.

First thing was to make certain our vehicles were up to the task. Ronnie's dad was the only one making any kind of money, so his bike was in excellent shape, and the one we could trust the most. Paul, Ernie and I had bikes held together with wire, sans gear and bumper guards. We had to put elastic bands around our pants legs so as not to get them caught in the gears. Our tires were the biggest problem. All of our tires had more patches than our pants, and that's saying a bunch.

Ronnie had a watch, so he was to time our practice runs. We'd start in Paul's yard because his mom was fat and always had a girdle on the line. The trick was to sneak up to the clothes line unseen, pull down on the girdle so as to get a good grip on the whole thing and quickly snatch a girdle stay from each side. The tricky part was to gently let go and not make the clothes line jump up and down for anyone to notice. No question about it, the operation called for cunning and nerves of steel.

We had discussed this operation for weeks. We had cleverly decided against taking the whole girdle, all agreeing that was stealing. Taking only the plastic stays and leaving the rest insured the fact that the girdle would still be usable by the owner, who might not even notice one of the many stays was missing (or so we hoped). Anyway, we were committed, ready and up to the task. Our desperate need required desperate action.

One might question why four kids might need girdle stays so desperately, but if one thought about it, they surely would come up with the correct answer. They were needed to catch fish – any dummy could figure that out. It didn't take us long.

All the lakes in New Jersey froze solid during the winter. The only way one could fish was through the ice. The only way at the time to fish through the ice was to use what were called "tip-ups." A tip-up consisted of a hinged wooden frame built to straddle a hole cut in the ice. A rotating spool was affixed to this wooden device, the spool being filled with fishing line. Also attached to this gadget was a springy metal bar with an open ring and a square, red flannel flag on top. When ready for use, a baited hook was lowered though the hole in the ice to whatever depth you wanted to fish. The line was then looped through the open eye and bent down to a catch, similar to that on a mouse trap. The idea was, when a fish took the bait, he would tug on the line and free the metal strip and flag, to signal the fisherman even if he was not close by. Every fisherman was allowed ten of these devices, so he could spread them pretty far apart. The only problem was that store-bought tip-ups cost about a dollar. Forty would cost forty dollars, and we knew for sure there wasn't that much money in the whole world. That's why our girdle fixation made so much sense.

Ronnie lived in an apartment house that, like all our houses, was heated by coal. His coal bin had an enormous supply of thin wooden slats, used as kindling to start the fire in the boilers. Forty of those were never going to be missed. Line, hooks and sinkers were no problem, we all had plenty of them. Paul hated his red flannel underwear, so he bravely donated them to our "flag" project. His mom never figured out who would want to steal them from their clothes line. Paper clips worked wonders for the mouse trap part. The only huge problem was to find a flexible, reliable strut to attach a red flag to, that could be bent and would, when released, jump back to its original form. Enter the girdle stay. Sure made good sense to us at the time and now, almost fifty years later, still makes sense to me. What I've never been able to figure out is the difference between mischief and Yankee ingenuity.

I was the fastest one, so it fell upon me to do the deed. Paul wore glasses so he wouldn't do for "spotting", so we just let him stay upstairs to keep his mom occupied. Ernie stayed in the alley to keep a sharp watch, while Ronnie sat on his bike waiting to speed off with the loot. Later, sitting in the apartment house basement with those two beautiful pilfered, plastic stays, we enjoyed the thrill of victory. Of course, we felt a little guilty; we all knew it but never spoke of it.

Paul's mother was dressed to go to the synagogue the next day and Paul had the job of trying to find out if she was wearing "the girdle." We were sitting on the porch watching the second story window, from which he would signal when his Mom left. He first and we, as we could, would check to see if we could detect any terrible lumps in her clothes as a result of the stays being gone. Paul leaned out the window, nodding his head up and down, indicating "yes" she was wearing it and "yes" she was on the way down. The front door opened and out she came but darn, she was wearing a heavy coat and we couldn't see a thing. "What are you boys staring at," she said. We were dumbstruck and all I could think to respond was, "You look really nice Mrs. Bergman." That was our first lesson in social grace and it carried a lot of weight in our later dating years. It worked! And on she went to her whatever she was going to do.

When Paul came down he assured us there were no tell-tale lumps under her dress that would indicate a few missing stays. Ronnie had been smart at figuring which ones to take – no wonder he would wind up being an engineer. At any rate, for the next week, the infamous "girdle gang" did its thing. In less than a week, we had our forty stays stashed in the basement hide-out. We spent many happy hours assembling our tip-ups and discussing exactly where we would try them out.

The Reservoir won the vote, hands down; it was unanimous. Of course, you were not allowed to fish in the reservoir. There were signs to that effect posted all over the place. But we knew special people could fish there, because we saw them. Whenever we trespassed, "Otto the Ugly" (our name for the security guard) would chase us away. We actually watched him talking to people he didn't chase and, more than once, saw people give him money. We fooled him some during the summer by splitting up. He couldn't get to all of us and all but Paul could outrun him. It was as much fun antagonizing Otto as it was fishing in that forbidden place.

The one thing we had not considered, the thing that made us most vulnerable, was that we would be out in the open, with no trees to use as cover. So excited were we in our adventure that we failed to factor that into our plan.

We decided somehow that the day before Christmas would be our best shot. Everyone would be busy doing last minute stuff and hopefully Otto would be off for the holidays. We had kept a cache of night crawlers all summer just for this purpose. Paul was the only one of us that had his own room, so he kept them under his bed in a newspaper-lined wooden box. We all contributed used coffee grounds to feed them, and when we got ready to use them they were in great shape. Again we congratulated ourselves on our perfect planning.

Morning came, bike baskets were loaded with stuff wrapped in shirts so no one could spot what we had. Ronnie borrowed an ice chipper and hammer from his dad's tool room, and off we went. The day was crisp and cloudless. There was lots of snow on the ground from past snow falls, but the streets were clear and dry. Perfect! We pedaled with strong steady strokes, making sure no one got too far ahead. We had about six or seven miles to go but were so psyched up, it could have been ten and we still would not have complained. We were on top of the world.

The gate to the reservoir was closed but not locked (it never was). One at a time, we slipped in, closing the gate behind us. From here on in it would be silence only, we'd use waves, whistles and body language to communicate. We were a well-oiled machine, getting ready to operate. The plan was to park the bikes in the trees and for Ron and me to go out on the ice, while Paul and Ernie watched. I'd hold the chipper and Ron would use the hammer. Once we had two or three holes in the ice, and were sure Otto wasn't around, Paul and Ernie would begin to bait and set out the tip-ups.

The ice was about five inches thick, but adrenaline was high and the work went easily. Turning around to check our two friends, we saw that they had five or six tip-ups in place and were going back to the bikes for the rest. We continued digging.

Before we got the tenth hole dug, one of the red flags began waving and Ernie raced over to it and pulled up a really nice yellow perch. We were all beside ourselves. Our plan was working perfectly. By the time we had twenty holes dug, we had almost a dozen perch on the ice. A quick conference caused us to decide not to dig any more holes, but to pay better attention to what we had already done as we had missed a couple of hits because we were spreading out too thinly.

Each of us watching five tip-ups was more than enough, the action being pretty steady. When things slowed down, and for the first time in a little while, none of the flags were waving, we made a corporate decision. Ron and I would watch all the tip-ups, while Ernie and Paul would transport our catch back to our waiting bikes. We'd fish for another hour or so and leave some for the next time.

With our two friends safely on the bank, having strung some forty perch and dragged them ashore, I turned to talk to Ron. At that moment, something caught my eye, some movement in the trees. The movement burst out of the trees and suddenly became Ugly Otto. He was screaming at the

22

top of his lungs and seemed to be spewing out fire and smoke as he did so. He was carrying what looked like a tree limb in his hand and he started toward us, waving it menacingly in our direction.

Retreat became the better part of valor and the silence part of our plan went up in smoke. We didn't discuss it but the thought of retrieving our tip-ups never occurred to us. Hollering for Paul and Ernie to get going, we headed for the bank and our "getaway" vehicles as quickly as the slippery footing would allow. Otto was behind us and gathering speed. The two front runners were already on their bikes and headed toward the gate when Ron and I hit the bank. Turning to see how close Otto was gave us great relief and tremendous joy. We had turned just in time to see him hit one of the holes we had dug, fight valiantly for balance, only to fall on his butt. It wasn't just any old fall, it was a stupendous fall. All his limbs were stretched to their limits. With both arms and legs pointing in different directions, Otto was airborne. He was in free fall for a long time before he bounced solidly on the ice. Then it looked as if someone were dribbling him, he bounced so many more times before he slid to a halt. There was no rush now. We slowly mounted our bikes and pedaled away. We knew Otto was done for the day.

Our folks never asked about the fish, or where we got them. All four families enjoyed a fresh fish dinner. Christmas came and went. I got new inner tubes for my tires. We never fished in the reservoir again, nor were girdle stays at risk any more. Clothes lines would be safe from attack and womanly figures would adhere to girdle guidelines, as long as directions were followed.

We wondered a lot about Otto and all those girdle stays and giggled at the thought of turning him in as the clothes line thief. Surely he still had the evidence that could jail him for life. However, righteously deciding in our kangaroo court in Ron's basement that bouncing Otto on the ice was punishment enough, we let it go.

Oh, how many years have passed since that glorious day on the ice. The one thought that stays, clear in my mind as if it just happened, was the sight of those pretty little red flannel flags dancing in the morning sunlight. Any time I hear the words "it's not over until the fat lady dances," I'm immediately transported to a different time and place. I suppose the smile on my face makes folks think I deem the remark cute, but they'll never know.

3

WHAT IT IS...IS BASEBALL

We knew it was wrong to steal, one of the deadliest of sins. We also knew it meant the belt, bed without supper, lifelong quarantine to quarters, and even worse, no more baseball. But when school was out and the weather hot and sticky, a bunch of seven- and eight-year-olds had to be creative if we wanted to get up a good game of stick ball. Ronnie Susserman was in charge of finding a broom stick, Paul Bressman had the assignment of finding something to hit, (preferably a ball) and I was given the job of rounding up trash can lids to use for bases. And so began my lifelong love of "the game."

It was a time when adults sat on porches to watch kids play in the streets. It was kick the can, hide and go seek, king of the hill, ringaleerio and stick ball. Stick ball was the top of the list. If you were good enough to make the block stick ball team, you were guaranteed a status that put you right next to Mr. Mirsky. He owned the candy store and treated winning teams to fountain sodas.

There was no such thing as organized ball in our neighborhood, so we made up our own schedules and tournaments. The "Crusaders" (that was us) were hot stuff and would take on the world and accept any challenge. We drank lots of free fountain sodas. We sure loved Mr. Mirsky.

I suppose that's where my love of the game began. We'd go over to the empty lot to watch the bigger guys play real baseball, and drool and dream about the time we would be old enough to join them. It was the right of passage we were paying our dues for in the streets. Dues meant skinned knees, torn britches, chipped teeth and scalp wounds. A bleeding elbow really helped the cause. And if you could hit, that was even better.

I turned out to be a fair hitter and a pretty good glove. By the time I got to the sixth grade, I was playing shortstop with the big dogs. When I was in the eighth grade, I was scouted by the high school coach who wanted me to play on the freshman team. Life was wonderful. Then I discovered girls. All of a sudden I noticed that girls were different from boys. What a revelation for an almost thirteen-year-old. I guess baseball had arrested my development, but I sure meant to make up for it.

I didn't play freshman ball but did go out for the team the next year. It took me that long to come back to earth. Only problem was, one of the girls I'd been seeing was the coach's daughter. He invited me to meet him behind the school one day just to "talk things over." I saw the punch coming and ducked. His hand hit a brick wall, broke three fingers and ended my high school baseball career. Things sure were different back then.

None of that really mattered, though. I loved the game and worshipped the men that played. I spent many wonderful hours watching the Newark Bears play. They had a catcher named Yogi Berra, who would swing at the worst pitched balls imaginable. He got more home runs by swinging at balls over his head than any player I have ever seen. I caught one of those homers and still cherish the ball with Yogi's signature on it. Yogi naturally went up to the Yankees and I became a lifetime fan. To this day, I remain loyal to the team.

Those were the days! Days when players had nicknames. Names like "Scooter" (Phil Rizzuto), "The Yankee Clipper" (Joe DiMaggio), "Doc" (Dr. Bobby Brown), just to name a few. It was a time when you had to toss a coin to see if Joe D. or Ted Williams were going to earn the unheard-of sum of $100,000 a year. It was a time a family could afford to spend a day and players actually came over and spoke to kids. It was a time when players were real heroes, and behaved like heroes. It was a time, I'm sorry to say, that has been lost. Baseball has become big business, as perhaps it should, but something so good is missing.

It seems as if I was a Little League coach forever. Both my kids, Susan and Mitch, inherited not only my zest for the game but also rather unique athletic talents of their own. They both went on to earn places on their respective all-star teams and both had storied Little League careers. I couldn't coach both boys and girls teams and I know Susan has never held it against me for choosing the boys. When Mitch turned eight years old (Susan ten), there was an opening for a team coach and tag, I was it. The team I inherited was the Pirates, the lowliest of the low. If there was a place below "last" they would have won it. Last place was the only thing the team had ever won.

Drafting kids for the team was interesting, to say the least. The other coaches had years of experience, knew all the kids and were aware of the "gene pool." They chose kids whose dads or brothers were athletes. My choosing confused them; I simply made a hopeful player run to a chosen point. If he didn't fall down, he was okay with me. The ones that fell were drafted last and I took any kid no one else wanted. Of course I got to draft my own son and chose as co-coach one Dave Allman who just happened to have two outstanding players as sons. We got to draft them, too. Dave was a male nurse at the Veterans Hospital whose work hours left him with ample time for practice and games. I had a fishing charter service and had afternoons and evenings free as well. Lots of practice and hard work by the boys let them finish in third place that year, and in first the next two years

Susan was our secret weapon that first year. She was cute with long blonde hair, flashing eyes, a ready smile and the fastest legs in town. We had her at every practice and allowed each of our players the opportunity to race her around the bases. No one ever came close. Our guys were at the "girl hater's" stage, but all had the competitive urge to beat her. The end result was because our boys were so clued into running, they made extra bases on single hits and had more stolen bases and inside the park homers than the rest of the league combined. I still remember the day when Ray Turner, the one player getting fast enough to beat Susan, stopped dead in his tracks at second base and just stared as Susan continued past third and on to home plate. I wondered if he had pulled a muscle, but suddenly saw the other boys watching too. Susan wasn't running exactly the same. Surely she was as quick, but it seemed different. POW! Susan all of a sudden had hips that swung as she ran, and the boys stopped thinking of her as one of them. She had crossed the line and had grown up to be a real, honest-to-goodness girl. She remained a Pirate fan but had to miss practice from then on.

It was around that time when I got a call from a nearby Chamber of Commerce, asking for my fishing services. It was customary for them or any number of businesses to call on my services, all for the same reason. When a prospective investor was expected in Nashville, it was a well known fact that Printer's Alley and all the other night life claimed the attention of many a visitor. I had sold my schtik hard. Give them to me and they'll arrive at planned breakfast meetings alert and sober. The thinking was, in order to meet with me at five a.m., a good night's sleep was necessary and night life was not a good idea. A five a.m. to nine a.m. fishing trip would allow for some wake-up adrenaline infusion and would get the party back to their hotel in time for shave, shower and usually productive business meetings. It had worked that way on almost every occasion I was called upon.

This time the outcome would be different. This time two of the most famous and gifted baseball players in the country were to be my guests. You'll forgive me if I don't use the players' names. Not only is it still (after all these years) a personal family problem, but it would serve no purpose to sully the names of two superstars. Those clever enough to know of whom I speak will surely agree.

My daughter was beside herself. Her adulation of her athlete heroes was akin to mine when I was her age. I had the opportunity to meet some great players and had even had the pleasure of fishing with Ted Williams, one of the most outstanding men I had ever known. So, when these two guys, living legends as they were, came into my picture, it was simply a job needing to be done. Of course I was excited and thrilled at the opportunity, but Susan was in orbit. Though I had taken her and her brother on many a fishing trip and, as a ten-year-old could hold her own with most adults, she could not understand why she could not come along. "After all," she pouted, "I am the oldest child."

No matter how painstakingly you try to explain to a ten-year-old, they seem to have an agenda which defies understanding. The best I could offer was that I'd have the two sign one of her all star baseballs and check to see if there might be a time in their scheduled visit to Nashville where she could meet them personally. She semi-bought that scenario and not very gently let me off the hook.

Morning found me in my boat, loaded with gear and ready to go, standing moored to the marina dock. It was still dark. Right on schedule, a stretch van pulled into the parking lot and came to a stop at the dock. I must admit to feeling some of Susan's heartbeat as I waited for my two clients. The driver went to the rear door and flung it open and there, framed in the halo of the dome light was one of baseball's premier sluggers. The driver reached out a hand to help him out of the car, but he briskly brushed it away. Holding the door frame, he stood in all his glory, took one step forward and pitched head first onto the ground. He was so drunk he could not stand. Around the other side of the stretch, the door opened and one of the game's premier pitchers got out and staggered around to ask his companion what the hell he was doing sitting on the ground. He was sloshed, too, but at least was walking wounded.

The wildest argument I've ever been involved in quickly began.

"Wha' ya mean I can't go fishin'?"

"Sorry, but you're not moving so well and I can't afford the responsibility of one of you two being hurt."

I knew having one of these two guys hurt in my company would not only cost me the family ranch, but put me in someone's cross hairs forever more.

"Hey, you know who I am?"

"Yessir, I know who you are."

"Well then, that's settled, lets go fishin'."

"Sorry, no can do."

"Hey you, how 'bout if I whip your butt, then I'll take your damn boat and go fishin' without you."

Those kind of words flew about for the best part of ten minutes until I tired of being nice and said to the driver, "These two guys are too drunk for me to take them out in a boat, why don't you take them back to town and let them sleep it off." Calling them drunk set off another angry tirade and I think if they had been a bit more mobile, the story would have made the morning news. I did not wait to see the cargo loaded, I simply took my boat back to the slip, unloaded the gear into my locker, hosed the boat down and went to the restaurant for breakfast. The stretch van was gone.

When Susan got home from school that day and saw my car in the driveway, she darned near took the door off the hinges getting into the house. "How did it go, Dad?" She was so excited, I dreaded telling her the truth. And since no one ever wrote a book on parenting through a trial like this, I was strictly on my own. "We didn't get to go today, (what's his name) wasn't feeling very well." That wonderful glow on an excited kid's cheeks and the gleam in her eyes turned instantly dull. I knew instinctively that she didn't believe me. "Did you see him…did you talk to him…is he as big as he looks on TV…did he sign my baseball…am I going to get to meet him?" The questions flew like shots out of a repeating gun, each one burning its way into my heart.

Lying was the wrong way, I thought. "We didn't go out Susan, because (you know who) was so drunk he couldn't stand up. As a matter of fact, they both were drunk."

Silence, that long accusatory silence. Then tears. Then anger. Then anger at me. "You're lying, they wouldn't get drunk, not them…it was your fault." The rush to the bedroom, the slamming of the door and the uncontrollable sobs of a child whose life would now be changed forever. Heroes fall hard…dads too.

I endured three days of silence, any attempt at a discussion avoided as only a kid can avoid. Then back to almost normal with the baseball season coming to a close, and games to win and pride to recoup. We won the league championship that year and both Mitch and Susan did well with their All Star teams. We didn't speak of the dynamic duo again and still, after almost thirty years, continue to skirt the issue.

Now, as I look back at me and baseball, it's with mixed feelings. I love it and I hate it. I love the excitement but hate the steroids. I catch myself holding the edge of my seat when a base is stolen, but hate the thought of a player's strike. I anger at the unfairness of keeping Pete Rose's records out of the Hall of Fame, but take it personally that he lied about betting on "the game." I loved it when Johnny Bench spent a few days at one of our events and acted the way baseball heroes should act. Talking to kids, signing baseballs, being the best spokesman the game could ever have. I am blessed to have been able to have shared that with some of our participants. Dozens upon dozens of kids went away from that experience without a shadow of a doubt that baseball was the greatest thing since M & M's.

They say there's no going back, but I wish my children could have been kids when baseball was a game, nothing more, nothing less. When the only confusion was were the players men wanting to be boys, or boys wanting to be men. When caps were things you fired in toy pistols and five bucks could buy two tickets, two drinks and two popcorns. I hope that someone was wise enough to put all that into a time capsule so that extraterrestrial visitors might someday learn how earthlings at one time in their evolvement really had a time when "it couldn't ever get any better than this." What it was...was baseball.

4

HOLY COW

It was the summer of 1951. I was seventeen and had just graduated from high school, and the world was mine. I had lived vicariously within the pages of every outdoor magazine I could get my hands on, from the time I was thirteen. Four years of living other people's adventures was about to come to an end. This summer I was actually going to go to Canada, and my best adventuring buddy, Ernie Lawyer, was going, too.

We had actually been planning this fishing trip for almost three years. Ernie had quit school in his junior year and had gotten a job with Easco Seat Covers. Two years earlier he had gotten his boss to take me on part-time after school and on weekends. I'd worked full-time for two summers, and along with Ernie had put all our tips in the "fishin' jar" until we thought we had enough saved up to make the trip.

Ernie had bought an old '32 Ford that had only one problem we could find – it overheated occasionally. We planned to bring extra water just in case. Our destination was Lake of the Woods, Ontario. We had our bedroom walls covered with LOTW photos, stories, advertisements and enticements, cut out of sporting magazines. It was definitely the place to go as far as our limited research could tell.

We had mapped out the route from Newark, through New York State, across the Thousand Island Bridge, into God's country. We had traveled that route so many times in our minds that, had we lost our maps, we could have gotten there without them. We had covered the being gone for two weeks part with our respective families, with zero opposition. Mom and dad were always telling me to reach for my dreams, so they were easy, only being concerned about safety issues. Ernie's situation was simple, too. His mom couldn't care less and he told his dad when he was drunk (which was most of the time), and got a "do whatever you want to" answer, which was enough of an OK for him. The only hitch remaining was Bill, the owner of Easco.

"You what? You want two weeks off in June, the busiest month of the year, Hell no!" We listened to Bill curse and berate us for fifteen minutes. The truth was, Ernie was his best installer and I was as good as any of the other help. His final remark was, "If you guys go, don't come back." At the time, we'd never heard of anger management control, but if we had, we would certainly have suggested it. Bill was terribly wrong in threatening us, so I thought it was pretty cool when Ernie looked at me and said, "Well I guess we leave tomorrow," and we did. How's that for threatening two kids who had worked so hard and for so long to reach a dream?

The next morning (two weeks sooner than planned) we had the car loaded, our $300 savings, our maps, and enough excitement between us to carry off this adventure with no hitches, or so we hoped. Gas was 25 cents a gallon, we had enough oil and water in the trunk, and had even gotten hold of an extra used tire and rim. We had planned for any eventuality. We had bed rolls so we could sleep out while on the way, thus saving most of our money for gas, food and lodging when we got to LOTW. Mom packed sandwiches and her signature cookies, enough to carry us over for a couple of days. We figured if we both drove, we could make the trip in two-and-a-half days. That meant five travel days and nine days to fish. Boy, did we think we were ever smart.

The trip through New Jersey and into New York State was a breeze. We had seen a little country on previous trips to Lake Hopatcong or the Jersey Shore, but nothing to compare with the vast areas of undeveloped land we were seeing now. It sure was awesome for a couple of kids who lived in apartments with concrete back yards to see so much greenery, so many trees and most of all, homes where only one family lived, homes with only one floor. We both lived in tri-level houses with at least one family in each apartment. It's the way it was.

When we reached the New York side of the St. Lawrence River, we stopped, finished off the rest of our food and just stared at the largest, widest river we had ever seen. The only thing that could possibly have been wider was our eyes. Standing near that great river evoked visions of those that stood on this very spot, before there ever was a bridge. The start of this trip was certainly living up to all we had expected.

Pulling up to the border checkpoint, we had no idea what to expect. A uniformed border inspector approached us with a big grin and a very happy manner. "Good cop," Ernie said. "I think we're in for it." He was dead wrong. Our first encounter with a Canadian National was to prove to be just one of many pleasant meetings. "Where you boys headed, and for how long?" We told him. "You sure you're not going to open up a business," he jokingly said. "You certainly got enough stuff crammed into that car." He gave us a copy of the Ontario fishing regulations and told us there was a bait shop about three miles up the road where we could purchase our fishing licenses. "Good luck, and have fun," he said as he waved us through. Ernie and I never knew it at the time, but I'm certain that now, with the threat of terrorism on everyone's mind, border crossings are not quite so easy. How sad.

The bait shop was located on a hill overlooking some sort of canal. The owner was the second Canadian we had spoken to, and was as friendly, if not more, than the first. He issued our licenses and eagerly answered the flood of questions we had about line, lures and tackle. Our enthusiasm made us ripe marks to be picked clean. We would have bought anything he suggested. "Just make sure you have plenty of spoons," he told us. "Most of what you fish for will hit one if you fish it right."

Of course, we had read that about a thousand times, so we had about fifty of those kinds of lures between us. The guy was so nice that we bought a few anyhow. "Are there any fish in that canal?" we both asked at the same time. "A fellow might catch a Walleye or two if he tried real hard," was the reply. After getting permission to leave our car parked in his lot, we virtually flew down the steep bank toward the water's edge. "Bring me back one," was what we heard as we slipped and slid, happy as two humans could be.

We flipped a coin to see which one of us would make the first cast in Canada. Ernie won. His lure never hit the water before mine followed. Within two minutes we were both hooked up to a fish. Two Walleyes that could have been twins were soon lying on the bank. We had never seen one before, except in pictures. There's no way to adequately explain the kind of joy we felt, or the camaraderie, or the feeling of success. You'd just have to be in that picture yourself and share with us vicariously, as we had done for all the years we were planning for just this.

We continued to cast, and caught and released more fish than we had ever caught before, in just one day. Before we knew it, the sky began to darken. We had fished the day away. We remembered to bring a couple of fish up to the bait shop and presented them to the owner. His thanks were to say, "You boys don't need to be traveling in the dark," and saying that, he offered to let us spend the night in a back

36

room of the shop. His living quarters were upstairs.

When we woke, he brought us upstairs and fed us a wonderful breakfast before sending us happily on our way. He refused any kind of payment, reminding us that not only had we given him fish, but had spent some money the day before. Yeah! Really! It was the second time that a person we didn't know went out of their way to be nice to us. It was a new experience to two kids that had city survival instincts which required being suspicious of kind acts.

We had almost a full day's driving ahead of us before we got to LOTW, so we concentrated heavily on that goal. That is until we crossed over a bridge with a stream running under it. "Wonder if there's any trout in that creek?" I said. Ernie was driving, and before the words were out of my mouth, he was looking for a place to park. We jumped out, headed for the stream, and began to cast without saying one word to each other until "I got one!" rang out in the morning mist.

The little creek was full of small, native brook trout. We happily caught and released several before we decided to move on. It was only then that I noticed blood all over Ernie's face and bare arms. He noticed the same on mine. We had been eaten up by swarms of biting insects and hadn't even noticed it happening. Within hours, we were both red and lumpy and itched like crazy. With all our preparations, we had not been ready for this; none of the stories we had read told about such an eventuality. If it wasn't for the itching, the rest would have been laughable.

An announcement over the radio made us pull over to the side of the road in total shock. A huge forest fire was raging around LOTW and most roads and lodges were closed. It was the worst fire anyone could remember and there was no way to tell how long it would be before travel in the area was safe. Boy, did that deflate our balloons. Standing on the side of the road, map spread out on the hood of the car, we heard an ominous hissing sound. A tire check showed we had a tire almost off its rim, losing whatever air it had left. By the time we had unloaded the trunk to get to one of the spares, we had a pretty healthy pile of stuff on the side of the road.

We had blankets, clothes, rain gear, boots, shoes, tackle boxes and, you guessed it, no damned jack! Now here we were, red faced and swollen, in a foreign country, in the middle of nowhere, with a flat tire and no jack. Ernie was s--t faced with embarrassment, but what could be done was anybody's guess.

It wasn't five minutes before we experienced still another act of Canadian kindness. A car pulled up behind us, and without a word spoken, the driver opened his trunk, took out a jack and immediately started to place it under an axle on Ernie's' car. He changed the tire, returned the jack to his trunk, smiled, waved, and without waiting to be thanked, drove away. The word "speechless" doesn't come close to describing the moment. We were absolutely awe-struck. It was obvious that aside from a fishing trip, we were getting a solid course on human relations. Those lessons have followed me, and I've been privileged to share them with my children.

While we were re-packing the car, we noticed a hand-painted wooden sign attached to a nearby tree. It simply said "John Brawley Fish Camp 5 miles", with an arrow pointing straight ahead. We made a corporate decision to follow the sign. We sighted four more signs, each with a mile figure smaller than the previous one. We finally came to the sign that pointed us off the main road, and followed its directing arrow. The dirt road led us to a huge lake and a sizable old house that said, "The Brawleys Live Here."

Before we could get out of the car, the yard and the front porch were full of people. A huge man, dressed in bib overalls and wearing that "Canadian smile" we were still having to get used to, approached us with his hand stuck out and said, "I'm Brawley, welcome to Dog Lake." He then introduced us to his wife, oldest son Pete, a pair of twin four-year-olds, and his two teenage daughters. We were so excited, it took us over a week to realize just how cute the two girls were. Our focus was certainly elsewhere.

After explaining our plans and our plight to Mr. Brawley ("Call me John") he told us about the lake and his fish camp. As far as fish were concerned, Dog Lake contained every species we had read about except for Lake Trout. We were most anxious to catch Northern Pike, and were assured that not only were they plentiful, but grew to over twenty pounds as well. And oh yes, "Spoons will work very well."

John went on to explain how things worked at the camp. There were six waterfront cabins with everything we needed. Beds, linens, towels, soap, etc. were all provided. Cabin rental, which included the use of a boat and small outboard motor (including gas for same) would be five dollars a day. It was okay if we wanted to cook our own meals, but if we wanted three squares a day, that was available also. "You'll have to eat what we eat, eat when we eat, and eat with us in the big house," John explained. "Meals will be fifty cents each, or three dollars a day."

"Oh, one other thing," John offered. "If you care to have a guide, Petey is about the best there is around here, and he gets two dollars a day. He also gets to keep any fish you fellows don't care to have so he can share them with some of our church friends that don't get to fish for themselves." Agreeing to all the above, we were shown a cabin, told to unpack our stuff, and hurry up to the main house for breakfast.

As we unpacked, we counted our blessings, but mostly our finances. Having had Mom's goodies to sustain us, the only money we had spent so far was about twenty dollars for gas, ten dollars for licenses and ten dollars for lures. We still had two hundred and sixty dollars left. Figuring on possible emergencies on the return trip, we allotted forty dollars for going home. What all that figuring led to was that at ten dollars a day, we could stay in heaven for twenty-two days, a whole week longer than our original plan. We raced each other up to the main house and breakfast.

Our first meal with the Brawleys was to be like every meal we had. John was in complete control. Everyone bowed their heads while he said grace. Guests and parents served themselves first. No two people ever spoke at the same time, yet everyone was encouraged to speak freely, even the twins. Ernie and I never figured out if there was more love than food at meal times, but one thing was for sure, there was an ample amount of both.

As dishes were being cleared from the table, John simply nodded to Petey, which was his signal to get us out fishing. Petey was a gangly-legged, freckle-faced redhead who looked kind of small to have such a large task. He proved to be more than just good, he was an expert. I've since fished with guides all over the world, even spent some years as a guide myself but, self included, never met one with more confidence, ability or enthusiasm as that thirteen-year-old.

I could write a book about our fishing experiences, but this is not just a fishing tale, so forgive me if I gloss through the details. Fishing was, day after day, a dream-fulfilling experience. We caught every species of fish in the lake, including many smallmouth bass over five pounds and countless numbers of Northern up to and even over twenty pounds. We practically filled the Brawleys icehouse with fish.

The icehouse was as big as a barn. It was named such because, during the winter, John and Petey cut huge, man-size blocks of ice off the lake and stacked them inside. The ice stack was from wall to wall, and floor to almost ceiling. It lasted from winter to winter, and acted as the Brawley refrigerator. Before we got a real refrigerator at home, I can remember the ice man delivering blocks of ice to our indoor ice box, but this...who would have believed it had they not seen it?

The routine was the same every day. Early breakfast and out to fish till lunch, then out to fish till dinner, then an hour or so of fishing until dark, and then exhausted to bed and sleep until breakfast time. We never tired of it and Petey seemed to have a new idea every day that kept us always at a high energy level. Sunday mornings the Brawleys went to church, but allowed Petey to stay behind to fulfill his obligation to us. He seemed to be genuinely glad to be given that choice, and from where we stood, we didn't blame him a bit.

After a week or so, Ernie first and then I started to notice that the Brawley girls were getting prettier and prettier each time we saw them...and friendlier, too. We'd both experienced city girls, and where we were in life at the time, figured nature would take its course. Probably the hardest decision we had yet made in our young lives was to agree to not allow anything physical to happen. Our decision had nothing to do with fear of John, but rather a combination of all the "people lessons" we had been subject to since crossing the Canadian border.

One day, after lunch, Ernie decided he'd take an afternoon off from fishing and ride with John into town to see if he could replace our ruined tire. Petey and I decided to fish off the bank until they returned. Standing in front of our cabin, Petey pointed across a large field and said there was a neat cove that we couldn't reach by boat that was full of big fish, just on the other side of the field. He had a few chores he needed to do but assured me he'd meet me there in a while.

Rod in one hand, tackle box in the other, I headed in the direction Petey had pointed out. Though it was still early spring, the grass was high, but not so tall as to obscure my vision. I remember I was whistling as I topped a little rise and caught first sight of the water ahead. It looked like I might have about a hundred yards to go to reach the cove, when a movement to my left caught my attention. Staring at me through the grass was a huge black bull with horns as wide as my arms could reach...and curved...and sharply pointed. Talk about being caught between a rock and a hard place.

With no knowledge of how to handle a situation like this, I did the most natural thing any city kid could be expected to do; I panicked! Holding my rod and tackle boxes as tightly as I could, I headed toward the water at a half run, half trot pace, keeping my eyes on that bull. The bull kept up with me, staying about twenty feet away. The closer I got to the water, though, the closer the bull seemed to be getting. I stopped as I got to the edge of the water and turned to face the bull straight on.

At that moment, with the bull less than ten feet away, everything suddenly appeared in slow motion. The bull dropped its head menacingly, snorting and staring right at me. He started to paw at the ground with one of his front legs. Waving my fishing rod at him did no good. Shouting threats at him did less. I took a step backward into the water; God, it was cold! The bull stepped closer, head still down, foot still pawing, nose still snorting, and those twin-pointed spears aimed right at me. I'd like to say it was the freezing water that had me shivering, but fat chance anyone would believe that.

The bull was now on the edge of the water, and I was in up to my chest, still hanging on to my rod and box, hyperventilating and probably turning blue. At that exact moment, Petey appeared, walking up behind the bull as if he didn't see him. I screamed out a warning for him to "Run Petey, it's a bull!" Petey ignored my warning, walked up to the bull, leaned against its side and calmly asked, "What are you doing in the water? Isn't it cold?"

"That bull was trying to kill me."

"Oh Sheila, she's harmless, she wouldn't hurt a fly."

"SHE," I screamed, "What do you mean SHE? Look at those horns."

With that, Petey calmly grabbed one of the horns and

turned the beast sideways. Like a school teacher dealing with an unruly child, he pointed to a spot under the animal and without cracking a smile said, "Bulls don't give milk." On the way back to the cabin for a change of clothes, Pete never mentioned the incident, nor was it spoken of during dinner. It seemed to be our secret.

The next five days were chock full of fishing and family fun, then suddenly it came to an end. There has to be a last day for everything, but this one was tough. We had packed the car and planned to leave after breakfast. We didn't want to go, we could have stayed forever. Breakfast was quiet, everyone felt the sorrow of parting, but life goes on and we had to be on our way. Just before we got into the car to leave, one of the girls handed me a box, a going-away gift. "Daddy made it for you to remember us by, and you can open it now if you want to."

I was quite taken aback with her genuine sincerity and eagerly opened the box. Inside was a perfectly carved replica of my "bull" with a note that said, "To Stu, our favorite Toreador." Instantly everyone started to laugh and clap and dance on the porch. It was a lively scene. At first I was embarrassed, and a little angry that Petey had told on me. But then, like a shot, I realized they all must have known for at least a week and avoided making any reference that might cause me pain. This was truly a love gift, along with still another important life lesson attached. We left the Brawleys and Canada much better young men for the experience.

Seventeen was, as Sinatra said, "a very good year." It was the beginning of my travels across the world and through life. I had seen my very first cow with horns, I had learned to resist temptation. I had seen kindness in its truest forms. I had learned how to share and to fully trust. I had begun the arduous task of "growing up."

Ernie's dad died the following year of alcohol-related illnesses, and Ernie moved away. I didn't see or hear from him for ten years. He showed up at my little marina on Shark River one day, sadly showing the telltale signs of an alcoholic. He never reached the age of forty. I never forgave his dad for visiting that genetic monster on his son.

I never visited the Brawleys again, except in memory. And, in retrospect, I truly believe our best memories are more valuable than money. You can spend money; sweet remembering lasts forever.

5

YOU'RE IN THE ARMY NOW

It almost embarrasses me to claim that I'm a veteran. Even though I entered the armed forces toward the end of the Korean conflict, what occurred between my induction and separation was ribald, hilarious, and eventually set me on the path to a fun-filled existence.

Growing up on the streets of Jersey City and Newark gave me lots of street-wise heads-up. It didn't do much for teaching me and my cronies how to take orders, but wiseacres notwithstanding, we were all products of our generation.

It was a time when dads were feared and obeyed without question. Moms cooked, took care of all the details, lent a sympathetic and wisely understanding ear, listened to confessions, and defied dads so quietly and efficiently, they never had a clue. Or did they?

Drugs were not a problem, nor was under-age drinking. Autos were few and far between, and TV was a new experiment none of us could afford. An evening's entertainment was listening to The Shadow or Inner Sanctum on the radio, while shivering under the covers and acting scared. On special occasions, mom played the piano while we all sang the happy songs of the time. Rap would have been a foreign language. As a matter of fact, it still is. It was friends and family. Family and friends.

For the most part, the gang that I hung out with were honest, industrious, and loyal. Even though Lefty grew up to be a thief and convicted murderer, we still remembered him as a helluva catcher, who could hit a stick ball over the rooftops, and into the next block.

The only trouble I ever got into, not counting the time I ran away for three months, or took on the gym teacher in an alley, was when mom and dad found out I was running a poker game. It was a good game, too. Some of the heaviest dudes in the neighborhood played at the tables. The local cops watched out for us and were pretty well compensated for their efforts. It wasn't like I was doing it alone. Dave and Al were just as guilty, but I took the heat and had to back out of our partnership. Going back to delivering groceries on my bike certainly played hell with my dating expenses, I'll tell you that. Oh well, I was only thirteen, and as dad advised, "You've got a lot of life to live." Boy, was he ever right on that one.

High school was a blur, with more rights of passage than I can count. There were a lot of "firsts." And then, all of a sudden, I was seventeen and out of school. I was the youngest kid in the class, having skipped a lower grade, with my parents' and teacher's permission. You could do that back then, for two reasons: one, you were smarter than anyone else in your class, or two, you were such a pain in the ass that your teachers just wanted to pass you on. I was both, so I'll never know on what premise the decision was made.

That put me in a funny spot. My friends were all draft age, and had tons of fun rubbing it in. We all grew up watching John Wayne killing our WWII enemies on the big screen. We all had brothers or cousins off to war at the time, and had grown up to be the next generation of patriots. That war was a righteous one and we all believed that our country could do no wrong.

46

So it was that I watched on an almost monthly basis, one or more of my friends either being drafted, or enlisting. It was Korea time, and we all felt that the South Koreans would be annihilated without our aid. Most of the guys were anxious to go, even though some motives were just to escape our confines. Memories of Second World War heroism was probably the prime motivator.

And then I was alone. For the first time ever. I tried college, but failed miserably. It wasn't that I wasn't capable, I just didn't give a darn. I drifted from job to job, holding at least four during those horrible years between seventeen and nineteen. I was a wreck. Finally, not being capable of making any other decision, I volunteered for the draft. A week later, I was accepted. I'm certain there were sighs of relief among members of both my immediate and extended family. I heard more than once the whispered words, "It'll make a mensch out of him."

The ride on the bus to Fort Dix was both solemn and silent. Solemn because all of my buddies were in Korea, and I imagined I'd soon have a chance to catch up with one or more of them. Silent because I had learned early on not to talk to strangers. Play it safe. Besides, everyone on the bus seemed to be gung-ho, which never was and never would be my style.

The dull bus trip ended as we entered through the gates of Dix. That was the last dull moment I was to know for the next three and a half years; I just wasn't aware of it at the time.

As we unloaded from our transportation, we were told to line up, short guys up front. That was me, almost always the shortest guy in the crowd. Facing us was the shiniest man I had ever seen. His uniform seemed to have sewn-in seams, and fit like an expert paint job. His shoes shined so glossily that we could see our images in them. His chest was full of medals and ribbons, glistening in the bright sunlight. His dark

47

eyes sparkled. His skin was as dark as the black keys on my mom's piano, and so help me, it also shined.

"Smith is my name," were the first words we heard. "Sergeant Smith, to be exact. It's spelled Smythe, you need to remember that. For the next eight weeks, ladies, I will be your mother, father, wife or girlfriend." And after a slight but effective pause he said, "I will also be your God, and you will pray never to invoke my wrath."

My adrenalin was pumping overtime, and my street-smart survival lessons immediately flashed through my mind. The guy spoke softly and confidently. That meant he could be dangerous. On the other hand the greater lesson learned in the streets was, "He who speaks first is usually the loser." I was going to really have to think this one out.

"Now before I begin the almost impossible task of turning you girls into cannon fodder, there is one rule you must be made aware of right now." He definitely had everyone's attention. "You all may think I look shiny," he said, "well the first word that I hear uttered about shiny or shine, or anything that smells like a racial slur, I will eat that person's heart and feed his bones to the Captain's dog. Do I make myself clear?" I could not imagine anyone in this group having the slightest doubt that Smith (spelled Smythe) meant exactly what he said.

The next few days were mostly orientation. My buddies had clued me in on how to get through the gas mask room, so that was a breeze. Not so for some of the other clowns I was thrown together with. It was kind of amusing to see them gag and cry real tears, some of them even calling for their mommas. Smythe noticed I had an attitude about it, and gently reminded me that I had a bit to learn about soldiering. I made a mental note to try to get closer to him, since he was definitely "the man of the moment."

Then came a round of training films, mostly "how to's." Though, when my old pals were home on leave, they did everything possible to prepare me for basic training, to a man, they failed to tell me about the one film I definitely needed to be prepared for. I later learned it had been a well planned conspiracy, that fifty years later, I'm still kidded about.

I should have guessed something was coming down as we entered the theater. We were all issued a brown paper bag as we filed into the room. Smythe was at his shiny best, as he introduced what we were about to see. He went into great detail, and quite graphically, about the evils in store for those of us who might be tempted to sample the wares of local ladies. Local meant here in the States or anywhere in the world Uncle Sam decided to send us. His message was loud and clear, but it was easy to see no one, including me, was going to be scared off.

It was a "no holds barred" movie. It showed in living color the ravages of sexually transmitted diseases on the human body. Ten minutes into the film, the first retching gurgle was heard in the dark.

Fifteen minutes later, the soundtrack of the movie was drowned out by up-chucking G.I.'s, hidden from each other in the darkened theater room.

Suddenly, the lights came on to a scene of utter chaos. Men were throwing up on each other, the desks, the seats, the floor and the walls. Those of us who were not affected by the movie were motivated to throw up just because every one else was. If one were to describe a scene from hell, this would definitely be it.

To make matters worse, Smythe and several other non-coms were standing in the doorway gagging with laughter and pointing at the mess. The thought passed through my mind that though the movie was a necessary training aid, we had been set up. Set up to be ridiculed. For a seasoned street kid, that was a hard apple to swallow.

Standing now in front of his gasping, panting and odiferous troops, Smythe announced that we should have used the brown bags instead of each other's uniforms to catch our swill. "You will march to the barracks to shower and change your clothes. Then you will launder those stinking uniforms. Then you will all report back here, where you will clean this place up." He finished with, "Ladies, you have disappointed me. I thought I was training a bunch of soldiers, and here I find I've been given a bunch of babies. Well, I've got several more weeks to make men out of you, and by God, I intend to do just that. Now get the hell out of my sight, and be back here in one hour."

As one might imagine, after clean up, we were a bunch of malcontents. Add to that, today was payday, it was Friday, and because of our "performance" we were to be denied off-post passes. It was a proper time for me to arrange a poker game, something I had become fairly adept at. Poker was about to change my life.

A tightly-made cot served as a table. Foot lockers made wonderful makeshift chairs, and voila, we had a seven-man game with a small waiting list. About an hour into the game, Smythe entered our space, supposedly to "check on his brown bag brigade." He watched the play closely, commenting often about how our poker skills were slightly less than our soldiering skills. Out of the corner of my eye, I observed him as he went around and around the cot, standing behind the card holders and watching the half-hidden hands, and how they were played. He was, of course, correct in one thing – there was not a man among the players that had the smallest inkling about the refinements of the game. None would have left my old poker room with even their pants, let alone their wallets.

It was easy to determine Smythe was a devotee of gambling, and an idea began to form in my mind as how to make life easier for me. It was a longshot, but my built-in survival mechanism forced me to take the shot.

It wasn't long before the seat to my right was emptied,

and it took hardly a few seconds to talk Smythe into occupying it. He did protest, explaining it was not correct army policy for a non-com to socialize with the recruits but, "in the interest of making you better prepared soldiers, I'll bend the rules a little." Smythe was a poker player. He knew how to bluff, and he knew when to use a large bet to scare his opponents. However, even with those skills, the cards still have to fall your way in some positive fashion. You didn't need great cards, only fair cards. On this night, Smythe's cards were worse than bad. To his credit, he held his own, and was only out about fifty bucks when "lights out" in ten minutes was announced. That gave us time to play two or three hands.

The game was seven card stud, and on the next deal Smythe had a pair of tens showing. Also showing were a pair of queens, a pair of sevens, three hearts, and no one knew about my pair of hidden kings. Two players were out, with two cards yet to be dealt. The player with the hearts was dealt a fourth, and his reaction indicated he had drawn a flush and felt he had the pot locked up. He bet five bucks, which was our limit, got a raise from Smythe who now had two pair showing and a re-raise from the flush hand. Two raises was the limit, so the final card was dealt, face down, so only the holder of the hand could see. My sixth card had been a king, which gave me trips. The rules allowed a ten dollar last card bet, and that's what the flush hand did. Smythe immediately raised ten, effectively forcing two hands to fold. I had drawn the fourth king, and had the best hidden hand one could pray for. I figured Smythe for a full house, but I played it cool and just called, so the flush hand could make the final ten dollar raise. I figured there was almost two hundred dollars on the cot, the biggest pot of the night by far.

Though it was out of turn, the kid with the flush turned over his cards to show his hand, whooped and began reaching for the pot. "Hold on just a second, kiddo," Smythe cooed through an evil grin, as he turned over his tens full.

All eyes turned to me as I dejectedly turned up a third king, purposefully keeping the fourth hidden from view. As Smythe was raking in and stacking his winnings, everyone but me left the table to prepare for lights out. As Smythe was pocketing his money, I motioned for him to look at my hidden card. His expression was incredulous, but immediately turned to one of both wonder and understanding. We both knew I had lost the money but had won the game.

I was awakened at five the next morning by an orderly sent by Smythe to "fetch me." Sitting behind his desk, as always, dressed in his shiny best, he affected a toothy smile and handed me my "reward." It was a three-day emergency pass. Neither one of us discussed what the emergency might be, I was told only that I had to be back by reveille on Tuesday. And yes, it was OK for me to drive back in my personal car. A special place to park that forbidden vehicle was arranged. It wasn't even necessary for him to explain the need for secrecy; each of us understood our boundary lines. I knew instinctively that somewhere in his youth he had been a street kid like me.

The orderly drove me to the station in plenty of time to catch the first bus out to Newark. The week-end away was a great gift for mom and dad, as well as the few friends I still had at home who were not serving overseas. A couple of impromptu parties and complete disregard for the new information I had gained from the "film," put me in the best possible frame of mind for my return to the reality of the army. The guard at the entrance gate to Fort Dix obviously was expecting me. I got a legal parking sticker for my car, and was instructed where my parking space was to be. You'd have to be a total dumb-ass not to recognize that no matter what your rank was in the Army, the whole deal was run by battle-hardened sergeants. And at the top of that list would have to be the shiniest ones.

Thankfully, none of my barracks mates asked about

my "emergency," so getting back into the swing of things was simple. But if poker had turned my army life onto a new road, what happened at chowtime that next afternoon was certainly the single factor that started me on a journey that could only be thought of as Walter Mitty-like.

As a civilian, I had been a pretty good hoofer. I had hooked up with a spectacular-looking redheaded gal named Marcia Weisenthal, whom I had met at a wedding. Seems like she wanted to be a professional dancer, and certainly had both the looks and the talent. People paid so much attention to us on the dance floor that we immediately decided to work out a routine or two, and see if we couldn't make a few bucks entertaining at other weddings, bar mitzvahs, or any thing else we could dig up.

Not only was Marcia the prettiest, sexiest human being in the whole world, she was also the niece of Jerry Lewis, who along with his partner, Dean Martin, was the biggest thing in worldwide show biz at the time. Dancing with Marcia, and having her on my arm in the presence of both friends and strangers, certainly elevated my ego.

At any rate, after our noon meal, we all went back to the barracks to prepare for the rest of the training day. Outside the barracks awaiting my return was a civilian delivery truck large enough to carry off all the garbage Fort Dix could provide in a month. It was huge. The driver announced that he had a package for Private Stu Tinney, and finding out I was the guy, he immediately asked for help getting it off the truck. The thing was as large as a double entry door, and was carefully wrapped in plain brown paper. It took four men, one on each corner, to unload and get it into the barracks. By the time I was ready to open it, the barracks had filled with not only its regular occupants, but officers and NCOs from elsewhere on the post. Word travels fast in the army, it would seem.

I guess in front of an audience most people react by hamming it up a bit. I was no different. Sucking out every second, I slowly and theatrically cut away the paper. To everyone's surprise, even mine, it turned out to be a larger-than-life-size photo of Dean Martin and Jerry Lewis, caught in one of their zany antics. The autographed inscription written blazingly across the bottom read: "Stu, our country is in good hands with people like you protecting our freedom, God bless and good luck." It was signed, "Your good friends, Dean & Jerry."

No one in the room ever found out that I had never laid eyes on the pair except in the movies. I had no way of knowing whether the signatures were valid or forged. One thing I did know for sure was that Marcia was the most awesome person in the world. When I got a chance to call and thank her, the phone had been shut off. I learned a few weeks later that she and her family had moved to California where it was rumored that her dad, Bernie, was going to take over the Mystic Tape Company, one of his nephew's holdings. I never saw Marcia again, but learned a great life lesson from the incident – that a single moment in one's life can change its direction forever, good or bad.

The rest of my training time was spent in the bowling alley, either keeping score for playing teams, or filling in for an absent member. I never marched again, or fired a gun, or slept in a tent, or was eaten by the local bugs. I didn't get to do any of the fun things my fellow trainees did, but I have to reluctantly admit that I hardly had time to dwell on the loss. When frequently asked about my friends Dean and Jerry, I avoided at all costs any discussion about private lives. That tactic created a mystique all its own. Smythe and I hooked up on several occasions, going into town together for meals, beers, girl watching, or just plain getting away for a while. I found him to be a larger than life hero. He was, surprisingly, a naturally shy man. I learned about the unfortunate circumstances of his youth that brought him to the Army. I learned about the things he did to earn the medals he wore.

In short, I learned to respect him as no other man who has ever been a part of my life. When the time came for me to move on, we were both happy at my future prospects, but saddened that our fun time had come to an end. We never wrote, never spoke again. I do not know what ever happened to him, but I am content to believe the time we spent together was an important part of each of our tapestries.

The old saying goes, "Time sure passes by quickly when you're having fun." Before I knew it, basic training was over, and it was time for the traditional two-week pass and the delivery of our orders. All but two of us were to be sent to Korea. I, along with Lou Shalitt, was assigned to Salzburg, Austria. Lou was the chemist who later was to develop the paint pigments used on automobiles. He did all that while working on a grant from DuPont. Lou was to be a company clerk; I was scheduled to be, of all things, a field wireman. I didn't understand at the time, since I had never had any training, but I supposed something had to be written into my records. I saw Lou two weeks later when we boarded our troop ship, and once again quite accidentally when we were both vacationing in Switzerland. That's the way it is in the service, people come in and out of your life quickly. I always remembered the advice I got from Smythe to "never get too close to anyone," since it makes it easier if they get offed. Tough philosophy, but it worked for him, and as far as I was concerned, he was one of the folks whose advice I was going to heed.

I'd never been aboard a big ship before, and didn't know what to expect. It didn't take me long to determine that this was the pits. My gut feeling turned into reality after the very first meal. In the dining area, dishes full of food were sliding all over the tables as the boat rocked violently from side to side. The reaction was the same as the one in the theater, with guys barfing all over the tables, the floors, and each other. There was little escape in our quarters which were far below decks, and more crowded than a New York tenement. Whatever food wasn't ejected in the dining room was finding its way down here. This was Hell, Part Two, and I knew I needed to be somewhere else, so I decided to try to find a place to sleep on one of the upper decks.

Standing by the rail, wondering how long a swim it was to get back to terra firma, and trying hard to hold my meal down, I felt a bit lost. I noticed someone else standing at the rail and decided, against my better judgment, to talk to a stranger. It turned out to be one of my better quick decisions. As a matter of fact, one of my most outstanding.

It seemed as if my new best friend was part of the crew stationed aboard the ship. He was a young officer, off duty at the time, and was quite willing to fill me in on some really great information. I learned that not only was the ship transporting soldiers to Europe, but also the wives and children of some of those already stationed there. He allowed that they were mostly pains-in-the-butt, since they had to be entertained constantly. Some of the wives were reported to have high-ranking officers as husbands. As I trust you can imagine, my little friend who holds a special place on my shoulder began pouring advice into my ear. To his credit, wrong or right, I have always taken him quite seriously.

Without hesitation, I explained to my new friend that I was a professional dancer, a personal friend of Jerry Lewis and his family, and if it were at all possible, I'd be more than happy to sacrifice my time to helping entertain his wards. Why, I might even offer dance lessons to the gals as well as the kids. That is if it could be made available.

My new quarters for the rest of the trip were cramped. Cramped was okay with me because I was the only one sleeping in them. I took my meals in the galley, quickly learning how to charm the cooks out of special treats. Everyone treated me especially nicely, and for the rest of the trip, I danced with some of the sweetest, loneliest women ever to step onto a dance floor. Teaching some of the kids to dance had its moments since it was all new to me, but overall, it beat the hell out of living in the barfing booth.

This routine of "all good things must come to an end" was beginning to wear me down. The next thing I knew was that I wasn't as special as I had allowed myself to feel. I was standing on a dock, in a foreign country, with a large number of men I did not know. All of a sudden, I was back to being a plain soldier, with no idea what was coming next.

As our names were called we were told to line up. I wasn't up front this time, as the names were called alphabetically. I guessed there were at least a hundred of us. It was ingenious how we were formed up. No one stood directly in front of anyone else, which allowed us all an unobstructed view of the people giving the orders. When I determined who the head honcho was, my eyes stayed glued to him so I wouldn't miss anything. Another lesson from Smythe, "Keep your mouth shut, your ears open, and never volunteer."

"I am Master Sergeant Steinholtz," the deep voice roared. The manly voice belonged to a pig-faced, overstuffed, green-toothed slob of a man. His picture would never grace an enlistment poster. The little guy on my shoulder whispered, "Man, I think we got trouble." I was feeling pretty uncomfortable. I had been able to quickly figure out Sergeant Smythe, but this guy was a horse of a different color.

"I want you all to pull your dog tags out where I can see them," he roared. "I will look at your dog tags and your faces, and I will never forget you. If you ever piss me off, I will know exactly who I am getting satisfaction from. And trust me gentlemen, I always get satisfaction."

The stark differences between the two men who, at different times, were to be my exalted leaders were so apparent, they blew my mind. Where Smythe could have graced the cover of "Soldier's Esquire," this new ape was a prime candidate for the centerfold spread of "Dump Your Dirty Linens Here." I felt a bit uneasy. It got worse.

Speaking about dog tags, I remembered when Smythe told me exactly what they were for. I had imagined we wore them so if we ever were in an accident, or were arrested, we could be recognized as army property. It had also entered my mind that it might be for some of the guys who couldn't remember who they were. Then again, if they couldn't read, what would be the difference? Not so. Smythe explained that the little groove at the bottom was so that it could be inserted between your teeth and pushed up into your gums. It made for positive ID if you were ever KIA. That was a happy thought. The single letter identifying your religious preference or heritage was simply to determine what kind of grave marker was appropriate. Just another example of government efficiency.

As Steinholtz casually walked between the rows of men, he took each set of dog tags in his greasy paws, looked each man in the face, read his last name and repeated over and over, "I know your name and I know your face." It was obviously to provoke fear and respect. It was also obvious that he was scoring at least one out of two.

I smelled his presence several minutes before he was standing in front of me. He was big. He was fat. His clothes were disheveled. I was later to learn the smell was a combination of beer and wurst. He looked directly into my face as he called my last name, while holding my tags in his fat, greasy paws. I was waiting for a repeat of his litany, but it did not come. I saw his scowl turn into the kind of smile you might see from a nerd in a singles bar. Lecherous and evil. The little guy on my shoulder was gone, and I was alone and scared. It got worse.

Instead of shouting out my name, Steinholtz stepped closer, and in a whisper no one but me could hear, said, "Welcome to Hitler land, Hebe, I've been waiting for one of you for a long time." The saliva dripped off his chin as he continued with, "You're here to learn about all the good things Hitler did for your people, and I have chosen myself to be your personal instructor. Some of you people survived, but I don't think you look much like a survivor to me." Without another word, he slithered through the rest of the troops, finishing his act, and directing us to the buses that would take us from Bremerhaven to Salzburg.

During the long ride, I tried to take my mind off what had happened at the dock. Growing up as I did, in a multi-ethnic neighborhood, religious backgrounds were never of any concern to us. Of course, there were derisive comments thrown at each other, but that was all in fun, and we would have beaten the hell out of any stranger that said the same things. I knew I had no friends to back me up here. I knew I had nowhere to run. I knew this freakazoid was as serious as a heart attack, and that I needed to watch my own back as I had never done before. Fearing for my life was a new emotion, but the fear had certainly taken stage front in my mind. I clung to that ever-present street survivor code that "no matter what comes up, there is a way to handle it." Right!

It was winter in Europe, and heavy snow dotted the landscape. I should have gotten a lot more enjoyment out of the trip than I did. The war (WWII) had been over for ten years, but there was still much devastation to be seen. There was lots of farmland and also lots of partly destroyed buildings. I knew that the spoken language in Austria was Hoch Deutsch, or the higher form of German. It was a language I had opted for in school, and one I had done pretty well with. Since many of my neighbors had been European refugees, it was a language that permeated much of the normal conversations I heard on a daily basis. I was fairly comfortable in the fact that I could communicate with the locals, in the event I needed to run and hide. The thought was paramount on my mind. At the moment, it was my only weapon, and I decided, for a time, to keep it to myself.

The Post, which was just on the outskirts of Salzburg, was almost a mirror image of Fort Dix. I suppose the Army made them all similar, to make us feel at home wherever we were. The barracks we were assigned to were also so similar, it could easily have been Fort Dix. I wished. After we were all shown our sleeping quarters, we were given an orientation to familiarize us with where the important buildings were located. We were then given bedding and foot lockers and told we would have the rest of the day to unpack, make our beds, and take a trip to the PX to purchase any essentials we might need. Day one wound up being pretty peaceful. That was soon to end.

It was still dark outside the following morning when some idiot turned on the lights, and while beating on an aluminum pan with a wooden spoon, at the top of his lungs shouted, "Hit the floor ladies, formation out front in ten minutes. And make sure your beds are made, there's gonna be an inspection." Butts and elbows flew in every direction, no one wanting Steinholtz to "remember" them. It was apparent, as we stood in formation, that it was winter, and that we had not been issued our cold-weather gear yet. We were all shivering with the morning's freezing temperatures, while Pig and crew were in the barracks, pulling off their inspection.

"Tinney," I heard, "come in here." Entering the barracks, I tried to think away the heavy feeling in my chest. It didn't work. What I saw made it worse. I had prided myself at how tightly and correctly I had learned to make up my bed, yet here it was, in shambles. Blanket and sheets were on the floor. My foot locker, so neatly packed when I left, was upside down, its contents strewn all over the room. "I knew you were going to be trouble the minute I laid eyes on you," came the Pig's nasty remarks. "When we get back from chow, I want this mess cleaned up." Without another word, he left me alone, while he and the rest of the troops marched off for breakfast. It took until they all came back for me to straighten things back up. Funny thing, he never checked.

Chow being over (I never did get to eat breakfast), we were lined up outside the barracks. "Tinney," the Pig oinked, "climb that pole to where the red mark is. I want to show these guys what a real pole climber looks like." He handed me a pair of climbers' spikes, not even trying to hide his evil smirk.

Living in a big city, one could hardly avoid seeing telephone company employees climbing poles. As kids, we used to watch them, and often emulated them (sans spikes) shinnying up poles. There were a heck of a lot more poles than trees where I came from.

I took the spikes and the offered safety belt and put them on as I had seen workmen do it in the past. My false show of confidence obviously disturbed Steinholtz, and I had a moment's thought that perhaps I had acted a bit cavalier in front of the men. Inwardly, I was scared, big time.

I secured the belt around the pole and inch by inch worked my way up to the red line and stopped as I had been directed. Steinholtz announced he was taking the troops to the supply depot to pick up their winter issue, and because I had been so slow in climbing the pole, "You can wait up there until we get back, and think about what a slow, lazy malingerer you are."

Where I grew up was cold in the winter, and not many of us could afford what you would call really warm outer clothing. We had learned, of necessity, to wear a sweater under our shirts, and two pair of socks. So I was attired that morning, and lucky for me, since it was at least an hour or more before my Company returned, arms laden with warm clothing.

"You can come down now, butt-head," he roared. "And you better make a better show of coming down than you did going up."

My limbs were stiff from the cold, but I managed to slowly work my way down to the ground. It sure felt good when my feet hit the dirt.

After a few comments about how much practice he would see that I got, orders to go pick up my winter issue were more than welcome. Because I was unfamiliar with how to properly don the climbing spikes, I had badly bruised both my legs. I remembered as I was walking to the supply depot how mom used to pay special attention to the many cuts and bruises I got while growing up. "Let me kiss them and make them better," she would say. It worked every time. I was sure wishing mom could ply her magic here. The little guy on my shoulder whispered, "Well, your mom isn't here, and you're on your own." As if I didn't know.

The rest of the week was mostly drill, and Steinoltz pretty much left me alone. He never missed an opportunity, however, to whisper a chilling reminder of how my time was coming. Of course, when weekend passes were issued, my name was absent from the list. It seems as if I was the only one who didn't earn one. Well, that was OK with me, since I had been waiting for an opportunity to find a local resident or two with whom I could practice my German on. There were several Nationals working on the Post for me to approach. My only plan, still, was to cut and run if it became necessary. I spent the entire weekend doing just that, talking German to anyone I could find, and making new best friends among some of the local residents. Each promised never to address me in their native language should they ever see me in the company of another soldier. To a person, I learned, the Austrians tolerated us, but did not necessarily care much about being occupied. After all, they were never the enemy, or at least they felt so. We were, however, a major part of their economy so they smiled, bowed, acted courteous, and talked about us behind our backs. Having been taken into their confidence because I spoke their language, I was made privy to many "ugly American" stories. I was absolutely certain that if I needed help I could find it among my new acquaintances.

Monday through Thursday saw me either cleaning up the mess hall, the latrines, or some other "punishment" for who knows what. Nothing happened that I couldn't easily handle until that fateful Friday.

It had snowed all day and all night on Thursday, and there must have been over a foot of new snow on the ground. Steinholtz was ready to play. He chose me out of the formation to go on a "special assignment" with him and his crony, Corporal Pesant. We were going to lay field wire under combat conditions, whatever that meant. The rest of the men were given their orders for the day, and were marched off to accomplish same. I was left with Steinholtz and Pesant, and felt this was the day of reckoning. I quickly determined neither man was carrying a weapon, and I could easily outrun both of them, even in the heavy snow. I was scared, but not terrified. Thankfully, I still had my wits about me.

We all piled into a jeep, a huge roll of wire and two field telephones the only gear aboard besides the three of us. Pesant drove off the post for several miles until he found the spot they seemed to be looking for. It was a narrow, snow-covered road that had been partially cleared. Huge drifts of wet snow lined both sides of the road, as far as the eye could see. Pesant parked the jeep, and he and his boss rolled the roll of wire out of the jeep. They proceeded to strap it on my back, and lead me off the road into the waist-deep snow.

Armed with only one of the phones, Steinholtz ordered me to follow the road, but to stay off of it and plow a new trail alongside of it. As I broke through the new snow, he slowly unwound the wire from the reel, carefully laying it on the road. He did not speak one word until all the wire was emptied from the huge spool. I was glad he didn't ask a question, since my whole body ached with pain and I couldn't have responded. With the wire off the spool, he attached the loose end to the phone he had been carrying and called Pesant, who was attached to the other end.

"Drive back to the mess hall and bring back some hot coffee," he said into the phone.

Though the weight of the wire was off the spool, my shoulders ached from where the straps had been carrying the load. Still, it felt considerably better now that much of the weight had been removed. I was not to be comfortable for very long. Steinholtz directed me to the other side of the road, where the snow was unbroken. As I struggled through the cold, wet snow, he re-rolled the wire on the spool. It got heavier and heavier with each step. Somehow, we managed to get back to our starting point, where Pesant, the jeep, and hot coffee awaited. I was allowed to remove the spool from my back, and to sit in the jeep as the two drank coffee. Not a word was spoken directly to me on the ride back to the Post. I heard many racial and ethnic jokes passed between the two red-neck idiots that were riding up front. Through the pain, I kept myself in check by beginning to formulate an escape plan. I truly felt it was an escape, because I really knew that I was both in prison and in serious danger.

I was dropped off in front of the barracks with the words, "The party has just begun, Hebe, it's gonna be a long winter." They both laughed crazily as they drove away, leaving my wet, cold, aching body in the road in front of the barracks. I took a hot shower, got to the mess hall in time for a much-needed meal, and fell into the sack and easily to sleep. There was no reveille on Saturday morning, since everyone else had a weekend pass, and I was the only one in the barracks.

After I dressed and ate breakfast, I headed for the PX where I knew I could talk to some German-speaking folks. I related my tale to Peter, a local resident, who made me laugh when he referred to my two antagonists by the names of Porky Pig and Piss Ant. I did not go so far as to ask for his help, but

I knew he was working the entire weekend, and that having worked more on my plan, I could then approach him. I just knew I had better not be here on Monday. I knew I was close to the breaking point.

As I wandered aimlessly around the Post, I began to remember some of the things I had done to survive when I had run away from home as a thirteen-year-old. Well, this wouldn't be for just three months, this would be a major, life-altering move. How would I get in touch with parents and friends, where to go, who to trust? The questions flew through my mind like shots fired from a repeating rifle.

When I looked up, I was standing in front of the JAG building. It had never occurred to me to ask for help or advice from anyone in the service. I had to assume, like on the streets, that army folks would take care of their own. Why would they even listen to my tale of woe, let alone help me? "What the hell," I thought, it won't hurt to sniff it out, since by Monday I figured I'd be long gone.

It dawned on me immediately that there was no one working this particular Saturday. All the lights in the building were on, but all office doors were closed and all visible desks were unoccupied. I did hear a radio playing somewhere and decided to follow the sound. I found the source at the end of a long hallway. Looking at a partially open door, over which a sign read Salzburg Rod & Gun Club, I not only heard where the music was coming from, but also sounds of things being dragged around.

As I tentatively entered the room, I took in the sight of what was obviously a store. Glass cases, now empty, covered most of the available floor space. Empty hooks on walls and ghostly looking clothes racks indicated much stuff had been on display here. The walls were lined with cardboard boxes, and a shirtless man was busily taping them shut. It was almost weird how he sensed my silent entry, because he immediately spun around to face me.

"Better be sure of what you're doing before you sneak up on a fellow," the man said. "And you damned sure need to get better at it," he continued.

"Sorry," I said, "I kind of got lost, and somehow wound up here. I sure wasn't trying to sneak up on you."

"I guess I'm sorry, too," he replied. "Guess it's force of habit. Twenty-five years in this outfit tends to teach you to always watch your back." As if I didn't know about watching one's back.

He offered his hand in a strong grip, introducing himself as Sergeant Hundley. He knew before I told him that I was a new recruit, and he behaved more humanely toward me than anyone else had since I arrived in Europe.

"I know all this stuff is packed up, but every box has an inventory, and it will be easy to find stuff. If you know specifically what you want, I can find it for you. You'll have the honor of buying the last item from the good old rod and gun club so, what'll it be?"

I had no idea what in the heck he was talking about, and told him so. Like I said, "I just got lost, and wound up here by accident."

He explained that several years ago General Hoye, Salzburg's commander, dreamed up the idea of a separate sporting goods store for any man who loved the outdoors. It was to be stocked with outdoor items not available in the PX, and were to be sold to servicemen at prices greatly reduced from what they were back home. There was even a rental section so that camping gear would not have to be individually owned, but could be leased to a family interested in camping.

"We're having to close it up," he continued. "I'm about to retire, and there's no one around here capable of running it, and God knows, I've interviewed dozens of wannabees."

The imp on my shoulder was jumping up and down, trying to get my attention. I got the idea. "Gee, that's too bad," I said. "I wish I had gotten here earlier, since I could run this thing standing on my head."

Hundley looked at me strangely, grabbed me by my upper arm, showing an enormous amount of hand strength, and said, "What in hell do you mean?"

I didn't hesitate. I didn't even check the water before I dove in headfirst. "My dad owns the biggest tackle store in New Jersey, and I've worked there every summer since I was ten. Before I got in the service, I was responsible for purchasing, display organization, and sales promotions." Looking straight into his gaping mouth, and hoping he didn't notice my body shaking, I continued with, "After that, handling this little thing would be a walk in the park."

I could almost feel the blood in my veins being restricted as Hundley's grip got even tighter. "Look me straight in the eye, soldier, and tell me you're not BS-ing me."

Somehow I managed to do just that. The thought of court martial, jail, or even perhaps the firing squad didn't enter my mind until days later. Desperate times demanded desperate measures. I forced myself to look directly into the man's eyes and said, "What in the hell would I have to benefit by BS-ing you?"

He relaxed his grip and said, "Pull up a chair, and wait right here. General Hoye is in his office, checking out my inventory sheets, and I want to tell him about you." And suddenly he was gone, and I was alone with little time to think this out.

"Just wing it," my imp said. "If you try to practice now, you'll fall all over your lies, and they will know. And then, for sure, you will have gotten out of the fire and into the frying pan." The quick decision to just let the lies build upon each other was easy to reach. I had done a lot of hunting, fishing and camping back home, and had actually worked in a small bait shop on the Jersey shore for one summer. I had a fleeting knowledge of name-brands, prices, display techniques, and cash registers. I prayed that would be enough to get me by.

I didn't have long to pray. Within twenty minutes Hundley was back. "Come with me" he said, "General Hoye wants to talk to you right now." As we walked through the labyrinth of hallways, I noticed my imp had abandoned me, and I was, as usual, on my own. I felt as if I was walking that famous last mile. Oh well, the firing squad would be a lot faster than what Steinholtz obviously had in store for me, so I was game to continue my little scam.

I have to admit my resolve was getting a bit weaker as we approached the General's door. Entering his majesty's office was like stepping out of a plane without the protection of a parachute. I knew only one thing, and that was I had to control the quiver in my voice and speak slowly and surely. I knew I would also have to look directly into the man's face when I spoke. I didn't think that one became a General without having seen almost all there is to see. This was to be either my finest hour, or my hour of doom. I took a deep breath and followed Hundley into the room.

The room was spartan, and obviously military. There was little furniture, and what there was of it smelled of utilitarian use. The walls were bare, save for a few maps of Europe and Austria, with some colored pins sticking out of them. The desk was neat and uncluttered, with only one framed picture on its surface. The back faced me, so I couldn't see whose photo it was. The chair that the General sat in was huge and comfortable-looking. The General absolutely fit the space he was occupying. *He* was huge and comfortable looking. Perhaps, under these circumstances, he might have appeared bigger than he was. I stepped up to his desk, stood at attention, saluted smartly, and announced that, "I am Private Tinney."

"Sit down soldier," he said, smiling warmly. "This conversation will be casual and unmilitary. Now relax, and tell me about yourself, all about yourself. I want to know about you parents, your siblings, your friends and your schooling. I want to know about your army experience up until now, and then I want to hear about how and why you feel that running our rod and gun club would be, as Sergeant Hundley has told me, a piece of cake for you."

The man exuded warmth and charm, with a confidence I had little experience with in my life until now. I knew as I began to speak that most of what I said had better be the truth. I had no plan as to when I would tell the big lie, but I knew I was going to have to throw it in there at some point.

I began my story with growing up in a loving household. I didn't leave out my friends, or Lefty. I told him about running away and about my run-in with the gym teacher. I told him about my poker room. I told him about German being my second language. I left nothing out. I even told him about dancing with Marcia. When it came time to tell about my army experience, I laid it all on the desk. He learned about the poker game, my car, and the giant photo of Dean and Jerry. I told him of my experience on board ship. I did not mention Smythe, and I left out Steinholtz. Nor did I say anything about the jobs I had held as a civilian. He listened intently, never taking his eyes off my face. Since I was telling the truth, the whole truth, and nothing but the truth, I remained calm and relaxed.

"Now tell me why you feel you can handle what has been one of my pet projects," he said. "And try not to leave anything out, since this is very important to me."

It seemed kind of odd to me that in all the time I had been there, the General had not asked me one question, or had in any way interrupted my dissertation. He simply sat in his chair, looking relaxed, and stared into what felt like my soul.

I really embellished my position in the summer tackle shop job, suddenly realizing that the experience had greatly added to my knowledge. I had, in fact, been allowed to do a little buying of merchandise we were low on. I also was responsible for running inventory. And since it was an extremely busy place, at the center of the ocean fishing scene, I actually had gotten some hands-on experience with numerous name brands. I told him of fishing trips to Canada and other places on the coast. In other words, I dazzled him with my fancy foot work. Or so I thought.

"Okay son," he said, "now tell me about your dad's store and everything you did there. By the way," he added, almost as an after thought, "what was the name of the place?"

Well, here it was, the moment of untruth. I felt as if I were sweating inside. I was hoping the sweat wasn't seeping through my clothes. Hundley and the General were looking at me intently, not a sign of any emotion showing on either man's face. And suddenly, without any warning, my little imp was on my shoulder, laughing his butt off. I said to myself, "Self, you have just signed your own death warrant." It had suddenly occurred to me that by making the summer job so important, I forgot that I had told Hundley that I worked every summer for my dad. I was certain he was aware, so the General must be on that same wavelength. I studied the men's faces quickly, but saw not a sign I could recognize on either one. Even though I was completely dressed, I felt suddenly naked. I was in serious trouble. My heart rate was higher than high, and my mind was racing around like a trapped animal, looking for an escape route, but unable to find one.

The crazy thought that came to my mind had no relationship to what was happening here, but somehow supplied the answer. I remembered the only time my dad ever spanked me. I had done something bad. I had stolen a box of caps, and been caught with them. I guess I was six. Dad made me return them, which was total embarrassment. He then spanked me with his hand, but hard enough to make me cry. When I had stopped sobbing, and was getting over hating him for the moment, he calmly looked at me and said, "The spanking was not for what you did, even though stealing is a sin. The spanking was for lying to me about it." He continued,

70

"Stealing is something you can stop doing, but lying is something else. Once you begin to do that, you are doomed forever, because it never stops. The truth, son, always tell the truth, it will be your best friend, even though at times it will seem not." He walked out of the room, leaving me with my thoughts. My thoughts at the time were, "Phew, I got away with that one cheaply, my butt doesn't even hurt." That was the day, by the way, that I met my little imp for the first time.

I hadn't thought of dad's words again until this moment. And, trapped as I was, they comforted me, and seemed to strengthen me for the disaster I just knew would follow.

I stood up, facing the General and said, "Sir, my father never owned a tackle shop, he's a butcher." I went on, looking at Hundley and continued, "I'm sorry I lied to you, Sergeant Hundley. I guess I was just trying to take advantage of an opportunity, and I'm ready to accept any punishment I deserve." It seemed as if I were standing for hours, though in reality it was only minutes. Both men were silent, and showed zero emotion. That was scary. I expected to be escorted out of the room, and without passing Go, be sent directly to jail. Instead, this is what I got.

"Sit down, soldier," came the command from the General. And sit down I did, and hard. Then, as I listened in awe, in the calmest voice I ever heard, he said, "I've known thousands of men like you. Men that learned how to survive in the streets. I have pinned medals on their shirts, I have watched them die, and they turn out to be the best damned soldiers I have ever had the privilege of commanding. They have won battles for me." Calmly, he continued with, "And so, based on those men that came before you, you get that proverbial second chance. I advise you to use it wisely. Now, I want you to tell me exactly what motivated you to make up this colossal story. I understand your survival mentality, so I'm sure there is some underlying reason." He finished by taking off his wristwatch, placing it on his desk where he could see the face, and said, "You have ten minutes."

The fat was in the fire, and I had no other way out. I related the story of my arrival in Bremerhaven, the greeting from Steinholtz, and everything that followed. The ten minutes were up before I completed my story, and I was abruptly stopped, in the middle of a sentence. The only thought I had was that this is where the army takes care of its own, and I was going to jail, or worse. I was wrong.

The General was emotionless the whole time I was speaking, though I thought I saw a slight sneer on Hundley's face. The General made it almost ceremonial, the putting on of his wrist watch. He never took his eyes off of me. I couldn't recall my thoughts or emotions at that moment if my life depended on it. I was paralyzed in mind and body. And the General just kept staring at me. Not smiling, not grimacing, just staring right through me. Then he drew in a deep breath, and directed his gaze at Hundley.

"Sergeant Hundley, take Private Tinney downstairs, and get him to help you unpack and restock your entire inventory. I want it completed today, no matter how many hours you have to put in. I want you to spend your last two weeks here, trying to teach this young man how to run the thing without a single hitch, ever." He looked directly at me and then, speaking in fluent German, asked me if I was ready to take on this piece of cake. I responded as best I could, in the same language, and seeing his smile, I knew I had just passed the most important test I had ever unwittingly taken.

Hundley was all business, from that moment until two weeks later when it was time to ship back to the States. He was a merciless task master. My work days were long, often stretching into the wee hours of the next. Many meals were missed, and through it all, Hundley did what was necessary to drum his total experience into my head in two weeks. He was not unfriendly, but he made no attempt at being anything more than an instructor. I was always "Private," and he was always "Sarge."

Steinholtz must have been ordered to lay off of me, and not to assign me any duty. On several occasions, however, he looked at me and winked as if he had a secret we both were in on. A couple of days before Hundley was to leave, Steinholtz approached me and said, "Your protection is leaving soon, and then it will be my turn." Ratting someone out was a thing you did not do in the street, that being an unspoken code. You just either took care of things yourself, or were joined by friends that would help. Since none of the above was available to me, I ratted him out, big time. That morning, when I saw Hundley, I asked if it were possible for me to speak to the General. "Why?" he asked. When I explained what had happened, he said, "That won't be necessary. I'll take care of it personally." Not another word was spoken about the incident, as we dug back into the task at hand.

On Hundley's last day, he informed me that I was to pack my personal stuff and move into the single officer's barracks. He gave me my room assignment, and let me know I was still to take my meals with the enlisted men. Nothing else was said on the subject. The next day, Hundley was gone. Disappeared. No good-bye, no good luck, no handshake, no job well done. He just wasn't there. I wondered whether ratting out Steinholtz to the General two weeks before had anything to do with his cool attitude toward me, or perhaps he was just a good soldier, performing a job he was ordered to do. Well, he did one helluva job, and got me as ready as I could possibly be to run the rod and gun club.

For the next four weeks things went along without a hitch, and I was really getting to enjoy my status. My customers ran the gamut of rank from lowly buck private to highly commissioned officers and warrant officers. First names were most frequently used, rank being left outside the door.

Our commonality was the outdoors, and outdoor speak was more important than rank. I got way too comfortable with that, and as a result, was ordered to report to the General.

"I've had a complaint lodged against you," he sternly addressed me. "More than one officer has told me that you call them by their first names while in the BOQ." He went on to say, "and this morning, a second lieutenant, who will remain unnamed, complained that you did not salute him when you saw him in the bathroom." His stern look and piercing stare notwithstanding, I just couldn't hold it in. I burst into laughter, and before I could pull myself together and apologize, I found the General not only enjoying my uproarious state, but joining me in laughing at the ridiculous situation. When we finally pulled it together, he got serious again, and said, "Tinney, you're doing a good job, and I'm satisfied I made a sound decision about you. However, this thing in the BOQ has got to be solved, so I'm having orders cut to have you live on the economy, and draw a per diem. That will solve the BOQ problem, and also allow you to meet people that can perhaps help our fishing situation." And so a small apartment in Salzburg, in a building occupied by military families, was arranged for. I moved in that very evening. My experiences there might draw the attention of a clever movie-maker, but more of that at another time.

The fishing situation the General mentioned was complex. Anyone could own a license to fish in public waters, like the river that ran through the middle of town, or get away places reserved for military personnel on leave. However, it was restricted to public waters, of which there were not many. In many cases, the best fishing was to be found on waterways that flowed through privately owned estates, and required a signed, daily permit to use them. The Austrians were very strict on that point, and since Americans were not very well thought of by the landed gentry, permits were hardly ever given, no matter what the promise of payment might be. Money was definitely not the problem.

Because I spoke the language, and because I had friends that didn't mind introducing me favorably to other Austrian nationals, I was able to have some small degree of success in opening up a few new fishing areas for GI's to utilize.

It was during the first few months of my living in town when I met the Baron. I vowed then, and will forever honor the vow, never to disclose the circumstances under which our first meeting took place. We were obviously in a place where we would both ought not to have been. Although we arrived separately, and unknown at the time to each other, we wound up leaving hurriedly in each other's company.

Funny how fate works. In defense of both the Baron and myself, against any dirty minds out there, neither wine nor women were part of the equation. Lets just say it was a sports venue that was not favored by either the Austrian or American governments, and let it go at that.

Baron Theadore Kramer-Klett Von Aschau and I quickly became good friends. I was often a dinner guest at his palatial home, centered on his enormous estate. The Baron had the best trout fishing stream in all of Austria, and a fischmeister that would shoot, on the spot, any one who dared to fish without a written permit. I was given such a permit and, when not alone, enjoyed fly fishing with my new friend on several occasions. Because he so diligently managed his trout population, it was a rule of thumb that any trout of eighteen inches or more that was caught had to be kept for dinner that evening. All smaller fish were to be released. The thinking was that the larger fish cannibalized the smaller ones, and were thus a detriment to that environment. We had several good trout dinners. I never once asked the Baron if he would open up the stream to American soldiers, I knew it would be out of the question, and would jeopardize our budding friendship.

One morning, while fishing alone, I caught a beautiful

brown trout that weighed close to eight pounds. The Baron was away for a couple of weeks and not available for a trout dinner, though he would have loved to have seen the end of one of his cannibals. I took the fish back to my apartment and kept it in the refrigerator overnight. I transferred it to the refrigerator at the rod and gun club the next morning, and offered it to the General when he stopped by to make his usual morning call before going up to his office. He was delighted at the prospect of having his cook prepare the fish, and invited a couple of his staff to join him for lunch. I was not included as an invitee. Our relationship, though friendly, was strictly based on military code. He was the General and I was the private, and that kept us miles apart socially. I have always wondered what it might have been like if our friendship were ever allowed to develop under more normal circumstances.

It was probably two days later when it was announced that General "Hap" Arnold was to visit our Post for a couple of days. Most of the Post personnel were to be on maneuvers, and the high potentates were coming from other stations around Europe to act as observers. General Hoye announced that his friend "Hap" was bringing his fly rod, and expected me to take him to the spot where I caught that huge trout. And since I had disclosed the location when I had given him the fish, he knew darned well where it had been caught. To his credit, he had never pushed me regarding my not being able to turn the Baron's mind in favor of opening up his trout stream for military use. He was, however, pretty emphatic about my pulling this one-time favor off, and let me understand that he was, of course, counting on me. I needed a pipe-fitter to help me ease the pressure he laid on my shoulders.

Even though I waited until Baron Ted had had a good meal and copious amounts of wine, and was in as good and friendly a mood as I had ever seen him, his "Nein," shook the goblets on the table, and made the wall tapestries sway as if in the wind.

"Nein, Nein, Nein," echoed through every corner of the room. The waiter, and the cook and his wife seemed paralyzed with fear as they entered the room, to see what was going on. The Baron went into a frenzy of conversation that was so angry, and so fast, that I had a hard time understanding all but the swear words. When the storm finally blew over, he was red-faced and exhausted. He was also apologetic, explaining that I was not "one of those." I didn't understand what one of "those" was, but I didn't ask. I didn't have much choice but to continue to try and get his favor on this. When he finally saw how persistent I was, the good Baron became the best negotiator I have ever known. The final bargain allowed me to bring General Arnold for one day only. I was never to ask again to bring someone, even if it were God.

The cost? Well, I can only hint, because it was not perfectly legal at the time, but it had something to do with a Browning Sweet Sixteen, and a twelve gauge over and under. Because the Browning factory in Liege, Belgium was not yet up to full production, those items were scarce, at any price. The story of how I dealt with that will never be told.

General Arnold and his driver picked me up at my apartment, an hour before daylight, on the appointed fishing day. The General refused my invitation to come in for coffee, saying he had had a breakfast prepared that we could eat on the way. He had actually brought breakfast for me. He was dressed in civilian clothes, as one might expect. His driver however, brought back shiny memories of Smythe.

The conversation over the next hour was completely un-military, save for the fact that the ground rules laid out to me were to address him as "sir." Had anyone listened in, they might have felt I was being super-respectful to my dad or grand-dad. We talked of many things, but mostly about the spot we were going to fish, and the man who owned it.

When we arrived at the spot, the Baron and his fishmeister were awaiting us, both dressed in waders and carrying fly rods. The Baron paired himself off with General Arnold, leaving me to fish with Fritz, with whom I had fished before, on several occasions. He was good company, but still I was a bit disgruntled at the pairings and just a little apprehensive of how the Baron would act, given his recent coming unglued over the General. The plan was for each pair to walk about a mile and a half in opposite directions, and fish our way back to the starting point, which should take us until lunch break. Fritz and I caught several nice trout, all of which we released. When we met up with our other pair, they were happily engaged in conversation (in German) and eager to talk about their experience. The General had caught three "keeper fish," which were immediately turned over to Fritz to have prepared for dinner. The cook arrived with a sumptuous lunch to be served stream-side, after which Ted excused himself, leaving me and General Arnold to fish the rest of the afternoon together.

The General decided that since the section that he had been fishing produced the biggest fish, that was where we would go. I suggested a section we had not fished, and one where the fish I had given to General Hoye came from. It didn't take two seconds for him to back off his decision in favor of my suggestion, and off we went.

I would have been perfectly content to let the General fish while I observed, but he wouldn't hear of it. We swapped places the rest of the afternoon. In other words, he got to fish one run thoroughly, and I got to fish the next. He was better than good with a fly rod and not only held his own, but if we were counting, I think he would have been ahead. When we reached the hole where I had caught my monster, it just happened to be his turn. We discussed the fly I had used to catch the big trout, it being a weighted nymph. The hole was fairly deep, and the fly had to be presented in a way as to make it go down into the depths of the hole. The General opted to put on a huge streamer, weighted with a small split shot sinker. His reasoning was, "If there is another big one living there, he might want some meat on his dinner table." I could see how Hap Arnold was responsible for helping win the war, he hadn't made a wrong decision all afternoon. This one was to be his best.

I won't poeticize his approach, his delivery, his focus or his hook set. I will simply say it was all picture-perfect. His calmness at handling the huge fish that took his streamer on the very first cast was awesome. However, his demeanor when we found the fish was too big to get into either of our nets, was something else again. I actually witnessed this man-among-men turn into a stammering, stuttering, excitable teenager, experiencing something wonderful for the very first time in his life. We chased that fish up and down the river for almost a half hour, before we were able to slide it up on the bank. For that half hour, the lowly private and the much-decorated General were transformed into two kids, splashing water all over each other, totally lost in the experience of complete joy.

We sat silently for a while, staring at the fish. When the silence was finally broken, the General said, "I can't believe it, Stu, I just can't believe it." I was quickly aware of the fact that General "Hap" Arnold (SIR) had called me by my first name. It sent a chill through my body that still occurs whenever I recall the incident. Like right this very minute.

Of course, the trip was over. When you reach the top of the mountain, there's nothing to do but climb down. There was no reason to fish any longer, since nothing we could do would top what we had already done. We decided not to wait for the Baron's driver to pick us up at the appointed time. We opted to walk the two miles back to the house. It was a fine walk, the conversation being totally about his catching that one fish.

Ted came down the front walk to meet us, having been made aware of our approach. He got all excited when he saw the fish, and immediately shook the General's hand, throwing his arm over his shoulder and escorting him into the house. We ceremoniously weighed the fish, and got Ted to admit that twelve pounds was the largest ever caught in his stream. And his record-keeping went back three generations of his family stewarding the river and its trout population.

The General graciously offered to add his trout to the dinner fare, and Ted just as graciously refused. "You must take this great fish home with you," he said, and immediately ordered that the fish be iced down to keep it in good condition until the General could transport it back to wherever he decided.

The General's driver returned in time to be invited to join us for dinner. The General was dressed in civilian clothes, and ordered his driver to do the same. For the rest of the evening we were just four guys enjoying good food, good wine, and good company. Lots of tales were swapped, in both German and English. Ted spoke excellent English, but preferred his native tongue. Both the General and his driver were up to the task. Ted's speaking English, though obvious only to me, was his way of showing acceptance. When it was time to leave, Ted said something that blew my socks off. "General Arnold, sir, you are welcome to return any time you wish. Just let my friend Stu know when you have such a desire, and we will arrange for your stay."

The trip back to my apartment brought me back to the reality of my position of PFC. The General was back to giving orders to his driver, in a very proper and military way. His discussions with me were suddenly on a different level, one of commander and order-taker. Certainly cooler than I had been experiencing all day. When we arrived at my apartment, the General got out of the car and walked with me to the front steps. Out of hearing distance from his driver, he shook my hand and said, "Stu, I want to thank you for one of the happiest days I have experienced in a long, long time." He went on to say, "Friends like the Baron are priceless, you do whatever you have to do to retain that friendship; he thinks the world of you. Those kind of relationships make America look good, and we certainly need more of that." He ended by saying that he was going to have that great fish mounted and hung in his office, as a constant reminder of the day.

His back was turned to me as he headed back to the car. The words came out of my mouth quite unexpectedly, and I was instantly ready to blame my imp for the indiscretion. "Hap," I said, "you turned out to be one helluva guy." He stopped in his tracks, turned his whole body to face me, and did something that made me know that it was really Generals and not sergeants who won the battles. He looked intently into my face, smiled a bright smile, threw me a casual salute, got casually into his staff car, and drove casually out of my life. But never out of my memory.

That night we had a small party at my place. Invited guests were all my Austrian friends who worked on the Post. I guess we were about twenty strong. It was Peter's idea to celebrate the sudden disappearance of Porky Pig and Piss Ant. As great a communication system as these folks seemed to have, no one, including me, had the slightest idea of where they had disappeared to. Hope sprang eternal, and each of us had an outrageous idea of where we hoped that they had been sent. Lots of beer was consumed, lots of laughter was shared, and it was made clear to me that everyone present just knew that I had much to do with getting rid of that pair of nogoodnicks, that were despised by all, for one reason or another. Nothing I could say in the way of denial could sway them from their hero worship. Finally, I gave in to the spirit of the party and took credit for their guaranteed discomfort, wherever they were. I silently wished the worst for them, and after fifty years, still hope that they reaped what they had sown. I guess that's my imp talking, but this time he and I are in full agreement.

The rest of my time in the service created a new story almost every day. My discovery of very talented Katarina Valenti, the deal I made with Mussolini's ammunition maker for shotgun shells for our skeet shoots, and the unreal deal I was involved in with Browning guns, are only a few. An aborted attempt to crash Grace Kelly's wedding and saving a friend from diving off the top of the Eiffel Tower. Some more "Army" tales will appear in this book; others I'm afraid, will have to wait their turn to be told.

The Austrians got their wish when an official peace treaty was signed, and all American troops were ordered to leave the country. Our occupation was officially over. Closing up the rod and gun club was like burying a friend, but the wild party we threw in a rented castle made it not only a bit easier, but created no less than ten hilarious stories to tell.

I only had a few months left to serve when all of this came down, and with not too many places to assign me, I wound up being a disc jockey at the army-run radio station in Karlsruhe. After being discharged, I became a European vagrant, so to speak. I wandered around Europe for more than a year, meeting new people, having great adventures, and supplying fish for some of the most famed tables imaginable. But that, too, is another story.

I don't know if what my family wished for me – the Army making a man out of me – ever came true. I do know this, though – it certainly set the stage for the play that has been my life.

6

FRANKIE AND JOHNNY WERE LOVERS

On a scale of one to ten, most folks would agree that Rudolph Valentino had at least the reputation for being the number one lover in the history of the world. On that same scale of one to ten, he would robably rate a low five when compared to my Army buddies, Frankie Colletti and Johnny Heinz. Whenever the three of us were on the town, mommas were wise to keep their little girls at home. Not that we ever meant any harm, quite the opposite. We were just three single guys, back in the 1950s, enjoying a European sexual freedom that we had not know back in the States. During the process, each of us learned to accept women as equals, another thing that was obviously not a life lesson to be learned in the States at the time.

Three is really a strange number when it comes to searching out female company. Usually, girls traveled in even numbers. Most of the time it was two, sometimes it would be four. Rarely would it be three. And the agreement between us was "all for one and one for all." If we couldn't hook up with three ladies, we would enjoy our own company for that particular day or evening. That wasn't really as strange a pact as one might think, since it was born not of loyalty, but rather necessity. I had the constant availability of an army jeep, which was at my disposal twenty-four seven. I used it to ferry myself from my apartment in town, to the rod and gun club. I also used it on my forays around the country, to find new fishing spots for my customers. When my mileage records were checked, it made it look as if I were doing a lot of "foraying." And in truth, I was able to discover, and make available, several new areas. We could cram six of us in the jeep, so it was an important part of our social life.

On the other hand, we had the use of John's MG touring car. It was a sweet little convertible with a small back seat. I always rode in the rear, since Frankie and Johnny were too big to even get a leg back there, let alone either of their entire bodies. We only used the MG when we went on ski vacations, and would be staying overnight at a hotel or a ski lodge.

Frankie Colletti was the handsomest human being I ever knew. He had a movie star face, blessed with ice blue eyes, a mouth full of straight white teeth, a smile that would melt away any opposition or inhibition, and an athlete's body, whose tightness could not be hidden even by loose clothing. Men thought he was handsome, women used the word "pretty." Put that whole package together with a personality that indicated a shyness and vulnerability, and you have the perfect girl machine. He was like a magnet to women of every age and size. And he adored and revered women. As far as a friend was concerned he, like me, was a street kid, and understood what loyalty meant. Frank was from Patterson, New Jersey. He came from a large and loving Italian family, that wrote often and sent many care packages. He was a home-town football hero, voted the man most likely to succeed. His only confusion at the time was one he shared with me: "What will we be when we grow up?"

Johnny was absolutely the opposite of Frank when it came to physical appearance. Standing next to six foot plus Colletti, both John and I looked almost midget-like. John was fat, but did not give the appearance of being obese. To tell you the truth, I couldn't have carried one of his arms or legs around for very long. He was a heavy dude, but could move as quickly as was necessary, drunk or sober. John was the only one of the three of us that ever drank enough to get tipsy. And he was a hilarious comedian, drunk or sober. He was the absolute king of one-liners, and could make up stories that had women laughing or crying, or even both at the same time. What he lacked in looks, he made up for in personality. Women seemed to want to cuddle him. John grew up in Indiana, where his family owned several night clubs. He threw money around with great disrespect for its value, indicating that, unlike his two friends, he had grown up in a privileged atmosphere. Though both Frankie and I were sticklers for everyone paying their own way, neither of us minded the many times when Johnny picked up the tab. Who were we to disappoint a friend? And besides, the allowance he got from home each month doubled the pay of all three of us.

Unfortunately, I could not boast of having any of the attributes of my two friends, even though I spoke the language better than they. Their methods of communication seemed so much more effective. That is, until the music started. Once I was able to get on a dance floor, the longest waiting line was always heaviest on my side of the room. My youngest sister, Myra, had seen a need to spend as much time as was needed to give me some sort of a chance at not being a wall flower. We wore the old Victrola out, practicing fox trot, rhumba, tango, and the jitterbug, which was the dance craze at the time. Though my routines with Marcia, back in the States, were built mostly around the sensuous Latin American beat, it was the jitterbug that the European ladies loved the most. I guess it's correct to say I jitterbugged my way clear across the continent. Any place we got the opportunity to go to a dance hall, it was my job to see to it that my two pals were introduced to available females.

Other than that scenario, it would be an honest

mistake for one to think that Frank, with his good looks, would be the point man. Frank turned out to be truly as shy as he appeared. Once formally introduced, he was comfortable, but until then, he might as well have been on a different planet. Women came up to introduce themselves to him by the droves, but he was unable to even return their greetings. Most of the time, they walked away either angry or sad. But once he was introduced by a third party, he immediately came to life, losing all shyness and inhibitions.

As it turned out, the most unlikely of the three of us wound up being the most successful at introductions. And his money-spending habit had nothing to do with that success. John just had the personality of an on-stage emcee. He said funny things, had a smile that would attract folks like moths to bright lights, and a sureness of self that made him a force to deal with. He was always positive, he was always happy, and people just wanted to be in his circle of light. And he knew how and when to either share his space, or deny same. He knew where he was at all times (except when tipsy) and he knew what he was going to be when he grew up. A wealthy night club owner, that was his future, and that was what he wanted, only not just yet. He was the only one of the three of us that knew he was going to Europe, even before he entered the service. He was taking his father's advice about sowing his wild oats before he was entrusted with one of the family businesses. He was definitely taking parental advice seriously.

Whenever we went on a ski trip, John was the one we turned loose in the lounge or bar. He was not the least bit interested in skiing, so that shoe fit pretty well. While Frankie and I wore ourselves out on the slopes, John was working his magic back at the lodge. The first time we stayed in Berchtesgarden, he hooked us up with triplets visiting from China. The odds of finding triplets were probably like one in a million, but the odds of finding triplets from another continent could hardly be calculated. But, that was our pal

Johnny, to whom the impossible was only a curve in the road, to be negotiated. Johnny was a genius at negotiating curves. Our short time with our three fortune cookies was more fun than a barrel of monkeys. They spoke neither English nor German, and we spoke absolutely no Chinese. Sign language seemed to suffice as far as communication was concerned. Everything was working out perfectly – that is until dad, who turned out to be an envoy on a military visit, showed up. Much Chinese was spoken, stiff fingers were pointed at us, fortune cookies disappeared, followed by an angry father. We howled when John said, "Funny thing about Chinese food, fifteen minutes after you leave the table, you're still hungry."

Frankie and I met when he came into the rod and gun club, seeking information on a particular rifle scope he wanted to buy. At that time, German-made scopes and binoculars were supposed to be the best in the world, and I had an inside track at procuring them. Because we came from the same state, it was easy for us to engage in back-home talk. I had relatives who lived close to where he grew up, and though he did not know them, promised to visit when he got back home. He was scheduled to be discharged several months before me. We took an easy liking to each other, and promised to get together sometime to either ski or fish. On a lark one day, I asked him if he would like to go on a "foray" with me, to scope out potential fishing areas. He of course agreed readily, but asked if his buddy John could go along. And that's how simple it is to meet special folks, when you least expect it.

With about five hours of daylight left, we began our drive into the countryside, to check out a particular stream I had heard of. It took us almost two hours to get to the spot, during which time I got to know my two new friends a little better. I was enjoying what I was learning. At my instruction, they were dressed in casual civvies, clean-shaven with combed hair. It, I learned, was a show of respect to let the local folks see us at our best. They were told, when we were negotiating for the use of the place, I was to do all the talking. They were also warned of the possibility that the land owner might not even invite them to do anything but wait in the jeep. And that was the case. Not only did the land owner have them stay in the jeep, he kept me there as well.

Normally, these people showed tolerance and the best possible manners. This fellow obviously had a personal axe to grind, and though he listened to my proposal, would not give an inch. I was not at liberty to offer him too much, but I think even if I could have offered more, he would still have remained negative toward the proposal. We spoke for the better part of half an hour, but always wound up with a resounding no. There was no way he was going to allow a bunch of strangers free rein on his beloved trout stream, particularly if they were Americans. He did apologize in some fashion, assuring me that no offense was being offered, and like most folks I met in this country, thanked me for taking the time to learn to speak their language properly. My two friends listened silently, as I had instructed, offering not one word of conversation. The landowner never acknowledged that he was even aware that they were there. He did not look at them, he did not speak to them. Just at the moment I was ready to extricate us from this impossible situation, trying to leave as good a taste as I could, Johnny broke his silence by asking a question.

In his best German (which was laughable) he asked, "Where can I go to the bathroom?" The land owner stepped back, a surprise and amazed look on his face. He looked as if he was noticing a picnic pest for the first time. He stared at John like he was looking at a two-headed monster, but was able to ask John to repeat what he said. John, of course, by this time was eager to make a second request, adding a word he had left out. "Where can I go to the bathroom, PLEASE."

The land owner hesitated for only a second before he

gave John a brief, but easy to understand answer. At least it was easy for me to understand. Neither of my two companions got the full drift of it, at the moment. As he turned his back on us, walking swiftly toward his house, it was obvious that we were dismissed. Before I started the engine, Frank spoke up and asked, "What was he so miffed about, John only wanted to use the bathroom." I didn't understand everything he said, did you?"

I was close to cracking up at the moment, and it took a few seconds for me to stifle it before I answered. When John asked where he could go to the bathroom, the answer had been, "in your pants." I wasn't quite certain, but I thought I had heard the word "idiot" in there somewhere.

As understanding and sympathetic a man as Frankie was, he could not stifle his laughter. It must have been catching, because I broke into loud laughter myself. You would suppose the indignity of his situation would make him angry, but he joined us in laughing at the absolute ridiculousness of his situation, pleading with us to "please find me a bathroom."

I had noticed a sign announcing a nearby town, less than two kilometers away. I assured John that we would be able to make it to the town in time, and while Frankie was still roaring with laughter, with tongue in cheek, I asked John to "hold his water."

So it was that we discovered Durmesheim, a little town that would become my own personal Brigadoon. For those uninitiated who have not the foggiest idea what Brigadoon means, I offer only that you try to find the old classic movie of the same name. In the movie, Gene Kelly and Cyd Charise created some of the most lovely, classic dance routines ever filmed. It was the story of a magical town that awakened for one long day every hundred years. The people never changed, were always happy and grateful for what they had, and never wanted to leave. Other than the hundred year thing, Durmesheim turned out to be exactly that kind of place. Of course, it didn't start exactly like that.

We drove into town unnoticed, since it was late in the afternoon, a time when most folks were sitting down to dinner. We immediately spotted the building so familiar in most small towns, that was the combination inn, restaurant, bar, dance hall, and meeting place. John bailed out before I came to a full stop, and disappeared through the entrance way. Of course, one could not drive an obviously military vehicle into any town without getting the feeling of being watched. Like in old westerns, the new arrivals always seemed to be looking up at windows to see if anyone was spying on them. So it was that we cautiously approached the door our companion had just busted his way through. It was obvious that John had found the herren's room, since the door was still slightly ajar. It was also obvious that we were no longer unnoticed. Three couples were dining, three single men sat at the bar, and five old men were sitting at a table, playing dominoes. There was a man and a woman behind the bar, and two waitresses working the dining area. Soft music was playing. Thirty-six pairs of eyes immediately turned toward us, and then, as if upon being signaled, immediately ignored us. No one nodded, no one offered a greeting, and no one smiled. I had learned that this was typical in towns where Americans were not appreciated. I was certain there was at least one ugly American tale to be told here. I was also certain that I did not want to hear it. We only wanted John to use the bathroom, perhaps purchase a cold drink, and head back to camp.

When John came out of the bathroom, smiling that smile of, "I'm going to live again," we walked up to the bar. In my most polite German, I ordered three beers. "We're out," was the response to my order. "Well," I continued, "could we order something to eat?"

"The restaurant is closed," came the reply.

Both Frank and John fully understood the words and

the implications. It didn't take a rocket scientist to recognize that we were not wanted here. Seemed a bit unfair, and a bit foolish to us, but then we did not know the reason for the cold attitude. We quickly agreed among ourselves that we would leave, being as polite as we possibly could, not wanting to add any more fuel to this fire.

Just before leaving, I stepped over to the table where the old men were playing dominoes. Funny I thought, how the gathering of old men everywhere I had witnessed it, had a sameness. In many places in the States, I had seen groups of old men sitting in a park, or in a town square whittling and sharing stories of family, friends, and past and present events. On city streets, in Italian neighborhoods, they could be found playing bocce. In France, it was a gathering around a table adorned with more than one wine bottle. And here in Austria and Germany, it was dominoes and beer steins. And every place you witnessed it, there was a sureness of self, a confidence of being, and a joy of life so evident, that it captured immediate attention, and taught the lesson that this was one of the best stops on the road of life.

None of the five seemed to pay any attention to me, though they were certainly aware of my presence. They were obviously playing for "loser buys a round," and were obviously not just starting. From the alcoholic condition apparent, no one was the champion. I had learned to play dominoes with several of my uncles at our once-a-month family circle meetings. I was certainly a better poker player, but every once in a while, I was able to win. Prior to my approaching the table, there had been much conversation going on. That all ceased while I stood and watched. I couldn't help feeling a warmth at the old folks gathering, even though we were being given the cold shoulder.

"Watching you gentlemen play gives me a feeling of being back home," I said. "Perhaps someday you would allow me to join you." It was a brash statement I knew, but it was really sincere. As I turned to leave, one of the men stood up and said, "Soldier, I have to go to the men's room, perhaps you will finish this game for me." I was stunned, but could not refuse. As he was leaving the table, with the aid of his walking stick, he turned to me with the look of a sly elf, and said, "Now remember, if you lose, you have to buy the beer." I knew instantly that I had been taken in, and that the hand I was about to play was a sure loser. I took the loss graciously, as did the recipients of the free beer. I even ordered one for the man whose game I finished.

They allowed me to lose two more games, and during that time, peppered me with questions about my family and my home. At the end of that final game, I was dismissed. It seems as if they were tired of "taking advantage of a beginner." I laughed along with them, but as I arose, expecting to be leaving with my friends, the eldest gentleman said, "You ought to try the schnitzel here, I don't think you'll find any better." Intent on their game, they made a special effort not to look at me.

I was kind of stunned, but turned to look at the owner/bartender, who simply nodded his approval. Neither John nor Frank had heard the old man's decision, and looked kind of perplexed when I said, "Sit down guys, it looks like we're staying for dinner." The rest became part of the three of our histories.

As usual, my friends worked their magic on all the women present. The cook, the waitresses, and even the three women dining with their husbands, came under their spell. It didn't take long before tables were moved together, and a party was started. It never took very long to get up a party in Austria or Germany, if you happened to be in a place where you were accepted. That all of a sudden was the case, and I can only guess it was as a result of the old men making the decision on behalf of the town folks. One thing was for absolute certain, it was the best darned schnitzel I had ever eaten.

We learned that day that Durmesheim had a large and public schwimbaad. In our lingo that's a huge public swimming pool. It provided both recreation and revenue for the town. It was a popular tourist stop, and everyone seemed to be proud of it.

When we finished eating dinner, the three guys at the bar insisted on buying our dessert. I was never certain how many beers were brought to the table, all I know is that we never paid for them. When we left the place, it was with a warm invitation to return, and just as warm a promise that we would. And we did, the very next weekend.

Being adopted by a town was a strange feeling for the three of us, but that's exactly what occurred. It was obvious, and it was unanimous, that we were to be the three "token Americans" that would be welcome here. The Burgemeister (mayor) did ask us, though, with a hat in hand politeness, to please not bring any one else with us. We were quick to agree, and never broke that promise.

Throughout that summer we spent many happy days in the pool. We became honorary uncles, adopted brothers, and invitees to every celebration that was planned. That included weddings, anniversaries, funerals, family get-together parties, and a multitude of other social events. Many of these parties were held at either the pool or the Inn. Needless to say, we ate much food and drank copious amounts of beer. We were three young men that had it made in the shade, and were enjoying every second of it.

Through those months, John and Frank shared their time with several young girls. They felt it was impolite to keep themselves to themselves. To their credit, they were not kiss and tell kind of guys, and most of the stories we shared with each other centered around the spectacular kindnesses we were shown individually and collectively.

As for myself, I had met Anneliese, and the many times I visited her town, I managed to put myself in her company. She had a boyfriend who was away for the summer, and remained loyal to him. Yet, when the music played, she wanted to dance with no one but me. We walked countless miles, hand in hand, discussing every subject under the sun. Up until that time, my opinion had been that you could never have a woman as a friend. I have been glad throughout my entire life to have learned differently.

The biggest festival in most German-speaking countries is Fasching. It is, for all wants and purposes, akin to Mardi Gras, without the floats. It's a beer festival, a food festival, and a reason to celebrate life festival. The only rule is that all inhibitions must be set aside, and if you don't want to have a happy time, you better stay home. In a word, it's absolutely wild. There was never any question as to where the three of us would be during that year's Fasching.

It was during that Fasching that the legend of "Fat Tuesday" was born, and our friend Johnny Heinz was immortalized. I don't think he appreciated it much at the time, but I'm almost certain that recalling the incident over ensuing years brought a smile to his face. Every time I think about it, I can feel my face stretch into a silly grin. I know that recounting the tale, I'll have to stop typing more than once, so that I can enjoy the mental image I've carried for almost fifty years.

The evening started as it usually did, calmly. Much home cooking, much beer drinking, many ribald stories, much hand shaking, much hugging, much gaiety, and much beer drinking. And much more beer drinking. Loud music, polkas, waltzes, and in honor of me, and the pleasure of the ladies in the crowd, several tunes to jitterbug by. That was particularly fun for me, since many couples in town had adopted the dance, and I was no longer the only one on the floor. At first they emulated my style, but eventually got brave enough to try it on their own, the results being much fun to watch. Since Anneliese's friend was in town for the holiday, I was able to dance with a lot more ladies than I was used to. I was passed around from partner to partner, and was enjoying the heck out of my status as the Fred Astaire of Durmesheim. Oh, right!

At some point during the evening's festivities, which included much toasting, someone decided it was time to toast we three. Frank was easy to find, as was I. John had disappeared, and no manner of hooting and hollering could bring him into the room. A search party was formed, and assignments were handed out by the Burgemeister. The ladies were to search the men's room, while the men searched the ladies room. The cooks were to search the kitchen. A group was sent to the pool to make sure he hadn't fallen in. In other words, a semi-drunk bunch of vigilantes was on a treasure hunt. What fun.

As usual, we had driven John's little MG to town. Early on, we had learned that the jeep brought unhappy memories to some of the folks here. In all the time we spent there, we never inquired as to what the problem was, and no one offered to tell us. To this day I remain curious, but firm in the knowledge that the decision not to tell us was a unanimous one, and probably a wise thing to do. We accepted that then, and I still accept it now.

After about a half hour of fruitless searching, a loud din arose from the parking area, which was a big empty field, about a block away from the Inn. "They're in the car," came the excited cry, followed by, "Come quickly, you have to see this." It was impossible for the huge crowd of people to approach John's tiny MG, as it was tucked between several other cars, making an approach by more than two or three people impossible.

The two or three people that were able to get close enough to see what was going on were babbling so fast it was impossible to understand. We heard the words "stuck," and "Greda, the Burgemeisters daughter." A call went out for people to move their autos so we could all get closer. That being accomplished, and John's car now being cleared enough for more people to see, this was the scenario.

It was difficult for Frank and me to comprehend that John had allowed Greda to drive his prized auto, but since she was in the driver's seat, we had to assume that's what had happened. Neither Frank or I ever drove the MG. John had obviously become a bit amorous after the car had been parked, and rolled over on top of the hapless girl to plant a kiss on her mouth. Somehow he had lost his balance or his footing, and got his big butt stuck under the steering wheel. Picture that scenario in the car, with at least a hundred folks well into their pints, surrounding said vehicle, and you have a sight destined to become a legend.

John was stuck so fast he could not move. Greda was screaming, "Get this pig off of me," and the crowd was howling good-naturedly, and arguing about what the best method would be to free the unhappy pair. Several strong men began to pull on John's arms, and when that produced no results, switched to his legs. That also brought only screams of agony from the car's inhabitants. One of the waitresses suggested that if we cut away his pants, perhaps that would create enough room for him to squeeze out from under the wheel. John protested, but to no avail. Several sharp knives were produced, and the owners gleefully took turns at de-pantsing poor John. All the while Greda's pleas permeated the air, only to be answered by her father's stern order to shut up and behave like a lady. Few of us in the crowd understood how that could be a possibility, and though we voiced our opinions, the Burgemeister stood firm in his instructions to his daughter.

Needless to say, cutting away Johns pants did not do the trick. Then one of the cooks came up with the idea to pour grease on John's butt, and then we could just slide him out. That seemed logical, so someone was sent to the kitchen to scout up a bunch of cooking oil. The cooks insisted that they did not want to use fresh oil, so they ordered oil that had been cooked with. And if it was hot, all the better, because it was determined that hot oil would probably get John to cooperate in a positive manner. You can see where this is going, it was positively insane, and more fun than any of us had had all year.

It was an awesome sight. John's super-sized buttocks glistening in the moonlight, hot grease running down both legs, and pooling on the floor at his feet. Still, all manner of tugging and shoving did not move his body one inch. Finally, with great oaths of protestation from John, a hacksaw was produced, and the steering column was sawed in half. With the wheel out of the way, we were able to roll John off of Gerda, thus freeing both of them. It took John a long time to catch his breath and regain his composure. It took Gerda only a second or two to get out of the car, straighten her dress and her hair, and ask if anyone had a cold beer. Everyone had a cold beer, and as if on command, raised their steins in a salute to John for accomplishing a feat that had never been seen or heard of before this night. They swore it would be a story that would bring many tourists to the town.

No one in town had a pair of pants that would fit John, but he agreed to wear a form-fitting skirt for the rest of the party, and made me and Frank promise to sneak onto the post and get him a pair of pants to put on before he passed the sergeant of the guard's station when returning to camp. Frank and I talked about leaving him in the woods in his skirt, but thought better of it. Our real concern was that his connections in Indiana would get even with us, and that was somewhere we definitely did not want to go.

When Fasching was over that year, John was presented with a formal proclamation. It allowed that each year at Fasching in Durmesheim, the first Tuesday would forever be known as "Fat Tuesday," in honor of John's magnificent greasy posterior, and the wonderful show he had put on for the benefit of all present. John took it well, and bought a keg of beer to cap off the celebration.

Two months later, John's service to his country came to an end. He got his orders to ship back to the states for his discharge. The entire town turned out at his farewell party. Even Gerda, who had been conspicuously missing for the past two months, came out of hiding to give him a farewell hug and kiss. The Burgemeister got drunk and cried, as did many other of our schwimbaad friends. It was a very touching farewell.

That farewell was repeated two months later, when it became Frank's turn to follow John back to the states. Though a happy event, as all parties in Durmesheim were, there was still a sense of somberness that one could feel, rather than sense. Frank got drunk for the first time ever. He laughed a lot, but he cried a lot, too. The people in this town had shown him great affection, and his honest emotional behavior indicated that the feeling was mutual. Not a soul, including me, was the least bit embarrassed by seeing this huge man in tears. And if the truth be known, he was not the only male in the bunch with wet eyes.

Before Frank left, we promised each other that when I returned back to the States, we would celebrate by picking a couple of weeks to spend together, fishing in Canada. Three weeks later, I got a letter from my favorite aunt and uncle, telling me that my friend had paid them a visit. Frankie had proven once again that street kids really knew how to keep their words.

Going to Durmesheim alone was indeed a sad state of affairs. All the folks in town, as well as myself, tried to maintain the old, free and happy spirit always present when there were three of us. Somehow, it just was not the same. I began to visit less frequently, and then not at all. The entire year I stayed in Europe after my discharge, I visited hundreds of cities, but never my Brigadoon.

During that year, a letter from Frank caught up with

me, detailing plans for his marriage. It said that if I could make it, a groomsman's monkey suit would be made available. I pulled every string I could think of, catching a flight back to New York, and was in time for the gala event. As handsome as Frank was, he seemed a shadow to the beauty of his new bride, Laurie. The wedding was a combination Italian/Greek Orthodox affair, that lasted almost two days. We were all exhausted when it was over, but I still drove the newlyweds to the airport, and saw them off on their honeymoon in Greece. When I picked them up at their hotel, Frank had to share with me a gift he had gotten in the mail. It was an ornate beer stein, hand painted, with the words Durmesheim on one side and Frank and Laurie on the other. We both stood in awe for a moment, more so because we could not understand how they could possibly have known. We agreed that it was "just more of that magic."

My flight arrangements had been for a return trip, so off I went to finish my European adventure. I thought often about returning to our little town for a visit, but though I was close many times, I always seemed to have some excuse not to go. Perhaps I felt that it had all been a dream, and it would not be there if I went back. I've heard, so often in my life, that there is no going back. Perhaps we should re-think that one. Perhaps we are cheating ourselves out of something wonderful.

As life continues, we set different roads to travel on than those we love. Sometimes the roads converge, and sometimes not. In this case, not.

I never heard from either Frank or John again, though I've made a few attempts to locate them. If either of you guys read this, I live in Columbia, Tennessee, and I'm in the phone book. And to steal a few words spoken by John F. Kennedy, when he visited Berlin, to all my old friends in my wonderful Brigadoon, "Ich bin eine Durmesheimer."

7

FESTIVAL OF EEL

The block was like a mini country club, and it was exclusive, too...sort of. If your name ended with a vowel, you were a charter member. Or, if it happened to end with *ein* or *berg*, and you shopped at Tabatchnik's Deli, you were also recognized as a member. Anyone else living on the block was eligible to participate in activities but would never get into the "inner circle." It was the times.

The block was actually three blocks, and for all wants and purposes could have formed the Italio/Israeli border. Everyone watched out for everyone. Kids coming home from school to homes of working parents were assigned to various families, to be cared for and watched until moms and dads got off from work. Offering to pay for that service was an insult. However, lots of pies and cakes changed hands. Food was more acceptable as a gift than money or anything wrapped in pretty paper.

The block was a living thing, with a life of its own. It felt the joy of births, the sadness of death, the happiness of a graduation or a return from service to one's country. Weddings were special, but no more special than anniversaries. Each of the things I've mentioned plus dozens more were cause for a "festival", or more specifically, a block party. No one organized one, no one was in charge, no one planned most of them, they just happened. Porches were set with tables and food and drink was available to everyone (on the block). Some of the festivals were named after holidays like Thanksgiving, Christmas or Easter. Special ones were done to re-celebrate the ending of WW II.

Tessie Malzone was the matriarch of the kitchen, and the odors coming from her house could make a person stop dead in their tracks. All the young girls on the block hung out there to learn the culinary secrets of the old country. Her husband Al had old country secrets also, but he did not choose to share them, though he was generous with the results. A dinner table at a block party was incomplete without an unmarked bottle of Al's basement brew. Al made the best wine in Monmouth County. It was allowable to make wine to be consumed by one's family, but no more. Al claimed the whole block as family and even allowed "outsiders" driving police cars to drop by for a laden brown paper bag. As I look back at those times when family meant so much more than today, I sometimes regret the rush to technological superiority where machine rules over common sense. The simple times ingrain themselves in heart and memory and, unlike machines, can never be unplugged.

The only splinter group (those not living on the block) were members of the mosquito fleet. Many of the members of that elite group of "nuts" lived on the block and paved the way for the acceptance of those of us who didn't. We all owned fourteen-foot aluminum boats, powered with small engines. We all dragged them across endless stretches of beach, to launch them into the surf when schools of stripers or blue fish were located within the limited reach of those boats. We had a communication system extraordinaire, a brotherhood to die for, and a competitive spirit that seemed to wash away the awesome danger involved in what we did.

The end result was that we made a few bucks selling fish to local hotels and markets as well as keeping "the block" supplied with fresh fish. Being accepted as a full fledged, card carrying member of the "block" I was entitled to all its benefits. Since, at the time, food, drink, pretty girls, fishing and partying were high on the priority list, membership in this exclusive club was easily accepted as part of the adventure that was my life. There'll be time for Mosquito Fleet tales, but for now, the tale of the eel continues.

The time was close to New Year's Day...every year. Preparations began a week earlier on the frozen ice of a nearby bay. Though the water was salt, every winter it froze over solid enough to walk on, and to catch eels through. Young men were not permitted to participate in the actual "catching" but were allowed to watch and learn. Young boys, however, were a necessary part of the ritual. It seems to me that the youngest catcher might have been in his mid-seventies. There were men on the ice well into their eighties and nineties. They were wrinkled, with skin like leather. They walked slowly but upright and proud. They smiled with their lips and their eyes and exuded an aura of health and well being. They were impervious to the cold and wet conditions and performed a physical feat that would be almost impossible for men half their ages. It was all in the technique.

They would fan out on the ice, find a likely spot and, with a hand-held axe, chop a hole that was a perfect fifteen-inch square. This was done without any measuring device other than eye. Each had a twelve-inch "gig" which was firmly attached to a pole of fifteen to eighteen feet in length. The gigs had eight or ten tines on them that were bent inward at the end. It created what looked like a hand with the fingers curled inward. It was how the eels were held.

The technique was to place the gig through the hole and push it down to the bottom, which was about three to four feet. Then, gently raising the pole up and down, forcing the gig into the silt-like bottom, the catchers felt for movement that was magically transmitted up the pole to their hands. When a signal was detected, the pole was raised hand over hand until the gig emerged, almost always with an eel. The eel was dumped on the ice, where he wriggled a bit and then almost immediately froze in place. It was the job of the young boys, pulling sleds with boxes mounted on them, to run from hole to hole, collecting the eels. The old men would laugh heartily as the boys slipped, slid, fell and got soaking wet. I supposed they were remembering when they were young and doing the same thing.

After concentrating on the area immediately beneath their feet, and getting no more messages, the catchers raised their hands a few inches on the pole and once again sought the bottom, but on an angle as opposed to straight up and down. Probing the bottom straight up and down was a job in itself but, at an angle, was a physical strain. Standing on the shore, watching poles rising and lowering was almost like watching a ballet. It was magical; it was rhythmical. And the children cutting through the scene were only part of the ritual being played out on the ice. The whole thing took the best part of four hours. That is, it took that much time for each catcher to carefully probe a fifteen- to eighteen-foot circle beneath the hole he had cut. The results were astounding. Hundreds of eels were caught that first day. The ritual went on for four days. No one counted, no one kept records, but sleds with boxes full of eels went directly to pre-chosen homes for what was to be done next.

It was the ladies' job to clean, skin and prepare the eels for cooking. New Year's Day was the time for it all coming together. Some folks eat black eyed peas for luck at that time of the year but, I can assure you, luck comes easier to those who work harder for it.

This particular year was to be my first eel party. I had used small eels for bait, but had never eaten one. I was cautious. The mosquito fleet guys were busy visiting houses where cooking was being done. Like the bad boys we were perceived to be, we were lovingly allowed to be "tasters." That is, we were allowed to taste everything but the eels which were cut into two- to three-inch pieces and were sizzling in pans full of hot olive oil. First taste of those delicacies was an honor reserved for the catchers. But we glutted ourselves on samples of hot homemade breads and sauces and soups and salads and desserts...and yes, of course, Al's nectar of the Gods.

Finally, it was time to serve the eels. We all gathered around the porch where the old men sat on their benches of honor. Each was served a heaping plateful of the delicacy they had worked so hard to capture. As one, they picked up a hot morsel, put it to their lips, bit gently and again as one, nodded in silent approval. A cheer went up from the waiting crowd, followed by the formation of lines leading to the cookers' kitchens.

"What do they taste like," I asked Frankie DiNofrio who was standing in line in front of me. "Tastes just like chicken," he replied. "You'll love it."

I've had lots of experience since that day with the phrase, "It tastes just like chicken." In Texas that's what rattlesnake is supposed to taste like. In the South, possum and rabbit magically assume that same taste. And I'm absolutely certain that the phrase has been used in every language known to man to describe a local delicacy to an unknowing stranger.

I innocently accepted the words of my friend Frank and allowed my plate to be piled high with pieces of eel. My first bite told me that this eel had never met a chicken in its life. It was not unpleasant unless your mind slipped back into remembering the darn thing slithering on the ice. Out of courtesy to our hosts and a great fear of reprisals, I ate the whole thing. I chased the taste with several glasses of wine, and left the party in the company of a lovely young lady who was visiting from Chicago.

A warm spell descended within the next few days and within a week, the ice had melted. It was almost eerie to look out on the water and remember that not very many days before, men and children were walking upon it. I thought, "What if the warm spell had come earlier, what if there were no ice, what if..."

I'm so glad the answer came to me so early in my life. If you allow the "what ifs" to take front stage in your mind, the adventure of life is doomed to be a dull one.

8

RED EYE EXPRESS

Let's face it, each of our lives is ruled by one or more philosophies. The dictionary description of philosophy is simple: A personal set of opinions of the basic truths and laws governing the universe, nature, morals, life, etc. In other words, the whole ball of wax.

The neat thing about philosophies is we don't have to make them up, they are with us from birth. True, the first ones we learn are filled with thou shalt nots, but as we mature, others as important are added, like all the thou cans, thou wills, and even thou musts. Philosophies are thrust upon us, first by parents, followed by priests, ministers or rabbis. Then there are teachers, instructors, professors and friends. The learning never stops..at least for most of us. It's almost like trying on a new pair of shoes until they are either comfortable enough to keep, or must be relegated to the trash pile.

On my adventurous walk through life, I have shared philosophies with untold numbers of people. Each individual I have ever met has freely discussed his or her personal thoughts regarding whatever subject was at hand. Sharing philosophies is as natural as sharing the air we breathe. They are like the proverbial "rear ends," everyone has one.

Freddie Gartner, from the time I met him until this day some fifty years later, has clung to the single tenet of an ancient Russian philosopher, Petrovich Pannitchka. When Americanized (as most foreign ideas are) it becomes simply, Peter Pan-ism. No human being is clever enough to instruct on its intricacies. No human being has the capacity to learn its rules. Only those fortunate few who are devoted followers can ever understand its joys and fulfillment.

Freddie is a man-child. He has the body of a man, yet retains all the joy, recklessness and abandon of a child. Some say it was the war, and cite the fact that he receives a "disability check" as proof. Everyone who knew him as a youth is gone now, so there can be no confirmation. He is well known amongst the fishermen along the Jersey Coast. The unanimous opinion is that "he's different" but also that "he's the best striper fisherman that ever was."

I met Freddie in the late 1940s. I was a teenage wannabee, Freddie was a veteran who was among those who fought not only in Europe, but in the island-hopping assault on Japan as well. In all the years I have known him, he has never spoken of those experiences. Our total conversation evolves around tides, moon phases, fish movements, and who did what last night. Last night and tonight are what Freddie can deal with. His love affair with the striper is legendary. To be with him when he catches one is a moment that can only be termed as "spiritual." He takes on a glow that lights up his features as if he had turned on an inner candle. He caresses his catch as a lover would stroke his partner, and then lovingly releases it back into the sea.

Freddie's dad owned a tackle shop in Newark that had a great salt-water selection, even though the shop was located over fifty miles inland. Freddy's job was to sweep the floor, take out the trash and accept everyone's derisive abuse. Freddie had a brother who was meaner to him than his dad, but both of them are gone now and Freddie is still here. All the folks that used to tease him are gone. He never talks about them and never complained. He just smiles knowingly and gets on with his life.

I was sitting outside of Dmorjian's Bait Shop on Shark River, trying desperately to figure out how to rig an eel. I was surrounded by people who knew, but was offered nothing but snickers in the way of help. I was frustrated and embarrassed and almost ready to give it up when a pair of hands gently took what I was working on away from me. Without a spoken word, the hands slowly showed me how to do the job, the face nodded kindly, then got into an old, rusted pick-up truck and drove slowly out of the parking lot. The conversation around me weighed heavily on the subject of "the idiot helping the stupid" but I didn't mind a bit. My skin was thick and I had the feeling a friendship had just begun.

Striper fishing on the Jersey Shore is done most successfully at night. Almost every other block had a rock jetty, built to stave off beach erosion. They became the platforms of choice for fishing activity. Countless storms and crashing waves over the years had skewed these platforms with pointed, slime-covered rocks that had to be negotiated in the dark until one flat enough to stand on was found. Those of us who fished these rocks had golf cleats galvanized into our boots to give us a small bit of purchase. Different jetties were available at various times during the tide, and great care was given to water movement so as not to be washed off. The most successful anglers are the ones with the least faint hearts. Obviously no heart fears less than that of a child, so Freddie was acclaimed the "craziest" fisherman on the beach. He took chances that no one else would dare and never, ever fished with any one else.

I'd be standing on a jetty and barely notice the silhouette of another angler on the next jetty. It had to be Freddie, because his truck was parked close by. Not having a hit, I decided to walk up the beach to the next jetty. When I arrived at its base, there was no one there. Usually a fisherman left the tell-tale spike marks in the sand around a place he has fished, but there were no such marks here, and no one in sight. It was pretty damned spooky because I was sure I had seen someone. It was then I discovered how sly Freddie was, and how really smart. He would walk in the water between jetties so the waves would wash away his foot prints. He was so keenly aware of his surroundings that when anyone was nearby, he would simply vanish almost into thin air. In all the years I've known him, no one has ever slipped up on him or observed the way he fishes.

In those years, we all augmented our meager salaries by selling the fish we caught to either hotels or fish markets. Freddie always had a truck full (never more than a limit of ten) and had regular customers who were eager to buy his catch. It was much later when he decided to release the fish. It took a long time for his passion to turn to inner peace with the idea of setting his catch free.

The many times I got to fish with Freddie were purely by accident, I thought. He would simply show up on a jetty that I was fishing and we'd spend a few silent hours enjoying the company. In the beginning, we never offered to gaff each other's fish; that was a ritual of "winning" to be savored. One night, a thirty-pounder broke off just as I was reaching for it with the gaff. I sadly watched it float away, hoping it would revive itself and be okay. When I left the jetty to move on, Freddie was standing on the beach, holding a thirty pound striper out to me. The fish had a gaff hole right behind the gill plate. I didn't ask, he didn't tell, but from then on, any time we fished together, we shared the victory by gaffing each other's fish.

I was smart enough never to ask Freddie "how" or "why." I don't suppose he would have told me anyway. He did, however, let me observe in such a way as to be explaining it to me but to make me feel I was learning it by myself. And

110

always, when I finally got it, was that twinkle in the eyes and the slightly drawn up mouth that was his signature smile.

One night I was on a jetty that had produced several fish the night before, but had yet to have a hit. Freddie suddenly appeared and said with authority, "They ain't here." I was used to asking unanswered questions, but I took a shot at it anyhow. "How do you know?"

"Can't smell 'em."

And he abruptly left. I could smell the salt air, other mixed aromas and my wet clothing. How the hell you could smell stripers in the water was the looniest thing I had ever heard. I did not catch a fish on that jetty though I stayed hopeful longer than I should have that night. I finally got two on another jetty and was not a bit surprised to see Freddie at the fish market the next morning with his usual ten.

Another night, I was ready to leave a jetty as Freddie was climbing toward me. I told him to save himself the trouble, I'd fished it hard and did not get any strikes. He smiled as he went past me and muttered, "I smell 'em coming," and continued on to the end of the rock pile. I moved north one jetty and took a fish on the first cast. It was the only one. I watched the silhouette on the jetty I had just left, but could detect only that it was occupied. I saw the silhouette leave the jetty and return almost instantly, only to climb back out again. My curiosity got the best of me, so I walked back to see what was up. What I found was Freddie with a fish in each hand, leaving the rock pile, walking a few feet up the beach to deposit the pair on top of those he had carried off in the last couple of trips he had made. All in all, he made five trips. He had caught ten bass, all over twenty pounds, off that single jetty where he "had smelled them coming."

Then there was the night I finally did sneak up on him. It had been rumored that he was slaying the fish in Shark River, but no one had actually seen him doing it. Rumors were rife among the striper clan, so it loomed as much a possibility as any thing else about Freddie. I knew the river fairly well and decided that I'd just fish it one entire night so I could put the rumor to rest. Outgoing tide was best, and the later at night, the better. Many of the prime places on "the terrace" had to be reached by gaining access to private property. It was easier done when the property owners were asleep. I fished every "hot spot", but no fish and no Freddie.

As I neared the old railroad bridge, I heard a noisy splashing, followed by a low but human grunt. Peering into the dark, I detected nothing. Five minutes later, I heard another huge splash that seemed to come from under the bridge. Crawling out on the railroad ties was dangerous, plus trains flew by at unannounced times, making this one of those places to be avoided. I couldn't help myself; I was drawn by my curiosity over those splashes. I inched my way to the center of the bridge and heard a really loud splash. Lying flat on the tracks, I peered over the side, and there he was. He had shinnied down a piling to a cross beam just wide enough to stand on just above the water's edge. He had tied himself to the piling with a rope, and was doodle-bugging under the bridge. Hanging onto another rope, I could see several fish strung, floating with the tide and occasionally making loud splashing sounds. I never told Freddie that I had found him, nor did I ever try that spot myself. My karma just wasn't right for it.

Over the years, I learned to park my vehicle off the beaten track so as not to be found. I learned to bury my fish in the sand, to be retrieved at a later moment. I learned that, no matter how large a fish I caught, never to drag it on the sand so someone else could know where it was caught. I learned to duck under the boardwalk when prying eyes were seeking. I learned so many tricks from watching Freddie that I could probably write a book on how best to keep your fishing secrets. I am convinced that half the fun in his life was getting over on all the folks that thought he was too dumb to know he was being made fun of.

The last time I fished with Freddie was the summer of '69. It was the summer of race riots in Asbury Park and the summer I decided to leave the coast I loved and do some adventuring in the south. That clear summer night, spent with a simple man, pursuing a simple activity, has happily haunted my mind for almost thirty-five years.

I was walking across the beach toward the Avon jetty to fish the second half of the incoming tide. Somehow Freddie emerged from the waterline, headed for the same jetty. Most folks fish it on the outgoing tide, but hardly ever on the opposite.

It's a high, flat-top rock pile for almost three quarters of its length, with living room-sized boulders in all manner of disarray at its end. The end is where the action was. As long as you were mindful of the waves, and were agile enough to hop to a higher spot until they swept across the front, you were okay. It was a lot to be aware of, but then faint heart never won the fair lady.

As quick as I was (and I was quick), Freddie was quicker. He seemed not to be touching the rocks as he went by me; he literally flew out to the end as I more carefully picked my way out from rock top to rock top. The next thing I knew, Freddie was on the end, rod raised ready to cast . The whole scene seemed painted in black and white. Silhouetted against a backdrop of white-crashing water, standing on the apex of the world, was my slim, unearthly-looking companion preparing to do battle with the elements. How very small he looked at that moment, and how very vulnerable.

That whole scene came instantly crashing down upon me as Freddie stopped his forward casting motion, spun toward me and quickly leapfrogged over that dangerous terrain, headed directly at me, as I stood frozen to the spot. He grabbed me with a strength I did not know he possessed and started pulling me toward the beach. His rod and reel were nowhere in sight. He had dropped them at some point during his flight. He had fear and desperation written all over him as he said, "They're after me, the red eyes are after me." There was no calming him down as I allowed him to pull me off the jetty and onto the beach. His eyes pleaded with me as he headed toward the boardwalk, staggering backward and waving for me to follow.

My car was the closest, so we headed for it. Safely inside, with two steaming cups of coffee poured from my always-present Thermos, and all doors and windows secured (at his insistence) he unfolded his eerie tale. As he stood on the tallest rock at the jetty's end, getting ready to make his first cast, he heard a sharp sound. It made him turn his head in the direction of the next breaking wave where he saw two sets of bright red eyes heading right for his face. "They were screaming at me, and they were after me," he said, and even with the hot coffee warming him, continued to shake in fear of what had just happened.

It took the best part of an hour for things to calm down and for Freddie to get hold of himself. I had convinced him that whatever the danger was, it had gone away and we were going to be okay. I thanked him for saving me from whatever it was, and got him to agree we would stay put for another couple of hours until daylight came and we could make certain the beach was safe. And then the miracle happened. Freddie began to speak to me in complete sentences. He shared things I had never heard him talk about. I'll never disclose the things we spoke of but he answered every question I asked until we came to his time in the Army. The cloud instantly covered him and he climbed back into his safe place and began to talk about bottle caps, tides, rigging eels and "red eyes" in the night. I knew then that a magic moment had passed and would probably never come back.

When it was light enough to see, we left the car, crossed the beach as we warily peered out to sea, and sat in the sand at the base of the jetty. The tide had filled and had turned, and the waves were now breaking on the beach, instead of on the end of the rock-pile. Freddie stiffened: "Did you hear that?"

"Hear what?"

"That sound."

He stood up, ready to take flight, and suddenly broke out into the happy laughter you might expect from a child arriving at a surprise birthday party. He jumped up and down, alternately laughing and pointing at the surf.

It took me several minutes to catch on to what was happening, but when I did, I'm afraid I behaved as nutty as Freddie, joining him in his absolute glee. What it was, was a school of seals, barking happily as they rode the crest of the waves toward the beach. During the night, the dim light of the moon made their eyes appear to be red. Freddie's red-eyed monsters turned out to be a group of "sea children" practicing their surfing lessons. Neither of us had ever seen seals on the Jersey coast, nor have I told this tale to very many folks, fearing they would think I, too, was "different." Freddie walked out to the middle of the jetty and retrieved the rod and reel that the sea had deposited there for him. He somehow did not understand my surprise, acting as if that was the way it was supposed to be.

I've not seen Freddie since that night, though I think of him often. I keep up with him, though, through a young friend who has become my adopted nephew. He's a young striper fisherman with a pretty healthy reputation for success with the bass, and has latched on to Freddie as I did. He tells me wonderful stories about Freddie, stories that make me feel like, "I've read that before." Seems like little has changed. Freddie still haunts the jetties and the Shark and Shrewsbury Rivers. He doesn't have a truck anymore; he doesn't drive. When he is spotted, he's pedaling his bicycle as fast as his legs can pump, with a basket full of stuff and a rod and reel in his hand. My nephew tells me that often he doesn't even hold on to the handle bars.

Freddie must be well into his eighties by now, but I've been told he looks the same as he did when I first met him over fifty years ago. Has he found the fountain of youth? I don't think so. What Freddie has found is a philosophy; the philosophy of Peter Pan. You can never die if you believe and live in "Neverland."

9

MOUNTAIN DEW TROUT

It was the best trout fishing I've ever known. I remember every fish, every pool. Almost every moment of that magical trip is deeply ingrained in my memory. Recalling it all evokes smiles and warm fuzzies. It concerns me only that I can't remember the stream or its exact location in the North Georgia Hills. I hardly think my mind made it all up, the mental pictures are too precise. And besides, I have a souvenir.

After graduating from The American School Of Broadcasting, I found myself in Carrolton, Georgia as a young, aspiring news director. Six months of reporting calf births, runaway horses, quilting bees and an occasional blurb for "college in the country," had me a little edgy for some solo time. I was finding it tough living in the smallest community I had ever been in. As "the voice of the news," I was the one under the closest scrutiny and, being the only "Yankee" in town made it even stickier. I re-fought the Civil War almost every day.

The one highlight of my life at the time was a chance meeting and occasional breakfast with Susan Hayward who, when not making movies, lived quietly with her husband on a nearby farm. I was in my early twenties and she was definitely my first serious fantasy. I carried a picture of her in my wallet and dreamed a time or two of saving her from the dragons, or some evil villain wanting to do her harm. It never occurred to me that it might be she that saved MY life.

Hiram Bray, our chief dee-jay, was an outdoorsman and a bit of a fisherman (mostly catfish). Hiram knew almost every inch of water in the state of Georgia. I had three full days of R and R coming to me after working 24/7 for six months, and I was chomping at the bit to get away. I needed to be somewhere else for a while. Somewhere I didn't need to talk to anyone, interview anyone or be on hand for anyone. In other words, I needed a place where I could fish, camp, pee in the woods, and reclaim my individuality.

Hiram understood perfectly what I needed. He described a hunting camp he and a couple of his buddies owned in the North Georgia mountains. It had a makeshift cabin equipped with cots, a stream for water, propane cook stove and gas lanterns. Pots, pans, eating utensils, toilet paper and a real out-house were also part of the inventory. Sounded like heaven to me.

"Does the stream have any trout in it?" I asked him. "Dunno," he replied, "we never fish up there; only hunt deer." Ain't deep enough for no catfish, though, I can tell you that for sure." Hiram drew me a crude map to the place and, even as bad as my sense of direction is, I managed to find it.

I stopped at a little country store/bait shop on the way and picked up a bunch of worms and crickets to use for bait. I also got a few last-minute food items, knowing there were no stores near the camp. I showed the proprietor my map and asked if he knew anything about the stream or if it had trout in it. "Dunno," he said, "I ain't ever fished for 'em, but them streams are all full of bass and brim." Encouraged, I thanked him and made my way to my home away from home for the next three wonderful, glorious, no other human beings in sight days.

I spent the next hour or so making the cabin as livable as possible. You have to imagine this place was in the middle of nowhere. No electricity, no phone, a dirt road barely wide enough for one vehicle with only a marginal place to turn around behind the cabin. I hadn't seen another dwelling for almost the last hour of the trip. This looked exactly like what the doctor ordered.

It was late in the afternoon so I decided to just scout the stream for likely places to fish the next morning. It was a dream stream. Boulders, fast runs, undercut banks, overhanging trees and, pool after pool after pool. The banks were rough and pathless but the stream looked safe for wading. And it was mine, I owned it (at least for the next three days). I went to sleep dreaming alternately about trout and Susan. It couldn't get any better than that.

Waking before daylight, I lit the Coleman lamp, started the stove and made coffee, bacon , eggs and potatoes. That was the limit of my cooking skills at the time, but it was the best darned breakfast I had eaten in six months.

I was standing in the stream up to my knees in cold mountain water just as the sun started to shoot rays of light through the tree tops. Forest sounds were all around me. Bird calls, squirrels leaping from branch to branch, movement in the leaves by unseen animal feet. Deer grunts and turkeys gobbling from the highest roosting places...what a morning! If your timing is right and your head is screwed on correctly, God will sneak one like this on you every once in a while. We just have to be ready to see it.

I wasn't sure about the trout thing, though if ever there was a "trouty" looking place, this was it. I tried a worm on my first cast, fishing the first pool I came to. Instant hit. Missed fish. Two more casts, two more missed fish. I had one of my cricket cages inside the creel I wore over my shoulder, and thinking perhaps the hits were from bream and the night crawlers I was using were too large, I opted to try a cricket.

Next cast produced the prettiest ten-inch brook trout I had ever seen. I happily released that one. The next five casts brought four more brookies and a rainbow, all about the same size. The fishing was so fantastic I felt I could catch enough for dinner any time I chose to, so I continued to work my way upstream, releasing everything that I caught.

It seemed as if there was at least one fish behind every rock, every snag and several in every pool. I happily wondered if the place was stocked just for my enjoyment. Alternating between worms and crickets, I must have caught and released fifty beautiful trout.

I'd made a couple of peanut butter and jelly sandwiches and my belly was beginning to growl. I looked for a place to climb up on the bank to eat lunch. Just ahead of me was a makeshift wooden bridge with a small clearing close to the water's edge. There were signs that someone had camped here, even had a fire going. The bridge was really interesting. It wasn't high enough to wade under and there was not a nail or a wooden peg anywhere to be seen. It just seemed to fit together like a Leg-O toy, but surely looked substantial enough to drive over. Strangely, there was no road on either side, only a well-beaten foot path. My thought was that some ambitious hunters had made it for whatever reason they had in mind.

As I was taking a second bite of my sandwich, I thought I heard a sound, then a voice. "Hey," the voice said, "You boy, look up here." Startled I guess is the best way to describe my immediate feeling. A little scared, but mostly surprised. I looked up to the top of the bridge, and the mood instantly changed from startled to scared...scared s--tless. Leaning over the edge of the bridge was a bearded face which I barely noticed because, directly under it, pointed directly at me, was a double barrel shotgun.

"Y'all c'mon up here," the face said, "and walk real slow." I wanted to respond but somehow my voice failed me.

"Step up here on the bridge" said the face. I did as I was told, and as I arrived on top of the bridge another voice behind me said, "He's a little feller, ain't he?" I turned my head slightly enough to see another face and another shotgun.

"What are you doin' nosin' around here, boy?" one of the faces asked. I couldn't answer. "Speak up," the other face growled.

"I'm, I'm fishing," I stammered.

"For what?" Simple question.

"Trout." Simple answer.

"Show us some." Simple demand.

"I've thrown them all back." Honest reply.

One face looked questioningly at the other, "You see any sense in throwing fish back?"

"Maybe he's lyin'," was the response. "Well, we'll see, won't we?"

"Throw me that basket, boy," he ordered, but not angrily. I did as I was told. "Nuthin in here but a sammich and some worms and crickets. Take them boots off, boy," he ordered and again I did as I was told. They turned the boots inside out and shook them and bounced them on the ground. They twisted the heels and squeezed the toes. I was wearing a shirt with no pockets. "Take off them pants, boy." Now I was really scared.

"How come?" I stuttered.

"Cause we say so."

"Okay. I don't have much money but you're welcome to it, only please don't shoot me," I pleaded in as manly a way as I could muster under the circumstances.

An evil grin appeared on the face as it responded, "Didn't say we was gonna shoot you." I did not want to hear it but I did: "YET."

My pants on the ground, standing in my shorts, shirt and socks, I felt as alone, scared and vulnerable as I had ever been in my entire short life. One face grew a hand that swept up my pants and methodically emptied the pockets. Pen knife, keys, change, map and wallet. After turning the pockets inside out, one face put down a gun and began to rifle through my wallet. Drivers license, family photos, press ID, twenty-one dollars and my picture of Susan Hayward.

"Who's the pretty lady here?" the face asked.

"Susan Hayward" I said. She's a movie star and she lives in Carrolton." My teeth were chattering with cold and fear as I went on and on about her movies and how lucky I was to just know her.

"She a Georgia girl?" the other one asked.

"I think so," I muttered.

"Georgia girls sure are the prettiest in the world, ain't they, Junior?"

Wow! One of the faces had a name. And all of a sudden the tone of the scenario did a complete one hundred eighty. "Put your pants on, boy, you look stupid standin' there half nekked on this bridge." I gladly did as I was told. "I'm Junior," the face said, sticking out a meaty, shot gun-less hand. "And this here is my baby brother, Virgil," and the other gunless hand reached out.

"I'm Stu," I said, "and I hope I haven't done anything wrong."

"No, we just don't see many folks up here and we don't trust strangers much. We thought you was a government man snooping around in our business."

When they learned I was a friend of Hiram's and was using his camp, they got even friendlier. They asked me if I needed any supplies, told me they had killed many a deer with Hiram and wondered why I hadn't told them all that in the first place. RIGHT! They told some funny stories, visited for about an hour before they left. "Save us some fish if you get any more, we'll probably see you again before you leave." And then they were gone.

I headed directly back to camp. I sure as hell did not

feel like fishing any more just then. I toyed with the idea of heading all the way back home but remembered how much I needed the mini-vacation, and decided to fish again tomorrow.

Morning broke not soon enough as I had a fitful night's sleep. Daylight brought clear thoughts but I still fantasized that having Susan's picture along was part of what saved my life. I started at the same pool as I had the day before and fished until I exhausted my supply of crickets. I had bought 150 and I swear I had a hit or caught a fish on every one. I kept about a dozen nice fish, some of them measuring sixteen inches long.

I slept well the second night and planned to fish with lures until noon, and then head for home. As I started getting ready to cook my last breakfast, Virgil and Junior showed up out of nowhere. I didn't have enough to feed them, but they did share a cup of coffee with me. "I can cook up some fish," I offered.

"We don't eat fish in the mornin," Junior said, "we just came to say we was sorry if we scared you on the bridge, and bring you a little token. We hope you ain't mad at us, being a friend of Hiram's and all."

Having said what they came to say, Virgil handed me what looked like a fruit jar full of water. "This is some of our best," Junior said, "it's for sippin, not for swiggin." Holy s--t, I thought, this whole thing makes sense now. All I could say was, "Thanks a lot, I'll carry it home with me."

"Don't give none to Hiram," Virgil said with a wicked grin on that face. "He don't know we make anything this good, and we don't want to spoil him."

I mentioned I had some fish, cleaned and ready for cooking and went down to the stream where I had them chilling and brought them back to the cabin. "You boys enjoy these, and watch out for the bones; wouldn't want you to swallow one and get mad at me."

We all had a good laugh, and in the blink of an eye, they were gone.

I fished the morning away and saved enough fish for my landlady and to show Hiram that there were really trout in his stream. On the way home I dreamed about breaking that mason jar over Hiram's head. Surely he knew I'd run into the brothers two and was probably busting a gut telling his cronies. Well, I could live on the energy of "get even plans" for quite a while. I finally did get even, really even, but that's another tale.

By the way, it's been over forty years since that adventure, and I guess if Guinness has a spot for it, I probably have in my possession the most aged jar of "Mountain Dew" in the whole wide world.

10

WILD BILL

There are people you enjoy because you like them but, on the other side of that coin, there are those you enjoy even if you don't like them. Think on that.

Bill Watterson was a guy I alternately liked and hated but, for sure, never a time we were fishing together passed without hearty laughs and gut-busting guffaws. Bill was a very funny guy and in a millisecond could make you forget the last time you noticed he was a class jerk.

He owned a "tote the note" used car joint that specialized in "re." RE possessing and RE selling. He had some goons working for him, the smallest of whom had hands the size of country hams. As I remember, the odor some of them gave off was reminiscent of an old smokehouse. At any rate, it was obvious to all that Bill was not to be messed with, even though he was only about five-six and weighed maybe one hundred and forty pounds, soaking wet.

Bill was a good customer; he hired me at least two or three times a month, so he was paying my mortgage. The first time he chartered my services was the trip on which I decided I could not always like him. I also was determined that he would never, not ever, catch a fish in my boat. Now, having confessed that publicly, I understand why some of my

Catholic friends could be hesitant at times to visit the confessional. It's pretty awesome to confront your own shortcomings, isn't it?

When Bill showed up for our first trip, his smile and enthusiasm were certainly disarming. Our trip was to run from five to nine, since he had to open his business at ten. "Grab my cooler" he demanded, "it's in the back of my truck." I opted to cooperate, rather than to tell him to get his own darned cooler. There was time enough to let him know that a guide's boat could have only one captain. He seemed to be a guy who enjoyed being in complete control and needed to be handled delicately. Oh well, it was only a cooler.

As I reached up into the bed of the truck to grab the cooler, I noticed the neck of a bottle poking out. It turned out to be a bottle of very good Tennessee whiskey. "Sorry Bill" I said, "no booze on board, it's one of my rules."

"You've got to be kidding me," he said, "just put the cooler in the boat and don't worry about it, I can hold my liquor."

"Well, Bill," I replied as calmly as I could, "that may be so, but I never break my own rules and I'm very firm where it concerns alcohol." Indicating I wasn't a teetotaler, I offered to have a drink with him at some other time, away from the water.

He got red in the face, indicating there was a real need for anger control classes here. In no uncertain and graphic terms, he told me where I could put my rules, my boat and our trip. At the end of that tirade, he sputtered, "And I'll take my money back, too." Calmly explaining that there was a last-minute cancellation charge that, as a business man, he could surely appreciate, I counted out and tried to hand him half the money he had given me for the trip.

Standing there in the marina parking lot, my hand extended holding the money, not knowing quite what to expect next, he completely disarmed me. A huge, face-splitting smile suddenly appeared where only seconds ago was raw rage. He threw his arm around my shoulder and said, "Hell, it's no big deal, we'll leave the cooler and still have a good time." There was that first millisecond where I stopped not liking him. But, I thought, "Would I buy a car from him?"

Once in the boat and underway, he said, "I'll handle my own gear and use my own lures; you just take me where the fish are, I'll do the rest." (Was he serious?) I had spent hours catching primo live bait since this was the time of year that the fish suspended in sizable schools and were almost always ready to take a lively fresh bait when properly presented. "You can let all that live bait go," he teased in an almost surly manner. "Live bait is for kids," he sneered. "I can catch any fish that swims on a lure."

I knew that Bill was an experienced angler; he certainly could talk the talk. His fishing tackle showed clearly that cost was not a factor. He had the best stuff that money could buy, some of it even custom made. Oh well, he was paying for the trip and I surely was not going to argue the point, even though I had a feeling what the outcome would be.

My depth recorder was showing a huge school of fish suspended from thirteen to twenty feet. They would have been easy pickings for a drifted live bait, perhaps even a properly fished lead head jig. But Bill was going to have it his way; he'd paid for the trip and was intent on controlling things to perhaps enhance his bragging rights. "Now," he said, "I'm gonna show you how to catch these dudes."

He opted to use a large crank bait. "I can get this down to where they live," he said. "Just watch me, Captain." Well, I just couldn't help it, the ugly crept back into me and here we were again. I didn't like him very much right then. To make a long story short, several hundred casts later it was time to go in. No hits, no runs, even though I managed to stay with that school of fish the entire time we were out. Bill left without a word (or a tip) and I figured that was the end of that.

Over the next week I had several successful trips and my good pal, Jimmy Holt, Outdoor Editor at the *Nashville Tennesseean,* was glad to publish photos of happy fisher folks displaying catches of huge fish caught locally. He liked to brag on the fact that you did not have to stray far from home to catch trophy fish.

Bill evidently couldn't stand seeing those big fish photos and was moved to call me and set up another trip. "I'll try live bait," he said reluctantly. "And maybe, just maybe," he dug, "you might try and think of some way to catch those fish on lures; you'll probably get a whole lot more REAL fishermen to hire you out." What a hard sell this bozo was. Well, I was prepared to teach him a lesson.

He asked me to fish so he could watch what I did and the first drift produced a nice fish. I tried to tell him how to measure his line to the proper depth, but he knew it all and figured out a better way. The wind picked up and adjustments had to be made for a faster drift. "I can handle that," he said, while I caught three more fish. "I need a fresh bait" he demanded, "put one on for me." Since he was sitting on the live well it would have been easier for him to choose the bait he wanted and hook it on himself. His control mechanism was now transparent and, once again, I didn't care for him very much. He sure had a way of making me think evil thoughts.

Prior to getting up to net a fresh bait for him, I rubbed my hand over the auxiliary gas tank, which always had some gas residue on it. Touching the gas and then the bait insured no sane predator would find it palatable. It was a mean trick, I know, but I was young, and convinced myself he deserved it. I caught and released twelve fish up to twenty five pounds. I kept the two largest for Bill to take home. The following Sunday, his photo was in the paper showing "his catch." I laughed so hard I had to run to the john.

He sure as heck became determined after that, but

the next three trips brought the same results. Bill never had a hit; his "captain" continued to clobber him. On the next trip, Bill brought along an acquaintance of his, Bobby Bare. Bobby was one of Nashville's hottest recording stars and proved to be a special kind of person.

I had later opportunities to fish with him and his son and watch them interact in a non-threatening environment that could only bring out everyone's best. As a further bonus, that chance meeting with Bobby led to trips with Mel Tillis and Bobby Goldsboro and their sons. Watching those father/son relationships first-hand and being privileged to be a small part of their growth spawned lots of fun memories, but those are other tales to be told. Isn't it amazing how even a bad experience can open doors of joy and wonder, if you allow it to happen?

But back to "the trip." Bobby took the rear seat, Bill the front and I in the middle where I could keep an eye out for both of them. Bobby was enthusiastic, relaxed, and listened open-mindedly to my directions. Before either Bill or I could get our lines down, Bobby had a fish on. Lots of laughing and good natured kidding ensued but despite all of that, Bobby handled the fish like a pro and soon it was in the boat.

Almost instantly after settling into the next drift, Bobby and I hooked a double header. Crossed lines and several trips around the boat had us breathing hard and our jokes and belly laughs (while Bill watched, actionless) must have driven Bill nuts; he was sullenly silent. "I need a fresh bait," came the demand. Of course I accommodated. Next drift, same results. Bobby was really getting off on catching so many big fish and the teasing rapport between us was natural and fun...must have stung Bill, though he appeared stoic, and grim.

"You need to sit in the back seat," Bobby quipped, "all the fish are back here." It blew our minds when Bill silently slid to the rear. I had stopped fishing since our bait cache was getting slim, and was really having more fun watching Bobby"s absolute kid-like joy. On the next drift Bobby caught and released two more stripers while he was sitting in Bill's old seat. Bill was silent. "Tell you what," Bobby quipped innocently enough, "must be the rod, let's switch; you use mine and I'll use yours." Bill agreed, mumbling something about voodoo and witch doctors that had us laughing so hard we had to reach for our next breath. No sooner did Bobby get Bill's rod in his hands, he had another fish on, and Bill had a fresh bait on, too.

"That's it," Bill said, "I'm snake-bit, that live bait just don't work for me." With that, he threw two of the nicest (and most expensive) rods and reels (his) a guy could own, into sixty feet of water. The gremlin on my shoulder said, "Oh-oh pal, I think you may have taken this thing just a little too far." When we hit the dock, Bill gathered up his belongings and split without a goodbye or a kiss my butt.

Bobby iced his fish down and offered to buy breakfast. Over bacon, eggs and coffee he asked, "What in the world did you do out there to keep Bill from catching any fish? No one can be that unlucky, the fishing was way too good for him not to get even a strike." I'd been caught. I never accounted for how sharp Bobby was. He knew darned well I was up to something and his natural curiosity was asking, "how?

After swearing him to secrecy, I laid out all the lurid details, even my feeble excuses for creating the whole scenario. In my ardor to confess my sins, I totally ignored the fact that the cook, waiter and several other fishermen were within earshot. The saving grace was that I had made a new friend and fellow adventurer, and that turned out to be a memory builder for me.

Two weeks later (no calls from Bill) at three a.m., I was awakened by my door bell chiming. "Who is it?" I sleepily called through the closed door. "I've had a bad accident and I need help," came the reply. Without hesitation I threw open the door and flicked on the porch light. My heart jumped past my larynx and lodged in my throat, my knees felt weak and my bladder was trying to decide whether to hang on or just let go. There, standing on my front porch, holding a pistol that looked as big as a cannon, was Bill. Wild eyed, hair uncombed and unshaven, he looked like the proverbial avenging angel. "I've come to pay you back you miserable bastard," he said, and pointed the pistol right at my face.

I'll never know what transpired over the next few minutes. I have to assume they were prayerful. The next thing I remember is Bill sitting on the front steps, laughing so hard that he was choking. To this day I'll swear the slight bit of moisture on the porch was early morning dew.

Bill came in for a cup of coffee which I laced with a very much needed toddy ingredient. I apologized, but didn't really have to since his "revenge" was sweeter to him than any admissions I could offer.

We fished together several times after that, but Bill always insisted on putting on his own bait. He never understood why I wouldn't let him put one on for me, even when he was closer to the live well. He caught lots of fish after that and turned out to be a pretty decent guy. He still retained some evil ways but, when you are trying to like someone, perhaps it's best to try and overlook what's bad and concentrate on what's the best. I suppose that's one of life's hardest learned lessons.

11

PUDGE

Pudgy Walton wasn't really pudgy, he was way past "walrus." Weighing in at close to 400 pounds, he looked more like a two-legged hippo dressed in a "brrr suit" complete with stocking cap, neck muffler, fingerless gloves and a pair of muck-luks any Eskimo would envy. If someone had asked me what color his eyes were, I'd have to try to remember if I noticed that he had any. To simplify the description, Pudgy was a huge guy.

He'd called my guide service just around Christmas-time and asked me to let him know when the top-water action on J. Percy Priest Reservoir got started; he was anxious to give it a try. He claimed he only needed one day's notice, so any time I called him he'd be ready to book a couple of days.

As a rule, mid to late April saw the onset of top water action. Generally I had solid pre-bookings for every day from April 1st through the end of August, but his name could easily go into the substitution file I kept to cover the last minute cancellations I was surprised with now and then. Stuff comes up, good and bad, so we were used to accommodating folks that either had or made up reasonable excuses.

Getting out on the lake to check conditions like

depth, temperature, bird and fish movements was an every day "business expense." So, even when I wasn't booked, I was out searching for schools of striped bass. Conditions normally predicted where the fish would be, but Mother Nature is a hard act to follow because she changes her mind so often. Winter is the most critical time since water temperatures are lower, as are fish metabolisms; hence much slower movement. A one degree change in water temperature, an early, even minute algae bloom could set the stage for early migration of small pods of actively feeding fish.

This particular year, the bait fish moved out of the shallow creeks and onto the main lake during the last days of February. After ten days of heaving a top-water lure that produced zilch, I finally began to see some results. Not having anything scheduled for the first half of March, I called Pudgy at his office in Birmingham and got an excited commitment for a three day charter the following week.

I'd never met the man, but he told me he would be driving a red pick-up truck and we agreed on a time to meet at the dock. He sounded like a fun-loving person and admitted he had never fished for stripers. He hurried on to let me know he wasn't a beginner, but rather an accomplished tournament angler with no small reputation among his circle of friends. Having heard that story before (only about a million times), I advised him that I'd supply the tackle and lures. I also told him to be prepared for extremely cold weather and to bring the proper clothing.

When he showed up at the dock at 5 a.m., dressed like a polar explorer, I kinda figured to myself, "here was a guy who listened." That was a good beginning. At the time, I was running a slim line Ouachita boat that bore a warning sticker limiting safe carry weight to 750 pounds. My 160 plus his estimated 400 plus the hoped-for four fish limit of close to another 100 pounds put us closer to the weight limit than I wanted to be. I began to think of what we could leave behind that was not absolutely essential to the trip.

M-m-m-m. Depth finder, 5 lbs...extra gas tank, 25-30 lbs...tackle box, 15-20 lbs...cooler with food, ice and snacks,10-15 lbs...anchor, 12 lbs. I even eyed the two fire extinguishers, but quickly vetoed the thought. Opting to keep the fish well dry of water, we pushed away from the dock at about daylight with only about a half mile to travel to where we would fish.

As light crept into the morning, I put a spinning rod in Pudge's hands. The reel was loaded with new 15 lb. test line and I had tied on a seven-inch Red fin, my lure of choice for early season top water fishing. I should have sensed impending disaster when he commented on having to use "sissy tackle."

"Should have brought my own tackle," he muttered. "My buddies would laugh me out of town if they knew I lowered myself enough to use a spin-rod." Making all the "guide" comments I could master to explain the why-fors, I blithely skipped past the issue and busied myself explaining how to work the lure.

There were specifics to follow, simple, logical steps, tried and true. I had designed the method years before and taught countless anglers how to latch on to what surely is the most exciting experience any fisher-person can have. Taunting and teasing a huge predator fish into abandoning caution to show itself in a frenzied attack is, at that moment, better than winning a lottery.

Rule one was to make an especially long cast to allow the lure plenty of retrieve time. Next, the lure had to be reeled very slowly to allow it to wobble on the surface and create a "v" shaped wake behind it, thereby emulating the prey fish that the predator fed on. The bait was really designed to swim under the surface, but its unusual buoyancy allowed for this subtle finesse.

It only took two casts for me to realize that Pudge was

more smoke than fire. The first was a beauty that sailed at least 30 yards. The direction however was slightly questionable. The lure sailed backwards over his head and landed behind the boat. Good trick, since he was sitting up front. The next was an Academy Award winner. The direction was certainly better but the lure wound around a limb, around the tree and bounced off the rocks. We retrieved the lure, minus the lip. Pudge understood that he had bought that one. The rules were, "You pay up front and you own anything you lose." I was later to rejoice pre-payment for the three day trip.

We'd lost the first half hour of prime time, so I asked Pudge to watch me make a cast, which I did. I guess if you live right good things are supposed to happen, so I wasn't a bit surprised that after traveling less than 20 feet, the bait was engulfed in a froth of boiling water. Offering to let Pudge take the rod to land the fish was obviously an insult to the man, and he refused vehemently. The fish was in the 20-25 pound class and went right into the waterless live well.

Here's the picture: Pudge was sitting on the front pedestal seat, his rear end practically swallowing it. His at least size 13 pacs were planted so firmly on the deck as to make him appear like a permanent part of the boat. Got to give him this, though, he mastered the casting routine in short order, and was really doing well in that respect.

Try as I might, I just could not communicate "slow down." His adrenaline was pumping so fast he couldn't coordinate keeping the lure on the surface and I knew unless he did, he would not get a hit. I took a second fish, slightly larger than the first, and that was my legal limit. And Hubert (his given name) now got my full attention. I begged, pleaded, cajoled, threatened and did all but stand on my head, but Pudge still would not keep the lure on the surface.

"The bait must be waterlogged," he said, which was followed by more excuses than I care to go into. I truly wanted him to catch a fish.

Suddenly the idea light went on in my thick noggin, and I simply replaced his lure with one that could not possibly sink. It would not have been my first choice, but since floatability (then speed) was the big issue, we had finally leveled the playing field. The new lure (a Zara Spook) had no lip, therefore it had simply to be reeled in with a slight movement of the rod tip supplying the side-to-side wobbling action that was necessary to attract the fish's attention.

Since the tackle-box was back at the dock, I dutifully thanked St.Elmo for magically having an extra lure or two stowed safely aboard. Miraculously, Pudge was great with the lure, he worked it perfectly. He was now animated, focused and wired for action. He seemed as tight as a bow-string, but under the circumstances, tight was OK.

Success breeds confidence, and working the lure correctly as well as consciously directing his casts, Pudge relaxed and became talkative (without missing a stroke). He spoke of his high school football days when he was a local legend. He talked about the injury that kept him from playing in college and erased his dream to turn pro. Going to work for his dad wasn't easy, he said sadly, but after his dad retired and turned the business over to him, he admitted to have come to grips with his lot. "I grew the business five times over," he smilingly said, and went on to talk of money matters with great zeal.

Neither of us was prepared for the Loch Ness monster that struck at his innocently moving bait. The viciousness of the attack, the suddenness of the mood change, white, sudsy frothing water flying everywhere; I had always felt there was the mystic "50 pounder " in this lake and surely here he was, knocking on Pudge's door.

Pudge responded with a strong hook-set and then, perhaps thinking he was trying to hook a marlin, planted his feet and set the hook again, again and again. Each time he did so was, if it were possible to visualize, stronger than the

137

time before. Finally, he set the hook so hard, he broke the pedestal supporting his seat right off at the base. Pedestal, seat, rod and reel, monster striper and Pudge went ass over tea kettle into the frigid waters of J.Percy Priest. Only Pudge came to the surface.

When he fell overboard he weighed around 400, but when he surfaced, wetsuit and water-filled boots must have added at least another 100 pounds. Try as we both could, it was impossible to get him back into the boat. He couldn't climb in and I couldn't drag him over the side. I managed to get a rope around him, and using the trolling motor eased him up to a concrete boat ramp which, fortunately, was only about 100 feet away. With difficulty he climbed back into the boat, loudly cursing me and everyone else he could think of. I didn't mind much, the imminent danger being over. I only now had to be concerned with hypothermia.

I couldn't gun the engine since the added weight had the water level pretty close to the gunnels. I did manage to get the bow up so as not to take in any more water, and headed back to the dock. Pudge was turning into a fudgesicle, with ice forming on his outer garments. I opted to head for my slip instead of the gas dock because the slip allowed for easy stepping onto the dock, the gas dock being higher than I thought could be negotiated by a water-logged giant. Being only ten slips from the parking lot and only 25 yards or so to the warm restaurant, I figured I was doing the correct thing. I hadn't counted on Pudge's impatience.

Pudge was sitting on the live well lid as I busied myself securing the boat in the slip. Since the Ouachita was narrow, and the slip wide, I started tying the bow-line so Pudge could step right up onto the dock. He wasn't having any of that; he decided to do it his own way. While I was bent over the bow-line, Pudge reached for the side of the slip, pulled the stern in crossways, stood up and stepped one foot onto the dock. Naturally the shift in weight caused the boat to slide sideways

138

in the slip, causing his legs (one on the dock, one in the boat) to begin to spread wider and wider apart.

I watched with horror and disbelief as the gap between boat and dock widened. It didn't take more than a few seconds and Pudge was, again, in the drink. Once again we were faced with the same situation; he couldn't climb out and I couldn't drag him out. Back to the old rope trick. I lassoed him and tied him snugly to the dock knowing the trapped air in his clothing would keep him afloat for the one or two minutes it would take for me to get more help.

It wasn't difficult to gather some folks from the restaurant, and in a short time seven of us were trying unsuccessfully to drag Pudge up on the dock. Someone came up with a bright idea and we formed a rescue line from my slip to the parking lot. Passing Pudge from hand to hand, pulling him from slip to slip, we managed to get him ashore. I didn't laugh when some smart remark about a "beached whale" began to circulate but, heaven help me, I did think it was hilarious. I later excused myself by blaming it on the tension of the moment.

He'd left his dry clothing at the motel so we got him into the heated men's room and collected his wet clothes. These we sent to a nearby Laundromat to throw into the dryer. Naked was definitely not Pudge's long suit, but there was no one large enough to loan him anything dry to put on. Ben, the security guard, suggested that Margie, a local bartender who lived on a houseboat on pier three was Pudge's size and maybe she could volunteer something.

She sure came through, and within minutes Pudge was in the restaurant wrapped in a fuzzy pink bath robe with lace fringes. It was really tough, but we all kept our cool. Pudge's clothes came back from the dryer within a couple of hours. He left Margie's bath robe on the men's room floor...what a sport.

"I'd like to cancel the next two days, and I'd like my

money back," he said...and he was serious. "You'll be hearing from my attorney, too," he went on.

"Well," I answered, "I'll be glad to give you a refund for day two and three, minus 5 dollars for the lure, 150 dollars for the pedestal and seat and about 90 bucks for the rod and reel. I won't charge you for the line since I get it for free." He sputtered, growled and got red in the face but taking in a restaurant full of folks that knew me, he decided that what he was thinking might be a mistake. He left threatening to tell all his friends what a miserable guide I was and, as the door closed behind him he let all who could hear know that he would never come back again. I must admit, I didn't spend a very long time mourning my loss.

About a week later I got a hang-up call at two in the morning. Since there was no such thing as caller ID at the time, I didn't have a clue. The calls repeated themselves for ten nights in a row and I was beginning to have a slight suspicion.

I had Pudge's address, so I wrote him a short note and enclosed a photo of him in his "designer" bath robe... "Thought you'd appreciate a reminder of our fun trip," the note said. Funny thing, those phone calls just stopped.

12

RIGHT IN THE KISSER

For the protection of any innocent parties involved in this tale, I choose to use aliases to describe the participants. All other details are exactly as I remember them.

Joe and Dan had booked a half day trip early in May. I had never taken them fishing before, but they dropped enough names on me to make me feel comfortable with taking them. They knew lots of folks I was familiar with, and had been recommended by more than one. After questioning Dan (he called to set up the trip) about their respective fishing skills, I found they had never fished before, but always wanted to learn. Since that was not a new challenge to me, I readily accepted, but told them to show up at least an hour early so we could do a walk-through on the use of tackle.

Fishing was hot, with giant female stripers banging top water lures savagely. It was my very favorite time to charter and I viewed with a bit of disappointment that I'd have to let these two use live bait instead of lures. Teaching a pair of neophytes how to throw a seven-inch lure with two sets of treble hooks with vicious strikes available, was not the safest way to spend a morning. A nervous newcomer could easily sink one of those hooks into a body part (his or mine) which would result in a trip to the emergency room. Had been there and done that, and didn't care for a repeat. So bait it was and I busied myself catching same.

Weather-wise, early May can be questionable. This particular morning was going to be clear, with a slight breeze. It was also going to be unseasonably cold with a morning temp of slightly over freezing. I hoped my clients were going to dress properly since everything else was perfect. The restaurant usually did not open that early but the owner remembered he owed me some favors and did not mind coming in early that morning. It was a warm and cozy place to drink coffee, get to know my clients and give them the basic lessons they would need to help them both enjoy the trip and get their money's worth.

Dan and Joe were right on time. They were both huge and healthy-looking guys, only they were wearing shorts, muscle shirts, tube socks and Adidas. I thought perhaps they had warm clothing in the car and had left it there until it was time to go. I found out a bit later that I was wrong; what I saw was what I got.

After introductions were done and coffee ordered, we set about the business of learning basic fishing one on one. They were both quick learners and I knew I'd have no unsolvable problems regarding their use of tackle. They caught on to how we were going to fish, how to use equipment, how to set the hook and play the fish. I wished all my clients that had limited experience could catch on as easily as these two did. What would normally have taken an hour took less than fifteen minutes. To the joy of the cook, we were able to order a big breakfast before we set out to fish; kind of made it worth his while.

During breakfast, I learned that both men were in the contracting business. One of them built substantially priced homes, the other erected office buildings, hotels and other industrial buildings. They were old college friends and both extremely successful. Both were health nuts and worked out regularly, letting me know their regular eight-mile morning run would have to be done this evening. I passed when they invited me to come along. In my condition, eight minutes would have done me in. These guys were sharp-minded and exuded confidence in themselves. I really looked forward to spending some time on the water and to seeing their reaction when they were pitted against a fish as strong as the ones we were hoping to catch that morning. I was a bit taken aback when I found that the clothes on their backs was all they had brought. They assured me it was no problem, however, so I put it out of my mind. It did not stop me from donning a light jacket. I didn't have to prove a thing.

As we left the dock, I noticed the kind of ripple on the water that a guide could only pray for. It meant a slight wind that could be used for drifting under the best possible circumstances. I was ecstatic. I felt that this would be one of those memorable trips to write home about. I was right!

It didn't take more than fifteen minutes for me to find a sizable school of fish. They were tightly bunched over a ledge that dropped off to a hundred feet deep. The fish, however, were suspended at fifteen to eighteen feet, over some very tall, submerged tree tops. Normally, my reels are spooled with fifteen pound test line but knowing about where the fish would be, I opted to use twenty pound test in case one of my new fishermen allowed his fish to get down into the timber.

I was running a twenty-one foot, center console boat at the time. Center consoles were brand new to inland lakes, but I had convinced my old buddy Earl Bentz that they would soon be the design of choice as fresh water striper fishing became more and more popular. Earl is perhaps the best boat designer in the industry as his success with Hydra Sports, Stratos and now his newest company, Triton, shows. The high sides he designed allowed for maximum safety and the hull design for maximum speed and comfort. The oval-shaped bait wells were pure genius as they allowed for keeping bait fresh and in excellent shape. All in all, my guys were going to have their first fishing experience surrounded by the best equipment available.

When we set up for our first drift, I had Dan in the seat up forward and Joe in the pedestal seat on the rear deck. I was in the center operating the electric motor and keeping my eye on the depth finder. With the gentle breeze we had, I figured we would be able to stay in contact with the school of fish for at least ten minutes, surely enough time to hook at least two. Dan asked me to fish also so that they could take a limit of six fish home with them. They wanted to mount two and have a fish fry with the rest. They really put the pressure on me by saying they had already scheduled the party and had invited guests.

While I was putting a bait on for Joe, Dan dipped his own out of the bait tank and hooked it on himself. This was getting easier by the minute. I instructed Joe to "count down" dropping his bait one foot at a time, until it was at sixteen feet, or right in the middle of the school of stripers. The introduction of a very active live bait into a suspended school of predator fish is most times enough to trigger their feeding mechanism. This time was one of those times.

I was closest to Joe and saw instantly that the minute his bait came close to the stripers, his reel spool began to rotate at a very fast rate of speed. He had a fish on. Instead of engaging the reel, he did what is not uncommon to newcomers, he set the hook. He did it exactly how I had shown him, however the disengaged spool, rotating faster now, turned into a backlash of major proportions. I added my two hands to the rod so it wasn't torn out of Joe's hands and just hung on until the line broke; there was nothing else to be done.

"My God, I had no idea they could be so strong," said Joe, and then to Dan, " wait till you hang one, buddy, it'll jar your socks." I opted to take the next drift far enough above the fish so as to have all our baits down to the proper depth and all reel spools engaged by the time we reached the strike zone. Both my passengers voted to have me catch the first fish so they could watch the entire procedure. They recognized the strength of the fish was more than they had expected and wanted to be certain of every detail that would insure their personal successes. I'd never had a pair of customers that were so willing to "do it right." I supposed that was the reason they were so successful in their businesses.

At any rate, it didn't take long to hang the first fish. I took my time, explaining how to pump and reel, pump and reel, while keeping the rod tip elevated in order to allow the equipment to beat the fish, as it was designed to do. It's hardly ever the equipment that loses a fish, but rather the misuse of same. The first fish we netted and put in the boat was a male, about twenty pounds. My customers' mouths were agape and they were obviously stirred up. For some strange reason, they asked me to repeat the performance, again, while they watched. Though in my book, the customer is not always right, I was more than happy to comply. The second fish in the boat was almost a clone of the first. I had my limit and now it was time for Dan and Joe.

They had their baits at the proper depth, we were just passing over the outer edge of the school, and both had a hit at the same time. Dan set his hook a bit soon and missed his chance, but Joe was fast to his fish and was doing just fine. He took instructions calmly and, in no time at all, had his catch ready for the net. His fish was a bit smaller, about fifteen pounds. Three down, three to go. As I turned to start the engine to swing above the school again, I noticed Joe was red in the face and seemed to be struggling to catch his breath. I voiced my concern, as did Dan, but we were both assured that the experience had him hyperventilating and he could control that. "You'll see, pal," he said, "wait till you hang one, you'll see."

And see he did. On the next drift, Dan hung a fish. It was easy to see that this one was bigger than any we had hooked yet. Dan, to his credit, was picture-perfect in his handling of the fish. He was seemingly calm, took directions well, and as could be expected, almost fell completely apart when he saw the fish for the first time as it neared the surface, some fifteen feet from the boat. "That one will top forty pounds," I said as I reached for the net. This was a time for extreme caution, since one error could cost the fish. There were no errors as Dan slowly eased the fish closer to the net. When the fish was near enough, I gently slid the net over her head and began easing her over the side and into the boat.

My position in the boat caused me to be blocking the passageway that was open from bow to stern. The other passageway had a huge cooler that effectively blocked that one. The next thing I was aware of was Joe, hurtling over the console and landing squarely on the front deck. He threw his arms around his buddy and said, "See, I told you," and then he planted a kiss right on his friend's mouth. At that moment, I was grateful that the fish was in the boat. I pride myself at not being easily shook up, but that spur of activity could easily have caused me to drop net and fish.

I deem myself to be a pretty sophisticated person. I grew up in a tough neighborhood with friends that could squash walnuts or heads in their hands. The "hood" was diverse as could be and people of "other persuasions" were not foreign to us. There was never any teasing or pushing and shoving; everyone got along well. If anyone had ever threatened our gay buddy "Smitty" they would have done so at great peril to themselves. But this one, this one got to me a bit more than I like to admit.

Dan insisted on immediate photos and we spent an entire roll of film in both of their cameras, each of them holding the fish in every conceivable way possible. By the time we were done with that activity, I noticed we had spent the best part of a half hour creating photo ops. It was time to catch two more and be done with it.

As I drove up to the marker buoy I'd tossed out earlier, I learned with dread that the school of fish had dispersed. They were nowhere to be seen on the electronics and a mile of circling the area didn't turn up even a single. My customers only knew they wanted two more fish and wouldn't settle for less. I was becoming a nervous wreck and had to reel myself in so I could finish this deal.

I had one spot I always saved as an "ace in the hole" and opted to give it a try. The Gods were good! In less than fifteen minutes, both had boated a fish about ten pounds each. They wondered if they could release them and try for larger ones and, with tongue in cheek, I told them that once they were in the boat, they had to be counted. We had our legal limit and had to quit fishing. They regretfully understood but seemed disappointed that one fish to be mounted was so much bigger than any other that might be mounted. I detected a bit of jealousy but did not push it any further.

After loading up their fish, both guys shook my hand and gave me a thankful hug, as well as a very generous tip. They never used my services again, but for the next two years, sent me a Christmas card. The third year I got two cards, one from Florida and one from California. For the first time, the cards were signed separately. I learned that the friends had split, sold their respective businesses and had moved as far away from each other as the continent would allow.

It embarrasses me now that the incident "spooked" me. Though I didn't show it, I felt it. Isn't it strange how easy it is to lose one's grip on things, even for a second.

I truly hope the fault of the break-up wasn't that one fish was so much bigger than the other. That would surely make me wonder if I had tried hard enough to help even the score. Isn't evening the score what it's all about?

147

13

NET PROFIT

Everyone has a Henry Blake in their lives; that's almost a positive. Oh, the name may be different but the game is the same. Henry, or whatever you choose to name your person, behaves as follows:

He (or she) knows EVERYTHING. If there is ever a doubt about that, just ask him. Henry knows all about the weather, the stock market, how to prune a tree and do dentistry on your dog. He also knows how many feet in a roll of toilet tissue, duct tape, and what was the longest leap on record for a flea or a frog. In other words, Henry is an expert's expert. And other than being at most times an annoying pain in the rear, Henry makes you feel somehow like patting him on the head so you can see him wag his tail.

Our Henry was, on top of all that, an imbiber, a true-blue and full blown alchy. He was not a sloppy drunk or a staggering drunk. Nor was he a slurring drunk or a mean drunk. Henry was an impossibly happy and impish drunk; the only kind you ever want to be near. I hate to say this, but Henry was more fun to be around when he was drunk, rather than sober.

In order for you to get the full impact of this saga, I need to set the scenario as it was the day Henry stepped onto the national stage with a splash heard around the entire fishing world. With but one act, he created a legend for all to talk about wherever tales were swapped. If you were actually a witness, you would forever be a part of the legend.

It was April, 1980. The location was Tim's Ford Reservoir, a 10,000 acre gem of pristine water tucked in a valley between Winchester and Tullahoma, Tennessee. It was the site of the very first *Striper* Magazine tournaments that would eventually lead to four hundred more such events over the next ten years.

Fresh water striper fishing was a new game in much of the country, and literally thousands of excited outdoors folks were struggling to find information on how to catch this wonderful and huge fish. When people are so hungry for information, it's only normal for the airwaves to be full of phony data. That kind of stuff results in serious damage to a resource and creates untold problems for fisheries biologists and managers.

I had been giving teaching seminars to fishermen all over the country, as well as being involved in several educational symposiums at state fisheries meetings, from 1977 to 1979. In 1978 I decided to form an organization of fisher-folks and *Striper* was born. Six months later we published our first bi-monthly magazine and in 1980 were ready to hold our first competitive event.

Our format was to be different and new. It allowed for men, women and kids to compete equally for all prizes. As a matter of fact, a thirteen year-old boy took second place. The fishing tackle world was beginning to take notice of what we were doing, and sponsorships were beginning to fall into place. Perhaps the most prestigious of these sponsors at that time was the Abu-Garcia Mfg. Co. They were so excited about our new concept that the CEO and owner, Lennart Borgstrum, decided to spend the week of this event with us to observe the results. He and his staff flew all the way from

Denmark specifically to be with us. All of this in the hopes that it will show, in part, the electricity and energy that was flowing.

Sharing information with each other was one of the basic tenets of the event. Trying to get fishermen to honestly tell where, how and when, especially during a competitive event, used to be a joke. Striper members were schooled differently. The health of the resource depended on it, and our members were more than willing. Information was flowing freely, and it was a joy for me and my staff to watch people with a common interest, meeting other people from other parts of the country, in what was in many cases the beginning of long-term and deep friendships.

The tournament schedule included a seminar and lake update on Friday evening, with starting time at daylight on Saturday. Fishing would run continuously through Saturday night with the final weigh-in at three p.m. on Sunday when winners would be announced and awards distributed.

By Wednesday all cabins and rooms at Holiday Marina were full. Cars from twenty-four different states were parked anywhere space allowed. There were jovial lines at restaurants and restrooms and information-hungry folks were everywhere, asking questions of anyone who seemed to be the slightest bit knowledgeable.

Enter Henry!

Lennart's headquarters for the week was a spacious, multi-deck houseboat, provided for his use by George Wagner, the then-owner of Holiday Marina. We chose that spot for our weigh-ins and award ceremony so that Lennart could speak to the competitors as they came up to the scale. He was keenly interested in how many folks were using Garcia tackle. His interest in the fishery was exciting for all of us, and the staff he brought along eagerly discussed new tackle and searched for info that would help them design tougher reels for this specific market.

At around noon on Friday, there were about thirty or forty folks gathered at the end of the dock. Lennart was on the upper deck of the houseboat watching and filming some of the activity. There was a young man, probably seventeen or eighteen years old at the very end of the dock, trying as hard as he could to master the art of throwing a cast net. He had someone reading directions to him as he tried again and again to keep the net fully extended when he threw it. Time after time, the net collapsed before it hit the water. He never gave up, though, and continued to try. It was obvious that no one in that crowd knew any more than the boy, since no one except the fellow reading instructions had a word to say.

Henry had been sharing his bottle of bourbon with some of the local folks and was well on his way to becoming happy. He was vocal, back-slapping and evidently endearing to his companions. The activity at the end of the dock caught his glistening blue orbs, and he immediately headed for the crowd, his favorite venue.

Pushing his way through the gathering, he mused, "Looks like you're having a tough time with that net."

"Of course I am," the boy said, "this thing has about got me whipped and I'm almost ready to give up on it."

"Whoa," said Henry, "I'll have you throwing that net just like a pro in less than fifteen minutes." Boy, did that get the crowd's attention. The boy looked incredulous; he'd been at this for over an hour and a half and here was an offer to learn how in fifteen minutes. He immediately handed the net to Henry, who instantly took control.

His movements and body language were slow, fluid and dramatic. "Back up please," he authoritatively pleaded to the crowd, "I need some room to properly execute this move." He spent the next ten minutes or so discussing the virtues of the cast net, the proper mesh size, the drying, repair and care. He even threw in, as an aside, the proper way to store it when not in use. Within that ten minutes, Henry had hypnotized his audience – he literally owned them. That included Lennart, who was watching from his perch over the water. When he was certain that he had everyone's rapt attention (and he did) he made ready to throw the net.

"I'm only going to have to show you this one time," he bragged. "It's so easy when you know how, you'll laugh at all the little mistakes you're making. And you can throw those directions away," he said, "they're all wrong anyway." He was so positive and so commanding, he even had my attention. I climbed on board the houseboat and joined Lennart top-side. He was so engrossed and busy filming, he barely noticed my presence.

"You hold it thusly," Henry said, gathering several feet of the net in his left hand, as he held the rest in his right. "You need to make it as compact as possible so you can handle an even bigger one than you have here." The boy looked on in awe, the crowd silently anticipating the lesson. Henry placed a small section of the net in his mouth so as to have none of it touching the ground. He artfully and gently swung the net from side to side once, twice, and with a deft twitch of his wrists and head, let it sail. The entire net popped open, just as it was designed to do, and traveled in an almost slow-motion arc until it settled gently and fully open on the water.

Applause immediately erupted from the watchers. Shouts of approval could be heard clear across the parking lot. As Henry turned to face his appreciative audience, sporting a how-about-that smile, a stunned silence fell over the crowd. Henry's smile was toothless. He had thrown his dentures, along with the net, into the cold waters of Tim's Ford Reservoir. Henry sobered immediately and without a word, pushed through the crowd and left the dock.

In the meantime the two boys who had been trying to throw the net were laughing so hard that they both fell off the end of the dock. A couple of onlookers attempted to help them out and slipped into the lake themselves. The score so far was the net and four folks in the drink. Everyone finally got out of the water and the owner of the net grabbed the line that was lying on the dock and began to retrieve the net. As the net emerged from the water, the watching crowd burst into hilarious laughter. There, still in the net, biting the line between two lead sinkers was Henry's set of uppers and lowers.

And then the jokes started. "I don't know if I want to throw a net that bad," someone offered. "Yeah," the reply, "that could get damned expensive." And on and on. The classic remark, however, was made by the young net owner. Claiming the ancient laws of salvage, he held his prize high in the air and proclaimed, "I'm gonna keep these, I may need them someday when I get old." Lennart and I were laughing so hard we had tears in our eyes. We joshed about showing his film at next season's festival in Cannes. Or maybe save it for some stag night hilarity. The possibilities loomed endlessly.

As for Henry, he showed up in time for the tournament. He wasn't smiling, so we didn't know if he had a spare; we never asked. He was spotted in several locations over the tournament time, but never weighed in a fish. Folks reported they had passed him, some even asked how he was doing. The consensus among all who saw him was that Henry was keeping his mouth shut.

14

RIVER RATS

There are streams and there are rivers. Fishermen that ply their skills on streams at times look as if they had just stepped off the cover of the latest Cabella's catalogue. Dressed in the sharpest outdoor wear, sporting form-fitting chest waders, and carrying pricey-looking fly rods, they all look so handsome. And forever, they will be known as "purists."

Those, however, who fish rivers could be bearded (or just unshaven), disheveled, odiferous, or any other shaggy description. They will never be seen on any catalogue cover but forever will be lovingly known as "river-rats."

I've fished rivers all over the country and in several places throughout the world. "River-rats" are apparent around every one. I claim the title myself. We don't use boats or waders, we mostly carry our lures in our pockets. We study eddies, generation schedules, water levels, clarity and dozens of other river sciences. There's no place to read up on that stuff, it's all hands-on and paying one's dues.

And best of all, when you become a full fledged "rat", you speak the language of the river. No matter what ethnic language another river rat speaks, you are able to communicate clearly. I must add, however, that much of the communicating is done through grunts, nods, exclamations and body language. More importantly, except on the rarest of occasions, this brotherhood takes special care of its own.

There are river rat rules. There are dues to be paid. All of this is unspoken, unwritten, but fully understood. For example, the river bank could be lined with a hundred fishermen yet, when the words "fish on" ring out, everyone acquiesces to the lucky angler. As he chases his fish down-river, all lines are reeled in to avoid tangles, and safe passage is allowed. Someone will always stop fishing altogether to follow and make certain there is no slip, and also to help land the fish during the last critical moments. Fishing a fast-moving river off the slippery rocks lining the bank is not only dangerous but, at best, an athletic endeavor.

And to the "rats" the river is Camelot. There is, of course, a hierarchy. Kingship, however, changes on a regular basis. The most and the biggest dictate who will rule. There are always squires; those anxious to learn, eager to pay their dues. They learn to operate within the rules and eagerly seek out those who are willing to teach. And teachers there are many since it's been long accepted as the only way to perpetuate the clan.

The river that flows under the dam at Keystone Lake has, like all other rivers, its devotees. It was here that I chose to film the first episode of a planned TV series to be called "Striper USA."

I loved coming to Tulsa. It housed the headquarters for two of our biggest advertisers, Zebco Fishing Tackle and Lowrance Electronics. Daryl Lowrance was and still is the CEO and owner of his company. He continues to this day to amaze me with new innovations that keep him on the cutting edge of an extremely competitive technology. At Zebco, adventures abounded. We had just completed a signature rod series that included myself, Bill Dance and Tom Mann. Some of the tales I have to swap about adventuring with those two will really have you rolling on the floor.

Jay Montgomery was the creative ad guy at Zebco and after the "rod deal" he invented a radio show that included the same trio. It turned out to be great sport for all concerned. Jay left Zebco (boo-hoo) and went out to the west coast to join the prestigious Saatchi agency. He now lives in New York, is with the same agency and is creative director for the Toyota account. Whenever you see a Toyota ad, think of Jay. I do. Whoops, I just got a call, informing me that Jay has decided to go out on his own, and free-lance. Ray Jay!

You'll have to forgive me for this aside, but it should be obvious to everyone that if you allow adventure into your lives, your story will never end, nor will it ever stop growing, nor will you.

Another Zebco regular was Bob Reid, marketing director and a most fun guy. Bob has since been marketing director for Daisy, Johnson, Berkley and currently is the number two guy at Ebonite. We still visit and continue to swap old and new stories. And then there was the genius that held all of the Zebco empire together, John Charvat. John was solely responsible for his company owning the largest market share in the industry. His talent led him to manage not only Zebco but the Brunswick Corporation as well as AMC, a giant outboard motor and boat manufacturing conglomerate. How thrilling it was for me that my life crossed and continues to cross the paths of such accountable and incredibly fine people. My mom always told me, "If you look for the best in people, surely you will find it."

But here we were, on the banks of the river, awaiting the siren that would indicate the generators were to be turned on and water would be rushing through the gates at incredible speeds. This action caused a re-generation of oxygen flow and mass movement of schools of bait fish in an upstream direction. More importantly, it almost always awakened the appetites of hungry predator fish. I guess you could liken it to passing a bakery when the ovens were just opened and fresh

157

bread was being taken out...yum.

Kings of the river this particular week were Tulsa natives David Clark and Johnny Furr. They were soon to become, in their words, "movie stars." David and Johnny were both self-employed in the building trades, and seemed to have no difficulty in arranging their time schedules. As a matter of fact, as I later learned, those work schedules were arranged around the generating schedule, which was almost always posted a day in advance. It was obvious they had taken over joint rule of the river kingdom, and meant to spend whatever time it took to retain their thrones.

The river below this particular dam had its own idiosyncrasies. No two rivers are really exactly alike, and each has to be thoroughly "read" before one can hope for success. Of course "rats" trade secrets, making it a bit easier on newcomers. One never knows when one will be visiting a brother rat's digs and will need the favor returned.

The fish at this time were holding mostly in the eddy emanating from the end of the first wing-wall. This caused a small problem in that the wing wall was probably a half a football field in length, away from the bank. Heavy sinkers were a no-no since they would easily snag on the rocky bottom. Add to that the fact that the fish were only hitting the smallest of lures and you have a technical snafu of giant proportions. Not to worry. The most innovative people in the world are those who fish. Present them with a problem and, sooner or later, an answer will be developed. Such it was in this case.

In order to cast light lures further, it would be necessary to use lighter line, a large capacity reel and a much longer than usual rod. What came off the drawing board were rods of fifteen to eighteen feet. And since there was no such thing available in the tackle world at the time, every one had to be custom made. It was almost surreal to look down the river bank on this misty morning to view a virtual rod forest. It's worth a trip to Tulsa just to see that sight.

At any rate, the film crew was ready and the would-be "stars" were champing at the bit. They promised we could get the fishing part done in less than an hour and the fill-in parts could be done at any time. They really did not want to tie up the river for more than that amount of time. They had walked the bank and worked the parking lot and had gotten approval from the nearly fifty other fisher-folks present to wait for that long for the filming to end. That was a major feat in itself and I doubt if they had not been co-kings could they have pulled it off.

The lures were all self-made, and each of the two had a folder of at least a hundred in their respective pockets. In other pockets, they carried light sinkers. The rigging was simple. The sinker went on first then about a foot above it was tied the first lure which was a hook tied with a colored chenille type material. A foot above the first, a second chenille dressed hook was tied on, thus presenting two lures floating down river, one above the other.

"What happens if you get two on at once?" I innocently asked. Johnny chirped in with an impish smile that, "We get to go home a little earlier." With that, Johnny climbed up on "his rock" (I'll explain that in a minute) and made a mighty cast with what looked like a skinny telephone pole in his hand. The lures arced lazily overhead and landed exactly where he wanted them to. As I turned to alert the cameraman, Johnny sung out "fish-on" and speedily headed down river. Completely unprepared for this, the camera crew stood dazed, staring at Johnny's back as he headed down river at an amazingly rapid pace.

In less than five minutes, Johnny was back carrying a ten-pound striper. Grinning from ear to ear he asked, "Did you get that?"

"No, stupid, if you want to be an actor, you have to wait for your cue to act...you blew that one, bub, now it's my turn." Johnny and David were lifelong friends, so one calling the other stupid was simply their way of communicating. It got worse.

I need to explain that every "rat" is dubbed with a name which may vary from river to river. Many of the names began with "The." For instance Johnny was known as The Carpenter and David, The Rug Man. I was to be known forever more on this river as The Bearded One.

At any rate, David climbed on the flat rock Johnny had vacated and turned, smiling to the cameraman. He waited till he got the nod and even though he was overacting, expertly cast his lure into the exact spot he wanted. The results were instant, and he even turned what he figured was his most photogenic side toward the camera while shouting in a rich tenor voice, "Fish on." The camera was able to follow the action while I was busy doing the voice-over. "That's the way it's done, stupid," he said to his pal with that wicked, impish grin.

"I wouldn't brag yet, idiot," smiled Johnny in return. "That peanut of a fish you just caught ain't big enough to keep in the movie, all you done was waste film and time. I'll show you what folks want to see," he bragged, and then went on to prove it by catching a sleek fifteen-pounder. The whole scene was captured on film. Between the two, David and Johnny caught ten nice fish, created a ton of laughs, and allowed us to get a great river show. Then the unthinkable. On camera (pre-planned, I am sure) they invited "The Bearded One" to try to catch a fish their way.

I grew up fishing the surf along the Jersey Coast, so longer rods were not new to me. By longer I mean eight to nine footers. But a sixteen footer? Hell, I'm only five foot seven in my shoes and that rod was three of me. Oh well, it was a dare and I sure couldn't pass that one up. The guys were patient with my fumbling and coached me into the ease of using this equipment. I knew how to read the river so it was only the technique I had to master. We had fifteen minutes left in our hour of grace and I managed to catch two fish. I thanked the guys for not busting my chops over the fact that they were the smallest two caught. But all that is on film and the letters we got in response were fun-filled and congratulatory.

We did our visit and interview section of the film in the parking lot overlooking the river and the wide angle shots were spectacular. It was truly a great beginning for STRIPER USA and I couldn't thank them enough. Johnny and David were a bit edgy to get back to their rocks and pleaded with me to join them for one more hour. They presented me with a custom rod they had made for me and were careful to let me know the rod was mine but the reel was a loaner.

Now about those rocks. It is an unspoken but firm "river rat rule" that possession of a rock makes it the fisherpersons real estate for that day. It's not unusual to see someone standing on a rock an hour or so before fishing begins, just to establish ownership. In the way of explanation, there are few perfectly dry and flat-topped rocks available, so competition for the best ones is keen. Even the "king" has to claim one on a daily basis. What gets sticky for newcomers is the "rock taboo." It is understood that when a fish is hooked and the fisherman heads downriver to land his fish, no one will occupy his rock...clearly it is his when he returns.

When we got back down to the river's edge, it was obvious to see that all of the near-fifty fishermen present were true, dues-paying "rats." The two rocks John and David were catching so many fish from were vacant, awaiting their return. How nice is that? In between the two was a really small Oriental man. His rock was a bit higher above the river but was flat enough on top for him to stand on. He was introduced to me as "Nimble Nim." His real name was Nim Ying. Nim owned a Vietnamese restaurant where some of the "rats" would bring their catch for him to prepare a meal from. Nim

161

was perhaps five feet tall and maybe weighed a hundred and ten pounds. It was incredible how this very slightly built person handled the long rod. It seemed an extension of his body and his movements were fluid enough to be almost poetic. He spoke halting English but his river language sang loud and clear, making him a member of the clan which, by the way, does not seem to be concerned with size, gender, race or religion. None of that stuff is ever discussed on the river.

"Fish on" sang out Nim as he set the hook and with great agility slid off his high perch and started hopping rocks on his way downstream. We watched, fascinated because it was obvious Nim had on a good fish. Several in the crowd quit fishing to follow and watch and encourage Nim, we three included. Jokes and gentle chiding and much loud advice ensued during the ten to fifteen minute struggle. Johnny was the one to get his feet in the water to allow Nim to swing his fish toward his outstretched hand. John deftly gilled the fish, which turned out to be just under forty pounds. It was the largest taken out of the river this year and clearly put in danger David and Johnny's rule. Without hesitation they sped back to their respective stations to try and protect their reign. They were so intent on getting back to their spots, they completely missed the fact that an unthinkable, despicable act had taken place in their brief absence. Someone, a stranger to the river, had claimed Nim's rock.

It took Nim a while to get back to his spot, having to drag a fish that looked at least as big as he was. When he finally got to his spot and noticed the stranger, he looked up and smiling politely said in his best English, "S'cuse prease, my loc." Everyone within earshot clearly understood except the stranger. He was big, probably six feet-two or more, and bulky. He looked like he might have weighed two hundred plus, muscular pounds. He sure as hell was tough-looking, and tough-sounding, too.

He ignored Nim completely and made a cast. Nim waited patiently for him to retrieve his lure and once again in a gentle and patient way said, "S'cuse prease, my loc." He didn't ignore Nim this time; he looked down and said, "Quit botherin' me or I'll slap you silly," and turned and made another cast. By this time the scenario was getting some attention and a few folks started to make their way toward the scene. Nim, again showing that wonderful Oriental patience, waited until the cast was completed and the lure was retrieved. Once again his gentle statement, "S'cuse prease, my loc." This time the stranger, now face red and neck bulging exclaimed, "Look slopehead, why the hell don't you go back where you came from before I climb down and break your damned neck."

Johnny and David started to move at the same time but their intervention was unnecessary. Without a word, Nim grabbed his rod in the middle and with that same artful, lithe and swift motion, swung it as hard as he could toward the stranger's midsection. The huge, heavy reel caught him right where his legs come together. In the instant before he doubled up, his arms flew straight up, throwing his rod and reel far into the river. He then fell off the rock and followed his rod and reel but, not nearly as far into the river. Hollering and cursing, he swiftly floated down river, not a soul offering to help. In a really short period of time he managed to climb out of the water some hundred and fifty feet from where he went in.

Showing zero emotion, Nim climbed back on his rock and, as he was readying to make a cast, mumbled under his breath, "My loc." The stranger never came back, at least that day. There was much discussion in the parking lot over who would have helped Nim out if it became necessary. It was muy macho, mano-to-mano speak, but it was all filled with admiration for "Nimble Nim" whose new name was now to be "Nim the Terrible."

Once again the river proved to be a singular adventure, one we all know will change upon each visit. We had met with our Tulsa friends, we had done business, we had shot a wonderful film, we had added to the "rat" legend. How much better could it get?

Not to be outdone, and needing to have the very last word, Johnny said with mock drama, "Boy, did I learn something today. We're doing this all wrong, hooking a fish and chasing him over those slick rocks, taking our life in our hands. What we need to do is, every time we hook a fish, just jump in the river and float down after him, just like Nim showed that guy how to do."

RIGHT!

15

JOE SHARK

The crowd at Bell's Marina in Eutawville, South Carolina, was as diverse a group as could be put together. The ones that come to mind are: Cholly Clark, Santee Hotel and golf course owner; Ray Oliver, a dentist and avid Clemson fan; Fuzzy Lambert, who at that time was area rep for Lowrance Electronics (Fuzzy's with Minnkota now); and Ray Watson, a successful fabric salesman from North Carolina and his lovely wife Dolly, a professional golfer. Add to that motley crew myself, Lindsay Sale, who was associate editor of *Striper* Magazine, and Danny Bell, wise-cracking owner of the establishment we were occupying at the time. Several other faces I'm unable to attach names to at this moment will hopefully forgive me when they read and re-live this oh so fun moment in our lives. We were all eating breakfast and swapping tales in Danny's restaurant.

With that many folks together in one room, you can imagine the stories that were flying around. It quickly became a contest of "one upsmanship" that got funnier by the minute. Breakfast all but forgotten, "the contest" was now way past believable, almost but not quite into the realm of fairy tales.

Into this melee of words, totally unaware of what was going on, walked Joe Drose. Joe and his brother were, among other things, fishing guides on Santee Cooper, and besides being a really good fisherman, Joe had a reputation as a story teller with a sharp wit. He was the butt of many a joke, but always seemed to give a little better than he got.

No one intentionally ignored Joe, it was just that this "contest" was in full swing, and since he had no part in it, no one even bothered to acknowledge his presence. He sat down at the counter and ordered his breakfast.

The conversation at that moment was, would you believe, swirling around felines. That's right, cats! The cat stories were flowing. Who had a six-toed cat? Who had one with fourteen? Someone knew of one with two tails and the one-up to that was one with two heads. "I swear, I saw it with my own eyes." That one made things slow down as if we all realized the thing was getting silly. It was at that moment that Joe spoke up.

"My next door neighbor had cats," he said, "a lot of cats." The following is as close to his narrative as I can remember. With everyone's attention glued on him and with as serious a look as he could muster, he went on. "Yeah, she had a lot of cats. As a matter of fact, every time I got ready to start my car, I had cats on the hood, on the manifold, on the roof, under the fender wells…they were everywhere. She sure had a lot of cats, must have been over a hundred."

"Anyhow," he went on, "I got this idea. I was doing a lot of shark fishing in the gulf; sharks were bringing a good price at the market. The only thing was expenses were killing me. What with the price of fuel and the outrageous price of bait, it was hardly worth the time. But seeing all those cats, I had an idea I could cut my bait cost to zero if I used one or two of them. And it wasn't as if my neighbor would miss them, her having more than she could keep up with. The next time I went, I just took a couple."

Wide eyes were carefully scrutinizing Joe's face looking for some hint that he was only kidding; there was none. He

166

went on, "We got some small wooden boards, and tied the cats to them. Then we wound some elastic cord around the whole deal and put our hook under the wrapping, but we didn't hurt the cat none. After that was all set up, we set the whole deal, cat, board, hook and line over the side."

He explained in lurid detail how they set the reel on free spool and watched as the cat floated further and further away from the boat. "Man, you should have seen the hit, it was better than using a top water lure," saying that with such glee as to have us all shivering with anxiety over what he'd say next. "Boy," he went on, "the darn sharks were actually fighting over that cat." We finally used 'em both and caught two huge sharks, and without the cost of bait, it was really worth our while."

I could see that I wasn't the only one getting a bit queasy as he continued his story.

"Anyway, we did that for about three months, taking more cats with us on each trip. One day I was mowing my lawn and my neighbor lady waved me over. 'Mr. Joe,' she said, 'my cats are all running away and I can't find any of them, have you seen any cats around lately, I can't imagine what's happened to them.'"

Joe's face was poker-player straight when he told how he answered her. "Yes ma'am, I know what happened to your cats; the sharks ate 'em."

Joe took a bite of his biscuit as the rest of us mulled the story over in our minds. We were horrified at the thought, and some of us (me included) were close to believing at least some of the story. No one could make up a whopper like that, or could they? The room was silent, all eyes on Joe.

Before anyone in the group could break out of our near catatonic state, Joe turned around to face us and said, "That ain't the end of the shark deal. Y'all know I guide some on the lake and the biggest pain in the butt is the free-loaders that follow me and my clients. I never thought that was fair to the people that were paying me to find them some fish, and have ten other boats ride along for free."

He went on, "I got an idea, the last time we went shark fishing. Bait was getting hard to find and the market price for sharks was going down. Anyhow, the last trip we only had two, a mako and a hammerhead that was about eight feet long. The markets were only buying makos, but I had this idea so we kept the hammerhead and carried it home."

We were all on the edge of our seats, Joe holding us on a tight rein. "I kept the hammerhead in the boat overnight and left for the lake really early the next morning 'cause I had a paying customer that was going to meet me at the boat ramp. I got my boat in the water way before daylight while the parking lot was empty. I laid off shore for an hour or so, and here they come, the followers. It was just getting light and I figured the time was right so I gunned the engine and run the boat right up on the concrete ramp; all the while hollerin 'SHARK!' as loud as I could. When I had everyone's attention I said, 'Look what I got," pointing at the hammerhead, "there must be a hundred of 'em right out in front of the ramp." Joe explained that it only took one look at that dead shark to empty the parking lot.

"I took that shark out and tied a cement block around him and sunk him where I could get at him and use him again. Picked up my passengers, had a great trip, and not one person followed me all day."

Joe turned back to the counter, quickly finished his breakfast, surrounded by absolute silence. He got up, paid for his meal and started to leave. Just before going out the door, he faced us all and said, "I guess I didn't figure it all out like I should have." After a slow, agonizing (to us) pause he ended with, "I went out the next morning to get my shark so I could use him again, but the damn turtles got to him first, now ain't that somethin'." As the door closed behind him, there was little to be said. In the sense of a contest, Joe surely had won hands-down but, was there the remotest possibility that there might be a smidgen of truth in his narrative?

I learned recently that Danny Bell had passed away and that saddened me. But every time we meet or speak to one of the folks who were there the story comes up. There is always the question of how much was fable or what part could have been real or, could anyone have a mind weird enough to have made the whole thing up.

We'll never know for sure, but the remembering brings images of old friends, fun times and life very worth living. Bye, Danny, we miss you!

16

ANDY'S STORY

As editor and publisher of *Striper* Magazine for almost eleven years, I received dozens of letters weekly. Some were happy, some angry, some downright disagreeable. They were from senators, governors, athletes, heads of corporations, leaders of industry and just plain folks, like most of us. One such letter prompted the following tale and created one of the most profound and humbling experiences of my journey through life. Much of it is reprinted from my magazine.

From *Striper* Magazine Nov/Dec 1980:

Andrew Hessington, Sr. is my friend. I don't take friendship lightly. It carries with it the responsibility of caring and unselfish sharing...it has to be earned and it is one of life's worthwhile experiences. Andrew is almost 74 years old. He has seen much of life. He is gentle and he is clever and has much of a child's awareness. His eyes are always bright and shiny, a smile ever-present and a wondrous way of always making you know he is there, without saying a word. He has enriched my life as I hope his story will enrich yours.

Andy's name first came to my attention over a

171

year ago. A scrawled note addressed to me personally indicated simply that he had heard of *Striper* Magazine and wanted to know more. I get lots of similar letters. I'm not much on divine providence but I often wonder what would have happened had I not told my secretary to put all letters addressed to me on my desk. I have this funny thing about wanting to or trying to answer all those letters myself...makes me feel good to be in touch.

At any rate, I dictated a short reply and included the standard information. Andy's membership application came back quickly, with a note telling me how pleased he was that I took the time to answer. His genuineness has remained constant. Two magazines later, another letter from Andy telling us how great we were and how he watched his mail box with hunger each time a new issue was due and also, the following which with great reverence we printed in our July/ Aug 1979 issue.

The following is a reprint of Andy's letter:

When I was a boy of about seven or eight years old, I used to hand net in the Delaware River for small fish and one species always appealed to me more than any of the others. This small fish had three or four stripes on each side. I did not know what kind it was then but in later years, learned it was a striped bass. I never knew just how big they grew until I was in my late twenties. By this time, I was fishing especially for them. I traveled all over the state of New Jersey hitting the bays and rivers and never did catch one, nor did I ever see one caught by any other fisherman. I would read about them being caught in the surf or at the mouth of rivers. By this time, my interest in stripers began to grow.

When my son was only seven years old, I bought an outboard motor and went to different places every Saturday or Sunday and tried my luck. My boy ran the motor and I fished. This went on from early morning until late in the day with nary a strike from a bass.

While on one of my trips, I met up with an old shad fisherman whom I had known for several years. I talked to him about the striper's habits, hoping that I would learn something which would help me in my quest. During my conversation with him, I thought I finally found a way to get results. He told me that in the spring of the year when the shad make their run into the bays and up the rivers to lay their spawn, the stripers followed and ate the shad roe. An idea hit me! If I had some way of using that shad roe on a troll line, I might get the bass to hit it. So in the spring of 1936, I bought shad roe in its natural form. My next problem was to find a way to keep it on the hook. I thought that cellophane bags would do the trick if I could find the right size, about three inches wide and six inches long. The mission was accomplished and the night of preparation was here.

We had set up another trip and the night before my son and I inserted the roe into the bags very neatly. A hook was tied to a piece of line and also placed in the bags with the barbed end piercing the bag. We then put them into the refrigerator until morning.

A beautiful day dawned and we gathered together the tackle and bait and were on our way. This trip was on the Mullica River in New Jersey. I had heard that stripers were being caught there at this time. I hired a boat and trolled the Swan Bay section all day long but still no luck – not so much as a nibble. I sure was disheartened but not too discouraged.

By now, my mouth was watering for the feel of a big striper on the end of my line! As the years rolled by, I would like to bet that I bought enough blood worms for bait that if I laid them end to end they would cover a mile, and then some. My enthusiasm wasn't dampened by my failures, though, for when I wasn't fishing for them, I was dreaming about them and I always managed to catch at least one in each dream but never on a real trip. Just about eighteen years gone by and not a striper to show for them.

Hauck, a great fisherman of striped bass, owned the place where I always stopped to buy blood worms when going to the Maurice River in New Jersey. After I knew him for two years, I began to hint around for him to take me fishing. He had a 28-foot boat and we could sure do some good fishing from that! Finally I arranged a trip with Hauck and a friend. We arrived at his store at 8 a.m. on a very brisk Saturday morning early in November. He had another friend with him so the four of us boarded the boat and were on our way. We arrived where Hauck wanted to fish. He had been at this particular spot many times and as recent as two days ago when he had caught thirteen bass in all. It was not impossible to catch one in this river, weighing fifteen to twenty pounds. My hopes were riding high and I guess you can imagine that I was sure getting excited by this time. I never felt so happy in my life.

We anchored the boat and started fishing with the blood worms. Hauck was a man who preferred fishing on the bottom for bass. It wasn't long after we were there that we noticed swirls in the water about 100 feet behind the boat. Then we saw fish breaking the water and Hauck said they were stripers playing on the top but would soon go to the bottom and start to feed. Sure enough, about fifteen minutes later he got the first bite and pulled in a bass of about three pounds. I was really keyed up now and thought that I would have a heart attack. My friend then caught one, then the other fellow pulled one in weighing about six pounds. Still, I did not get a bite. By now I was beginning to think that they just wouldn't bite on my line, I hadn't as yet even felt a nibble. I got so worked up that I broke out in a cold sweat. Just then I felt a tug at the line! It became taut! I knew that I had hooked into a big one! I couldn't reel it in I was so excited. About now Hauck and the others were getting a little concerned. Hauck started to give me instructions as to what to do as he took the landing net in his hands to help me. I was never so thrilled in my whole life. I could only imagine a big striped bass on my line after about twenty years of fishing for them. Hauck was saying to me, "Take it real easy, you sure have a big one on your line by the way it's pulling." Then came the moment I had been waiting for. I brought my catch to the surface. Hauck was set with the net in the water. I was reeling and he netted the catch and pulled it into the boat.

Well, lo and behold, there on one hook was a three- pound catfish and a gallon paint can on the other. I was sick! The others were just dumbstruck! They said that they never would have believed it if they had not seen it.

I am still chasing stripers all over the waters of New Jersey and this story is positively true. Signed Andrew Hessington, Jr.

Andy was beside himself that we would honor him so by reprinting his story. He was not aware then, nor is he now, of how much joy he gave us here or how his sharing his experiences affected many of us. He became our hero, we fell in love with him...we prayed for him to catch his striper.

How did Andy react? Like Andy! Several days later, a gift arrived at headquarters for me. Opening it was like Christmas for a kid. Ten pencils, a half dozen ball point pens, a roll of note paper and a roller holder, a neat pocket calendar and a small cedar box that smelled so good. The treasures of a child...the desire of one man wanting in his simple way to say "thank you" to another. No single gift in my life has ever pleased me more. Andy and I became pen pals, though I must admit my busy schedule has caused me to be a bit inconsistent in answering.

In one of Andy's now newsy letters came the information that he and his wife of over fifty years were planning a drive to Florida. He wanted to know of a good striper lake on his planned route and all the information we could give him so that he could perhaps stop and give it a try to catch his first striper. My answer was sort of blunt, as long as he was coming south, if he didn't stop in Nashville and give me the privilege of seeing this miracle happen, I'd never forgive him. Plans began to gel. We chose two days on Andy's return trip from Florida. My tournament schedule had me out of town a bunch and the timing had to be perfect. When I arrived at home, it was to a message that Andy's wife had become ill and he thought it best to get her home...poor Andy was thwarted again.

More letters and soon another tentative date was set. but really tentative...it's a long drive from Villas, New Jersey to Nashville. Enter Sir Lancelot in the form of Andy's son, Bud. The thought of his dad fulfilling his dream and the availability of that possibility made him take positive action. Like his father, young Bud is a gentle person and he apologetically requested that he be able to come, insisting that he wouldn't fish or get in the way, but only take photos. There was no way in the world I could refuse. This was becoming a real thing in my life, too.

I suppose two dozen phone calls were executed and plans were finalized. I'll back off for a minute and let Andy take it from here:

I guess the proper name for this story is my 56-year-old dream. I planned this fishing trip with Stu Tinney in Nashville, Tennessee. My trip was arranged to drive, but due to circumstances I changed my plans and decided to fly. I have never stepped inside a plane before, so my son decided he would take me. Well, to tell you the truth, I was scared to death.

When the plane took off it just seemed to me to be just hanging there, and I could not see or hear it moving. I thought for sure we were falling down backwards and I thought to myself, my God, we are going to crash and I'll never catch that striper.

Well, I was wrong, thank the good Lord for that. If anyone looked over at me, and did not know it was my son sitting next to me they would have thought there is something funny about that old man, as I was holding my son's hand and squeezing it tightly, and holding onto him for dear life. But I sure enjoyed the rest of the trip.

We arrived at the Nashville airport at 10 p.m. and took a cab to the Hyatt Regency Hotel. After checking into our room, we took a walk to the State Capitol Building. We were really impressed by the beauty of the lights, and the cleanliness of all the streets.

We decided to get a good night's rest as the next day would be the fishing trip. Monday afternoon we were sitting in the lobby of our hotel when someone tapped me on the shoulder; it was Stu Tinney. I had been corresponding with Stu for a year over this trip, but I had never met him. He was everything I expected him to be, just a wonderful person, and later turned out to be a perfect guide. We then drove out to Percy Priest Lake in his Striper Van, and wasted no time in getting started. What a beautiful lake, and a wonderful feeling just to be on it. Stu's boat is equipped with the latest sonar equipment, and gadgets for lake fishing. Well, I caught my first striper; it was about two and a half pounds.

Stu asked me if I wanted to keep it, but I told him to release it. My mind was made up coming this distance to catch something larger. However, I didn't catch any more that day as the wind kicked up and was blowing very strong, and made it very difficult for drifting, so we quit for the day. Stu took us back to the hotel, and told us he would pick us up again at 4 a.m. Tuesday morning. He wanted us to be at the marina and out fishing by daybreak. The wind was still blowing but not as strong as yesterday. It is now 7 a.m. and after fifty-six years of waiting for that big thrill, it was now at the other end of my line. I was shaking like a leaf, I'm so nervous, and I'm trying to do everything Stu tells me. "Now Andy, don't point that rod at him...keep it arched...now put pressure on him...now pump him...now a little pressure," and so on.

Oh great! I see him splashing, don't let me make a mistake now. Stu is netting him. OH MY GOD...the net broke! The end came out of the handle, but Stu is grabbing the loose end as he nets him and lifts him into the boat. THANK GOD! I'm so nervous I can't talk. Later I found out my son, who had been taking pictures of me during the trip, had captured this whole event on colored movie film.

You would think a grown man of 73 years old

wouldn't get all worked up over a fish, well I did. The fish is going to be mounted, and sent to me. Oh, by the way, I never told you what the striper weighed; he was almost thirteen pounds. To me he is worth his weight in gold, and I will hang him over my fireplace until I pass on, then he will go to my grandson 'Andy' just to remind him that if he wants something bad enough in life, never give up hope. No matter how long it takes, his dreams will come true, just as mine did after all those years.

Now before I finish my story let me tell you what helped to make this trip perfect. First of all, Stu Tinney of *Striper* Magazine, with all his skills and experience and love for striper fishing, would personally take time out of his busy schedule to help me make my dream come true. Then manager Bill Griffin of the Hyatt Regency Hotel who personally arranged for our accommodations. It was the nicest hotel I was ever in. They had the finest people working there, and treated us like a couple of VIPs during our stay. And to the taxidermist who is preparing and mounting my fish. And last, but not least, to my son who took me. What a wonderful time and companionship we shared together those few days as father and son.

Andy Hessington, Sr.

It would be almost fitting to end this tale right here, but some of the stuff Andy left out is worthy of mention. Through this entire episode, several people reached out to touch us. Lindsay Sale, our Special Projects Director, was in on it from scratch. She suggested that perhaps Andy was an "old 73" and might need special attention. None of us could have known that Andy was more of a kid in body and spirit than all of us put together. At any rate, because she has special training in such things, she insisted on hopping aboard, to be there if needed. The plan was to drift live baits which was the most consistent method for catching fish at that time of the year. And can you imagine the pressure we felt about catching just ONE fish? Lindsay, because of my tournament and seminar schedules had to see that we had the proper bait available...all this on her own time, too. The plan was for us to put three rods out, each guarded by a pair of watchful and hopeful eyes and as soon as any activity was detected, Andy was to be clued in to that particular rod.

Andy was right about the wind; he left out that it was almost 20 miles an hour, which forced us to fish in places other than we knew would be most productive. The front that had swooped in was responsible for the fish being scattered so, at best, we would have to work on single fish rather than the hoped-for school. You might know it but it was Lindsay's rod that began to dip and as she handed it to Andy, the fish decided to take....as a matter of fact, when it made up its mind, he damned near took the rod away from Andy. This was an especially vicious fish, stripping off yards and yards of line. I keyed in on Andy, perhaps shouting directions a bit louder than I meant to. I knew the fish had gotten too much line. I was in worse shape than Andy because I wanted so much for that fish to be in the boat, knowing we might not get another shot. A quick look to see that all was clear in the boat in the event we had to move, brought a lump to my throat. Lindsay was sitting tailor-fashion in one corner, unashamedly crying while Bud, eyes wet as well was standing on the console seat, his camera recording the whole event. Andy was the calmest one and HE looked as if HE was coming unglued. Yes, the net did break. That was an absolute first in thirty years of striper fishing but, by josh, that beautiful fish was in the boat and we had a helluva time keeping Andy from diving on top of it. The look in his eyes at that moment will no doubt be among my most treasured memories.

There is no way of telling here to what extent Bill Griffin, manager at the Hyatt went to make Andy and his son welcome. The suite was comped, the concierge was instructed to treat them like the President, and a special elevator key to the VIP floor was provided as well as special snacks and meals. It was rumored that Andy rode the glass elevator for hours. The time that Ralph Dallas, our staff taxidermist will take to mount Andy's fish, also at no charge, is another small part of the picture. Andy, by the way, sent Bill and Ralph a box of treasures, too.

The hug Andy gave me was warm and sincere. It will be remembered.

In February of 1981, I received the following letter:

Dear Friend Stu:

I received my mounted striper on Friday, and Saturday I got my magazine. Nothing could have made me happier than those two wonderful gifts. I just love my fish and my story and I'm proud of what you did for it. I would not swap my fish for all the tea in China.

I am sitting in my living room writing you this letter. My wife is sitting across from me reading her bible, my husky and collie (that's one dog) is at my feet. I'm in front of my fireplace with a roaring fire in it and over the mantle is my beautiful striper.

Can you realize how happy I am thanks to you and all my new friends in Tennessee? Stu, please send me Miss Lindsay's address as I want to send her a gift for all her kindness to me.

Your Friend
Andy Hessington, Jr.
Vilas, New Jersey

Not too long after, another letter followed:

My Dear Friend Stu:

Today marks a year ago that you first came into my life. The year has went by so fast but like all wonderful events in my life they just pass on. Stu, how are you making out with your new boat? I sure hope you are catching a lot of stripers.

I can't get my mind off Nashville or Percy Priest or you this week. Having my second attack of ticker failure was bad enough, but now I'm trying to lick a bout with pneumonia. I sure hope and pray I win out. I don't think I'll be working anymore. It is a beautiful day. I am sitting on my sun deck overlooking Delaware Bay. Now and then a small boat goes by hoping to have a good day's fishing for weaks or flounders. My nephew is catching lots of fish now. I sure hope I can get out at least in August, Lord willing. Stu, you don't have to answer this letter as I know you are a very busy man and I have nothing else to do but you told me to drop you a line now and then and I get a nice feeling writing to you now and then. I'll close now, Stu, God bless you and your family. If you run across Bill or Ralph tell them I said hello. I haven't forgotten them. And Miss Lindsay, too. They were all a part of my wonderful trip. I hope I'm around to write you again in a couple of months. Bye now.

Your Friend, Andy

And finally the last and most dreaded letter:

Dear Stu:

I'm sorry to inform you that my dad went home to be with his Lord on June 19, 1982. I tried to call you a couple of times but was unable to reach you.

Stu, I really don't know where to start as I'm not much for writing letters, however I know how my Dad loved you, as a close friend, and I wanted to share with you some of his feelings.

Our trip to Nashville, meeting you, Lindsay and Bill and all those other wonderful people, had to be one of the greatest highlights of my dad's life. I know it was one of mine. He told me he cherished being your pen pal; your letters made him light up like a candle.

I had known of dad's dream to catch a striper ever since I was a small boy and when a real opportunity for him to do so appeared, I couldn't help but become involved. When I went to the president of my company to ask for some time off and explained why, he said he couldn't believe it when I told him my wife and mom were staying behind and that it would be just me and my dad. He shook my hand and said he was proud of me because he always wanted to do something like this with his father but because of the business there never seemed to be time. And then his father passed away and it was too late. He said the memories dad and I would share together would remain with me the rest of my life. How right he was.

I cried unashamedly while I was filming dad catching that fish. I saw through my camera lens the smile on dad's face as you netted and lifted his fish into your boat. I saw the smiles and tears on Miss Lindsay's face and, though you might have thought turning your face would hide yours, it didn't work.

The movie and photos, as well as the mounted striper, will be passed along to his grandson, Andy.

My family will never forget how you made this miracle happen and though "thank you" seems so small, please know it comes from our hearts.

Andy "Bud" Hessington

And so ends Andy's story...or does it?

17

REDD'S REVENGE "?"

Redd Foxx was an American icon, long before I ever had an opportunity to meet the man. Like many an avid fan, I spent lots of hours in front of the boob-tube, roaring in appreciation of his junkyard antics. Through all the years that "Sanford and Son" entertained my giggle reflex, I never once suspected that some day I would share the same space with the man. That being the case, there was no way for me to be prepared for the fact that our chance meeting would wind up consuming over a month of my time and energy.

Ron Whitehead and I were at the point where our business relationship was beginning to turn into a truly meaningful friendship. We had walked the walk and talked the talk enough times to have formed a solid bond of mutual trust. I met Ron at a tournament I was putting on at Lake Havasu, in Arizona. He had driven all the way from his home in Las Vegas to try to convince me to hold a like event on his home turf, Lake Meade. He was so convincing, when our Havasu event was completed, I changed my flight and accompanied him back to Vegas. I spent two lovely days as a guest in his home, working out the details of a possible Las Vegas event.

Ron and his wife Linda raised and showed German Shepherds. Ron was, at the time, a well respected dog show judge. He also owned a small fishing tackle store, in an equally small strip-mall. His place of business was a magnet for lots of local sportsmen. It was there that he and a slew of his cohorts got me to agree to bring what they called "my dog and pony show" to Nevada. It was also the very spot where, two years later, I was to meet Redd Foxx face to face.

Needless to say, Ron did everything he agreed to do in order to make our event a success. He got us together with the Las Vegas Visitor and Convention folks. He personally introduced us to the management of Sam's Town, who would turn out to be our hosts. He took care of marina arrangements, publicity, press releases and tournament entry applictions. All this out of that little tackle shop. There is no telling how much personal time and energy he spent to see this project through. When I offered to compensate him for his sterling effort, he flatly refused. His reasoning was if he accepted payment, he would not feel it would be correct for him to be a tournament participant. Talk about ethics, what a breath of fresh air that was.

At any rate, over the next two years I visited Vegas at least five times. Each of those trips included much time on the lake in Ron's boat. We wound up spending lots of personal time together. We shared a lot of personal stuff. It's kind of extraordinary how deep friendships happen. There has to be a lot of trust, a lot of truth, a lot of consistency, and lots of stuff even psychologists can't figure out. Whatever the mix, we seemed to have all the right ingredients, and were really enjoying the hell out of our together time.

After our second annual tournament had been completed, it being so wildly successful, I decided to extend my stay for a couple of days. We'd had a truly great morning's fishing on Meade, stopped off for one of those sumptuous Vegas breakfasts, and headed for the tackle store. I was heading back to Nashville later on that day, and had decided to spend the time between helping Ron run his store.

The store, though small, was well stocked with almost everything a Nevada sportsman might need. The walls were decorated with posters, enlarged photos and several fish and wild game mounts. It was a typical hangout for outdoor enthusiasts. Ron, being the jokester that he was, had the head of a desert jack rabbit mounted on a very ornate piece of driftwood. He somehow managed to attach to the hare's head a pair of antelope horns. I have no idea how he accomplished it, but it looked really genuine. He called it a "jackelope." He and his cronies spent lots of fun times making up riotous stories about the critter.

It was that morning, while Ron and I were enjoying a cup of coffee and swapping fish and other tales, that the bell over the door jingled and in walked the man...Redd hisself. I don't remember if Ron was training a dog for Redd, or perhaps trying to sell him a dog, but they seemed to know each other and were having a lively conversation. Ron introduced us and as we shook hands, my immediate thought was that "this guy is for real." His handshake was strong, he looked me square in the eyes and smiled that same smile I had seen so many times on TV. He appeared to have life by the throat and was choking every last bit of fun he could get out of it. Why not? He had a successful TV show, a successful lounge act and a monumental base of fans of which I happily admitted to being a part of.

During the three-way conversation which, of course, as you could expect, was laced with risque phrases, cuss words and street talk, Red looked up and spotted Ron's jackalope.

"Whassat?" he said.

Ron replied as if everyone ought to know. "It's a jackelope."

Redd was not going to just let it go like that so he once again inquired, "Whassat?"

I had known Ron long enough to recognize that twinkle in his eyes, that tightly-curled lip, and that slightly exaggerated professorial stance. Redd Foxx was about to get a lecture on jackelopes. Redd Foxx was getting ready to be had.

With an amazingly calm and believable countenance, Ron began his dissertation.

"The jackelope is the rarest animal in all of America," he explained. "It only lives in the deserts of Nevada, never comes out during the day, and is rarely seen by human eyes; a sighting would be like one in ten million." He went on to say, "It's the result of the rarest of unions between a desert jack rabbit and a special desert species of antelope. They have to mate on a full moon or nothing will come of it." He continued, "They have long been considered endangered and it's against the law to kill one, or even have one in your possession. The last one I ever heard about anyone seeing in the wild must have been at least twenty years ago."

"Well, how come you got one?" Redd asked.

Warming up to his subject, Ron said, "Years ago, special permits were available to have one on display. My grandfather had such a permit and was allowed to pass it to my father and then to me. I'll be able to pass it on to my daughter, but if I didn't have any children, I'd have to donate it back to the state of Nevada."

I wish I could say it ended there, but Ron, like any good fisherman, once having his prey hooked, kept a tight line on him. He went on and on and on, making his jackelope as important as the second coming, winding Redd in tighter and tighter.

In the meantime, watching Redd, I could see a quiet resolve set in. He squared his shoulders, almost imperceptively planted his feet a bit more solidly, looked Ron square in the orbs and asked, "How much you take for it?"

Though caught slightly off guard, Ron recovered quickly and said, "Gee, Redd, I'd like to sell it but it's against the law and I can't afford the kind of trouble that would bring."

"Would five thousand get it?" Redd asked.

"Sorry, it's just not for sale," replied Ron.

Redd continued to look at the mount on the wall, seemingly disappointed. Shaking his head, almost sadly, he left without another word.

My mouth must have been agape as Redd exited, I remember how quiet it suddenly became. That is until Ron started to giggle. That small sound soon turned into a crescendo of laughter that left us both aching and out of breath.

"Was that fun, or what" Ron said as tears rolled down his face.

I have to admit, I got into the spirit of the joke and regaled him about his delivery. We spent the best part of the morning re-living the fun episode (fun at least to us) until it was time for lunch. My plane left at four, so we planned to eat, spend another couple of hours at the store, and then I'd split for the airport.

Back at the store, appetites for food satisfied, we were doing a little strategizing about next year's tournament. We were so deeply involved in the project, had the bell over the door not sounded, we would never have heard the silent entry of the person coming in.

"How 'bout ten thousand? That's a lotta money for a damned rabbit," were the first words we heard.

Redd had obviously decided that this incident was not over yet.

Ron's adam's apple did the two-step as he took in that remark. Ten big ones would go a long way toward his little girl's eduction. Regaining his misplaced composure, he immediately decided to continue on with the gag.

"I'm really sorry, Redd, but as I told you, there's no way in the world I can sell that jackalope."

"I got to have it man...money ain't no object. Just tell

me what it's gonna take for that thing to change its address?"
Redd was serious as a heart attack.

I could tell Ron was begining to have second thoughts,
but still he persisted in arguing his case. Over the next hour
there were promises to "make it right with the man," "not
tell a soul," and finally, an offer almost doubling the last.

The last straw had finally been broken, as was Ron's
will to continue on with the farce. He was facing an opponent
whose will was obviously stronger than his own, and seemed
committed to have his way whatever the cost.

It was tough watching my little buddy's game come
back to bite him, but I grew up learning you had to sleep in
the bed you made for yourself, so I sure wasn't going to put
myself in the middle of that mess. Ron looked to me for some
support and seeing none there, made his decision as to what
was the best thing for him to do.

"Redd, I'm really sorry, but I guess this has gone far
enough. I need to apologize for this whole thing. What you're
seeing up there is a joke, a phony. There's no such thing as a
jackalope, I made it all up. It was just a harmless gag."

Redd looked incredulous. At first he didn't believe
it, and looked at me for confirmation. I remained dead-panned
and stoic, while Ron broke out into a visible sweat.

"Are you b–s–ing me?"

It was hard to read Redd's face at that moment. I
couldn't tell if he was amused or angry. He put on his famous
junkyard grin, shook his head in disbelief, stared at Ron
intently, looked at me quickly, and just as quickly returned
to stare down a completely deflated Ron. He slowly shook
his head from side to side, grinned widely at us both
individually, and without uttering a single word, left the store.

"Boy, he really took that well," said Ron. "He turned
out to be a real good sport."

It was just about time for me to leave for the airport,
and that little imp that occasionally sat on my shoulder

appeared to suddenly make me aware of an opportunity for me to have a bit of devilish fun. So I said, "I'm not so sure, pal, he looked awful perturbed to me, he'll probably burn the store down, just to get even."

I had rendered my otherwise wordy friend speechless. For the remaining hour of my stay, not one word was spoken about the incident. I knew darned well my tongue in cheek remark had hit a sour note and that he'd ponder on it for awhile before he caught on to my stab at being cute with words.

My trip back to Nashville was pretty uneventful unless you count the heart-in-the-mouth feeling you get when you fly out of Vegas. It always looks like the runway is too short and the mountains too tall to ever make it out safely. Each time you do, you feel almost like it's "one for the Gipper."

The next morning (Wednesday) the message light on the answer-phone was blinking merrily, the numeric counter letting me know I had twenty-three calls to return. The first one was from Ron. It sounded urgent, so I called him immediately.

"You're not going to believe this Stu, but my coffee pot has come up missing. No, no sign of a break-in, nothing disturbed, nothing else missing except my coffee pot."

I asked him if he had called the police, and agreed with him that that seemed silly, since there seemed to be no actual break-in, no damage, and nothing was stolen. He was a bit concerned the Vegas cops would frown on a missing coffee pot call.

I must say here, however, the coffee pot in question was no ordinary coffee pot. Ron had ordered it large enough to serve forty cups. It was the centerpiece of his store, and the reason his many followers stopped by his place of business. By Ron's admission, it was going to take at least three to four weeks for him to order and receive a new one. I commiserated with him over his loss and agreed that it was a really spooky mystery. He promised to keep me posted as we said our goodbye.

The phone was ringing as I walked into the office the next day. Of course, it was Ron.

"You're not going to believe this," he stammered. "When I came in to open the store this morning, there was this huge guy standing by the door waiting for me. His arms were as big as tree trunks. He looked like he was ten feet tall. He had tattoos on top of his tattoos. He was a really bad looking man."

It took me almost five minutes to slow him down enough to have a normal conversation. When he was calmed down enough I asked him, "What did the guy want?"

"Damned if I know," was the reply, "he didn't say a word. He handed me a hot cup of coffee, and just walked away. Man, was I spooked."

"Did you drink the coffee," I asked.

"Hell no," he answered, "who knows what could have been in it."

I sensed the beginning of paranoia in my pal, and offered that up to him for his appraisal.

"Hell yes, I'm paranoid, wouldn't you be if you were in my shoes?"

"If I were in your shoes," I offered, "I would not have screwed around with dumb jackrabbit stories."

After what seemed like a minute of silence Ron asked, almost in a whisper, "Do you think it's him?" (with an emphasis on HIM.)

I felt Ron's concern and instantly made the decision not to screw with his mind any further. My friend was beginning to act a little strange.

"Not to worry, it was probably one of your nutso customers not wanting you to miss out on your morning caffeine hit."

I continued to offer those kinds of positive possibilities

until I felt he was calmed down enough for me to end the conversation and get to work myself. From time to time during the day I occasionaly wondered what all of that was about, but I surely didn't dwell on it for any length of time.

The next morning was a repeat of the one before. A call from Ron with a report that there was a steaming cup of coffee on the floor in front of his shop door when he arrived that morning. The only difference was there was no delivery boy. Ron didn't drink the coffee but poured it down the sink.

Every single day, for the next three weeks, a call from Vegas confirmed the early morning delivery of the coffee gift. Every morning, it was poured down the sink.

"Man, I don't know how much more of this I can take," Ron told me on that last day. He didn't dare call the police for fear of being required to take either a sobriety or a mental fitness test. He was losing both sleep and weight, and was even considering leaving the country.

As quickly as all of this began, that's how abruptly it came to an end. When Ron opened the store on Monday, it was to be greeted by the UPS delivery man, bringing him his new coffee pot. He had no coffee cup awaiting him. His phone call that day was the happiest I had heard in almost a month of daily calls.

The next morning was another strange one. Ron called to tell me that when he opened the store on Tuesday morning, his missing coffee pot was sitting in its old location. No sign of forced entry, nothing missing, and whoever returned the urn was kind enough to make a full pot of coffee. Ron, of course, poured it down the toilet, proving he was still a bit spooked by the whole scene.

Things got back to normal after that and Ron never spoke about his jackalope adventure. He never brought up any names or voiced any suspicions. That is until about three months later when he called me to say, "You'll never believe what happened this morning."

The conversation was a long one, filled with questions, suspicions and theories. The long and short of it was, when he opened the store in the morning, both coffee pots were perking and his jackalope had come up missing. In its place on the wall, mounted on a fine piece of driftwood was the head of a fox, sporting a perfect pair of antelope horns, artfully attached so as to make the creature look real. In its open mouth was an envelope. Ron read me the contents:

"I am a Great African Horned Jungle Fox. I once freely roamed the Veldt, feeding exclusively on jackalopes. Unfortunately my food source disappeared and I was unable to respond to the loss, and so I became extinct. It has become an International Law to prohibit the ownership or display of any member of my species. Anyone discovered doing so encourages the wrath and disdain of any human being that does not report this dastardly act. Legend tells us that any person owning a member of my species is doomed to a life of much uneasiness."

I had to hang up the phone, I was gagging and laughing so hard, I couldn't hold it together. I called Ron back later that day and led the conversation into the realm of it being one of his nutty customer/friends with a morbid sense of humor. We agreed it was a master comedic stroke. If I hadn't succeeded in taking that route, Ron probably would have gone nuts. After all, over the years, he had himself perpetrated tons of practical jokes. I tried to convince him that he had finally been had by someone a little more clever than himself.

Over the years, though, whenever we had an occasion to be together, I stuck a barb in him, just far enough to make him wince. We never really came to any conclusion, seeing there were so many possible explanations. I have to admit, though, it sure was fun to have something in my bag to wave in front of my friend whenever he thought to get over on me...and that was often.

ADDENDUM

Ron passed away as 1982 came to a close. I honored our friendship by penning an obit for *Striper* Magazine, thus sharing his fun spirit with all our members. I'll repeat that obit here to share with all my new friends the simple fact that though life must come to an end, spirits live on forever, as long as there is someone willing to pass on the stories.

As reprinted from *Striper* Magazine, Jan/Feb 1983:

The quality of our life is equal to the quality of our sharing. To those fortunate enough to have learned the secret of giving, come the vast rewards of love and friendship.

I meant, by beginning as I have, to sort out the thoughts that would make the task of giving my words more meaning...more depth. I would have enjoyed being able to simply deal with the death of a friend in short, concise, and neatly tied up phrases and put it to rest...but I can't.

Ron Whitehead is gone, forever, and I haven't yet taken a moment to mourn him. I don't even know if I can. I want to be angry at the unfairness of it, to throw a rock, to break somthing or scream out in high-pitched mourner's wail. I know if I do it won't make it the slightest bit different.

Ron and I became tight friends as slowly and as surely as first light creeps into day. By sharing time and action together, we learned laughter; we could depend on each other's moves; I trusted him with net or gaff, as much as I do my own son. That comes only from sharing. Ron was more than equal to that task.

We made many thousand casts together, and joked and carried on the way that only two men totally involved in an experience can do. We competed for the "most," the "first," the "biggest," and never really cared who won. A Richard Pryor special on TV gagged us both with laughter, more at each other's shortness of breath, than at the dirty jokes, and he was quick to throw a bait behind mine at the moment of truth and "snatch" away my fish; his mind was that quick, too.

Tournaments and seminars in Vegas were made easier, details taken care of as they should have been, by one who cared about the outcome of important things. His little tackle shop was a hub of activity, making available all sorts of new surprises. His following was immense, and loyal.

He shared his family with me....his home....his warm jacket on a chilly morning on Meade....his last cup of coffee and a drag from his cigarette when mine were wet....before I quit. I couldn't convince him he should....he was a three pack a day-er.

When the news of the cancer was given him, he straightened his back and stated simply, "I'll beat it." That was one for us, to boost our sagging hearts. I'll always believe he knew, but that was Ron's way, to make life more livable for everyone else.

I'd been inviting him to visit home plate for several years. There was always the thought that "someday." Someday came when he arranged to have his chemo at Vanderbilt Hospital. We got to spend some time on the dock, fishing for bait under the lights. He got to see me catch a few on my lake; big, night-time stripers, and I wonder, was I so competitive that I denied him some pertinent information....it was my turn to win, anyhow....I guess. I wish he had gotten one, though.

He took Vanderbilt by storm as he did everything else in his life. He whipped through a miserable medical treatment without a whimper, encouraging all in sight, others, too, who were not taking it as well. The staff fell in love with him, and believed in the miracle we all knew would happen. Ron was a great hypnotist. He wanted us all to be comfortable.

The massive heart attack caught us all by surprise. We really believed his treatments had effected a turn-around. Days of life support followed....dreary days. When the decision was made to unplug, Ron let us know he was not ready....each machine that went into down-time was replaced by his system taking over for a little while longer. I think what Ron did was to give us a bit more time to become comfortable with the final outcome; that was definitely his kind of stroke.

I hope none of you have told your sons that "men don't cry." That's a crock. When we forget how to shed tears, we become less than men.

Nothing can happen in the course of a day when many of us won't have a flashback that will include Ron; he touched our lives so. I shared sunrise and sunset, wind and rain, and surface so calm it was eerie. Small things like putting the boat on the trailer will conjure up tricks I played. Or quips he made.

The biggest school of surfacing stripers I have ever seen in my life was, as Ron and I discussed in hushed terms with each other (we were afraid no one would believe us), at least five miles long. As far as our eyes could see. We tested it out later by seeing how far we could see on the road from point A to point B, as recorded on an odometer. And we caught the you-know-what out of them. We were all by ourselves, not another boat in sight, and, if that's what heaven is, for a moment we were there together.

In Europe, it's not unmanly for one man to hug another, or drape an arm over another's shoulder in camaraderie. It's a special kind of love. My son tells me often, "Dad, I love you." For some unknown reason, we here look down our nose and feel uneasy.

Well, as I love each day from end to end, as I love the quality of my life because many of you see fit to share it with me, and as I love the out-of-doors I am sworn to protect, so did I love Ron Whitehead...pity is, I never really told him.

18

UNCLE GOO

It was the looniest idea that had ever been presented to me. I must have had a short circuit in my brain to even consider it, but I did. And the longer I thought about it, the less crazy it seemed. That's the way it is when an adventurous spirit is confronted with the possibility of a new adventure; it's hardly possible for reason to win out. The right questions are never asked, because somehow asking the right questions seems to make proffered hands shrink back. And then there's the fact that there was no one with enough knowledge to even know which were the right questions.

I don't even remember how I met Al Gannaway, but I do remember much of what transpired after we met. Al was an entrepreneur's entrepreneur. He owned, among many other things, a TV recording studio. I'd been in enough filming studios, doing interviews or whatever, to know that Al's was "state of the art."

Cable TV was a brand-new idea and being as unmechanical as I was, I had little understanding of how it worked or what the possibilities were going to be. But, for what was being proposed, I could be stupid about the dynamics, as long as I could produce the results. And the producing-the-results part was the loony thing I was wrestling with.

Al had leased an enormous amount of time on an orbiting satellite and was using it to sell products of various kinds. He was producing "shows" (if you could call them that) designed to attract attention so that his merchandise could be hawked. He claimed to have seen me and Lindsay doing something, somewhere, for some reason, on some TV show. That was totally believable since, in my travels, doing outdoor seminars, I was called upon to do lots of TV interviews. It could have happened that way but, I'll always wonder.

At any rate, the idea was to create a fishing show to be called, of all things, "Stu Tinney Outdoors." He would have a crew go out and solicit "sponsors" who would provide cash for expenses and merchandise to be sold. Sounded a bit "greasy" to me, but I'm a bit slow about business stuff and the rest of the idea sounded great. I was simply to travel the world, seeking fishing opportunities and filming same. I would be provided with "living expenses" and a small (very small) salary and a film crew. I would be able to pick my spots (within reason) and be totally responsible for show content, other than products to be sold. That is, after the first shoot, location to be chosen by Mr. Gannaway.

It seemed that Al owned a hotel on Caicos Island which was nowhere to be found on the map of my geographical knowledge. He wanted to put me and the crew up at that hotel and leave us for a week to work out the show. He knew absolutely nothing of fishing but assured me I could find whatever I needed in the way of boats, guides and information. He was totally familiar with the island and posed an interesting challenge. The immediate story line that came to me was, "How many different species of fish could be caught around an island paradise in five days?" WOW, I was hooked. Al also suggested that he hire Lindsay as "fluff" to appeal to the females he thought would be satellite shoppers. That tickled the hell out of me because "fluff" to Al appeared quite differently to me. Lindsay was an accomplished outdoors person with an enormous talent for seeing to even the smallest details. Nothing ever got by her sharp senses. She was a writer-photographer with lots of credits and I had learned to trust her judgment. She would certainly be an asset if Al could get her to agree to go along with the plan. I was not privy to those discussions but, fellow adventurer that she was, Lindsay decided to go along for the ride, at least until after the Caicos thing was in the can. Then there would be time for further negotiating.

Al was in a hurry to get this project started so he gave us just a week to get our stuff together. "There are no stores for you to buy any gear, so you better take what you need." That sounded simple enough to me. I had grown up fishing the salt on the Jersey coast and was familiar enough with both in-shore and off-shore gear as to make a realistic list of fishing tackle we might need. I opted for all light to medium spinning stuff, making certain I had a large supply of jigs, spoons and top water lures. And plenty of extra line. I was certain that if we wound up doing any deep water fishing, our boat captain would have adequate big game stuff on board.

As Lindsay and I went over the list, she innocently asked why I had not included steel leaders. Since I didn't consider that a "must have," I shrugged my shoulders and went on with the inventory. "Humor me," she said, and went off to buy a gross of assorted size steel leaders. For any of you that are smirking right now, as I was then, I can assure you the smirk will be wiped off. As usual, her decision to "do something" was absolutely on target.

The plan was to fly commercial jet to Miami, hop a commuter to the Turks and then another commuter to Caicos. Everything would be arranged for us in the way of travel tickets, transfers and accommodations while on the island. The rest would be up to us. Our film crew would already be in place, and would meet us at the hotel. Since it was the only hotel on the island, the crew would be staying there, too.

Things began pleasurably. The flight to Miami was non-stop and the commuter was awaiting our arrival. When we landed in the Turks, we were feeling pretty smug. We had obviously chosen the correct wearing apparel for this trip and since everything was going so smoothly, we could assume nothing but a positive attitude. It was quite dreamlike...at least for a little while. We had an hour to wait for our island hopper to be ready to leave so we enjoyed a lovely tropical meal in a laid-back, scenically beautiful atmosphere. Adding to the ambiance was the fact that everyone spoke in that lovely, melodious, almost sing-song British accent.

The first hitch came in the form of a grease-covered pilot who approached us at our table and indicated we were ready to go. He had crammed our luggage and tackle onto his plane, leaving barely enough room for me and Lindsay, but assured us the trip would be a short one, so our discomfort would be a minor thing. We didn't know anything about aircraft but this one was small, the ocean we were to fly over was large and we, to say the least, were a bit, shall we say, concerned. That concern turned into what seemed like a lump of concrete in the pit of our stomachs when a fellow on the ground showed up with a gadget on wheels with battery cables attached and connected them to our plane. "Need a bit of a boost," the pilot said as he started the engine and immediately taxied to the runway. "Have to get off the ground before it stalls out." Now that was just the confidence booster we needed.

Unfortunately, I can't report on the blue, blue sea or the exotic sights, because the rest of the half-hour trip we had our eyes shut tight so we couldn't see the end coming.

Looking back, I have to say the flight and the landing were pretty smooth. After going through customs, Caicos-style, which was simply asking where staying, why here, how long and good day, we went in search of a cab. A really smart-looking policeman pointed the way and told us it was OK to leave our stuff where it was until we had a cab to pick it up. He assured us no one on the island ever stole anything and our gear would be safe. He was absolutely correct. The only cab we could find was a four-door Chevy, probably twenty years old (or maybe even older) that had so much rust on it, the driver had to kick the door to let us in. He was amiable enough and gave us the history of the island as we headed for the hotel. Seems as if this was a thriving place at one time, until the salt petered out and the mining operations stopped. Now, the only industry was a conch processing plant where most of the women worked while the men went diving.

Holiday Inn was the sign on the hotel, but it was unlike any Holiday Inn I had ever stayed in. The land we had crossed to get here spelled poor, the housing for the islanders we saw spelled poor, and the hotel looked like the rest of the landscape. But, we were here for the best part of a week and were going to be busy, busy, busy, so a seedy-looking hotel was not going to interfere with that. The desk clerk, a rather stout islander, was happy to see us and her smile made us feel welcome. She turned out to be the cook and the housekeeper as well, and assured us she would spoil us and, dear soul, went out of her way to do just that.

We were shown to our respective rooms and went about the business of unpacking suitcases and arranging gear. A scream brought me running onto the balcony of my room. Standing on her balcony was Lindsay with a look of horror on her face. "There are roaches in my room as big as mice," she said, and calmly went on, "Would you see if someone has a gun?" The thing to admire about Lindsay is her sense of humor and her sense of self. I would have gone coo-coo; she simply wanted someone to take care of the problem. It turned out that these were not roaches at all (though they looked like them) but rather typical island pests that were difficult to keep out. Whatever our housekeeper did, we were not bothered by those guys again.

When we came back down to the lobby, we were met by a smiling young man who introduced himself as Clarence. "I'm your cameraman, what's the schedule?" Since we had yet to line up a boat and guide or look at available places to fish the beach, we had no schedule. Clarence said he was familiar with the island and would use the hotel vehicle to drive us around so we could put all that together and perhaps begin filming the next morning. He let us know he had already arranged a second boat for him to film from and was sure we'd have no trouble finding one we could fish from. Down to the waterfront we headed.

When we arrived at the "marina," a vise gripped my lungs and squeezed the breath out of me. There was no dock, no gas pump, no buildings and nightmare of nightmares, no boats. Excuse me, there was one boat, pulled halfway onto the shore. It was about fourteen feet long, looked like a Boston Whaler that had been cut in half. It had no seats, had enough patches on it to resemble a quilt, was powered by a rusty fifty horse who knows what and had a small islander sleeping on board. So much for the Caicos Marina. It was obvious that this was not the sport fishing mecca I had imagined, and that we were going to have to back up and punt.

First things first, we had to have a boat and a guide. Clarence explained that all the boats and men were out to sea diving for conch and wouldn't be in until dark. He said that the man sleeping in his boat was too old to dive as deep as the conch were located now but could probably guide us, since he was the one that supplied fish to the islanders. With our permission, he went to awaken "Uncle Goo."

As if on cue, the man in the boat opened his eyes, stretched his arms, and in a flash was completely upright. "Whatever his age," I thought, "he was even more spry than I." As we approached him, his eyes lit up with a glow of excitement and he lithely jumped out of the boat and came forward to meet us. It was obvious that he knew Clarence, who introduced us by name and he by "Uncle Goo."

"Is he your Uncle?" Lindsay asked.

"He's everybody's Uncle," was the reply, "everybody claims him. And now, he's your Uncle, too."

Goo and I shook hands and he turned and bowed courteously for Lindsay. I couldn't help but notice the roughness of his hands, the signature of hard work. His skin was as shiny and as dark as the black keys on a piano. His smile was broad and honest. His eyes sparkled with what could only be the hint of impish mischief and a joy of life. His skin had the leathery look of one who lives outdoors. For a guy only five feet tall and maybe a hundred pounds, he was one heckuva package. I instantly hoped he would be able to deliver what we needed, I wanted to spend some time with him; surely it could not be anything but great fun.

Apologizing for his boat, he explained it was really the best we could hope for. Well, hell, we didn't need a fancy rig if it could take us where we needed to go, and if he knew the waters well enough to guide us to the best locations. He assured us he could guarantee showing us bonefish, snappers, yellowtail, groupers and barracuda as well as any number of fish whose names he did not know. His enthusiasm and hypnotic voice convinced us, so we hired him on the spot, and arranged to start in the morning with the bonefish.

After breakfast, we loaded our gear into the hotel wagon along with Clarence's' cameras and recording equipment, and headed for the boats. Goo watched with great interest as our tackle went into the boat and said he had never seen that kind of stuff to catch fish in his whole life. All we really had were three medium-weight spinning rods, three Penn reels loaded with ten pound test line and a small tackle box full of various and sundry jigs and spoons of different weights, shapes, sizes and colors. Clarence "miked" us up and hopped into his boat which, by the way, made ours look like a cruise liner. Goo had brought a couple of wooden milk boxes for us to sit on and those, plus us, plus the small cooler with snacks and drinks, left zero space for anything else. When Lindsay asked about life jackets or a fire extinguisher, Goo behaved as if he didn't speak English and busied himself with pushing us off the beach.

I'd never had the opportunity to fish for bonefish, but all the magazine articles I had read prepared me for a fish easily spooked and somewhat difficult to catch. I had never heard of them traveling in great numbers, but rather in small groups.

The water was gin-clear as we slowly worked our way to where Goo promised would be the place to catch a bonefish. Nothing was in view as far as we could see but clear water and sandy bottom. Then suddenly Goo cut the engine and pointed to a spot in the water that was black. The spot was easily the size of a football field. "Bonefish," he said, pointing again at the spot. It did not take me long to understand that what we were looking at was acres and acres of fish, all of which were slowly moving directly toward us. Clarence, in the other boat, did a quick sound check, readied his camera and let us know he was ready to shoot. We opted to let Lindsay have the first cast and her lure fell expertly into the target area. Before the jig could sink more than a foot or two, she was fast into our first bonefish. It screamed off line for about ten seconds and then the line went slack. Thinking she must have lost the fish, she speeded up her retrieve and pulled a half of a bonefish into the boat. "Cuda," said Goo, our man of many words.

Each of us made three more casts, all with the same results. We'd hook a nice bonefish, only to have a barracuda attack the struggling bone and cut it in half. That made for an interesting minute of film, but we knew we had to solve that problem or come up with another game plan. Lindsay, ever thinking, came up with the thought that if we could catch the barracudas that were herding the bonefish, we might have a better chance. We'd also get a barracuda film and add to the number of species we would catch. Great idea! And we had a good supply of shiny spoons to throw which, we were certain, would attract the 'cudas.

I attached a spoon to each of our lines and took my turn to cast first. Voila! Instant fish! For a second my line screamed and then suddenly went slack; it had broken. Same thing happened to Lindsay. "This is not going to work," I said. "Those sharp teeth are just cutting right through that line."

"It'll work," replied Lindsay as she reached into her jacket pocket, pulling out a cellophane bag, "try one of these." And there were those dumb damned wire leaders I had smirked about. She was gracious enough not to say it, but that imp on my shoulder said it for her: "She told you so, didn't she?"

Lindsay made the first cast with a spoon attached to her wire leader and instantly hooked a barracuda. They're pretty spectacular on light tackle and an alert Clarence filmed at least three jumps by the fish. I'd been smart enough to pack a hand-held gaff so getting the fish in the boat was no trick. The fish weighed a little over thirty pounds, but before I could release it, Uncle Goo dispatched it with a wooden club he had hidden somewhere in the boat. We knew instantly that there would be no catch and release where Goo was concerned. We continued to catch barracuda over the next hour or so and wound up with ten or twelve before it was done. When we stopped getting hits, we switched back to throwing jigs at the bonefish and succeeded in catching twenty or more of those before the school broke up. It had been amazing to learn that the barracuda were actually herding that bunch of bonefish. At any rate, it had been a successful morning, we had gotten two great action films and had caught two species. Time for a lunch break.

Our friend at the hotel had packed us each two

sandwiches, some fruit and lots of sodas. Lindsay and I carefully folded the wrapping paper and put it with the empty cans back into the cooler to be disposed of when we got back ashore. Goo watched us with obvious curiosity and then threw his trash over the side. I instantly reacted, perhaps a bit harshly, criticizing him for littering. He looked at me blankly and I suddenly understood he didn't have a clue. He and his fellow islanders had been throwing trash into the ocean all their lives, and saw nothing wrong with it. What Lindsay and I were doing was simply a waste of time to him and proved once again that white people were a little crazy and over excitable. It's so neat to try to understand someone else's culture and not try to foist one's own upon them. For the rest of the time we were there, we did our thing about trash and had not a word to say when Goo did his.

Goo noticed a storm forming and allowed that we had better head on in. He was right on target and we barely made it to shore before a tremendous wind came up. We had lots to do the rest of the day so we arranged to meet again the next morning to fish a reef Goo knew about for whatever we could catch. Returning to the hotel, we washed up and changed clothes and decided to walk on the beach to look for places to fish and to film background stuff. While we were walking, a native woman approached Lindsay to offer her a gift. It was something she made for "the pretty white woman who came to visit." Lindsay was visibly moved by such sweetness from a stranger who, without another word, fled from the beach. All of the islanders we came in contact with, though very poor, were so eager to visit with us and so desirous of making us feel welcome, they certainly made us glad we had come.

We got back to the hotel just as it was getting dark and decided to go right to the dining room. The only other guests were two white men who immediately invited us to join them. We found out they were father and son, lived in

Florida, and owned the conch processing plant. They came in once a week to pay everyone and check on the catch. We enjoyed a nice dinner and, while having a drink, Lindsay decided to go upstairs and freshen up. We three guys decided to go outside and enjoy some fresh air and a bit of guy talk. The sight that greeted us was almost carnival-like.

There were about forty or fifty islanders, dressed very colorfully, standing around what turned out to be the island musical group. The instruments were obviously handmade with sounds that were more like bells than any thing else I could describe. In the center of all of this was a large man, holding a large drum directly over a large fire. He explained that he was tightening the skin. No one was playing until Lindsay stepped outside and then all heck broke loose. The band started to play, people started to sing and dance. When she asked me what this was all about, all I could think of was a smart-ass reply. "Looks like the prelude to a sacrifice to me, and since you're the only white woman on the island, it looks like you're it."

In truth, as we soon learned, the whole deal was put together at the urging of Uncle Goo, to give a proper welcome to the "pretty white woman" who came to visit.

We were told that was a rare thing, indeed, at the time, and we have no way of knowing if that had changed. The business owners were certainly impressed. The older of the two remarked that not only was he paying most of these folks, but he had been coming here for over twenty years and no one did a party for him. We were sure his words were in pure fun as we partied together into the wee hours. Lindsay danced with so many people I thought she would not be able to get up in the morning to fish. She's a trooper and when dawn came, she was ready to go.

As we were heading toward the reef, I asked Goo about what kind of bait we were going to use. He gave me that "be patient, silly person look" and concentrated on wherever we were going. He suddenly cut off the engine, grabbed a short steel rod that resembled a post for a wire fence, and jumped out of the boat, disappearing beneath the surface. Here we were, afloat in an almost boat, God knows where, with no shore in sight. As Ollie would say, "What a fine kettle of fish this is."

Goo broke the surface with that s...t-eating grin on his face. Impaled on the end of his steel rod, was a pretty darned good size lobster. "Bait," he said. "Bait, hell, DINNER," said I. He and Lindsay both laughed but I was as serious as a heart attack. Lobster for dinner sounded awfully good to me. Goo promised when we were finished catching fish he would get us some lobster. Amazingly, without depth finder, land marks, buoys or any other help, Goo dropped his cinder-block anchor directly over the reef he had promised to take us to. The first few fish we caught were easily recognizable as Yellowtail. We also knew what the Grouper, Snapper, Jewfish, and Puffer fish were. Since Goo did not believe in catch and release, the bottom of the boat was soon covered with nine various species of reef dwellers, all of whom we could identify. Then Lindsay caught an especially pretty, multi-colored fish with rather large eyes. When Goo saw that we did not know what to call it, he immediately sang out in his soft British accent, "Popeye Uncle John." Since we couldn't argue the case, Popeye Uncle John it was.

A few minutes later, I hooked a really large fish that had the rod bent to the reel seat and the gears of the reel screaming loudly. With all the fishing skills I could muster, and a bunch of luck thrown in, within fifteen minutes or so, I had whatever it was close to, but deeply under, the boat. Since we were fishing for smaller fish this day, I had mistakenly left the hand gaff back at the hotel. I had to work the fish from the far side of the boat, so I couldn't see what it was when it hit the surface. But when it did, Lindsay reached over the side, grabbed it by the tail with both hands and somehow managed to flip it into the boat. As soon as Goo saw the fish, he jumped into the water. So here we were once again with no captain and a huge Nurse Shark flopping around in the boat. It was obvious that Goo was not getting in the boat with the shark, so we rolled it back over the side and watched it swim away. Goo got back in the boat, pulled the anchor, started the engine and in his own special way, let us know the trip was over; we were heading in for the day. We did shoot some super film and, counting the lobster, were able to add twelve more species to our count.

The third day was a repeat of day two and, all told, we had now captured thirty-three different kinds of fish and were working on having almost half a season's shows in the can. We did a lot of "takes" on the beach which included intros and promos.

Walking the beach with Lindsay and Clarence after each day's fishing allowed us to discuss the filming and plan for the next trip. Tomorrow would see us learn to fish native style. That meant leaving rods and reels on shore and using only hand lines. The islanders wrapped twine around a stick in such a way as to allow them to cast it remarkable distances. When a fish was hooked, they retrieved it slowly, re-wrapping the line on the stick as they did so. It was as much an art form as the dance. There's no way to adequately detail the beauty of motion, the sheer athleticism, the total concentration that went into every throw. We were so engrossed in watching that morning that it quickly became Uncle Goo's show. We knew we could learn the art somewhat but decided not to film us this time. Why mess with perfection; it sure couldn't get any better. On the way back in, this fourth day, Goo decided to keep his "lobster promise" and shut the boat down over an obviously rocky area. He offered one of his "spears" to each of us, Lindsay excitedly accepting, me graciously refusing. Looking at the stuff Clarence shot later on was the only way to convince Lindsay that she had speared more lobsters than Goo, whose on-camera remark was "I teach good." What a lovable character he was.

Our walk on the beach that fourth afternoon was interrupted by a stranger. A man, carrying several bags and boxes stopped us in our tracks. He immediately emptied the bags and boxes and displayed native wood carvings he claimed to have done and wanted to sell. The stuff was fascinating and beautifully done. Dark and light woods combined, showing intricate details of fish, animals and people. Our favorite was a "turtle box" that Lindsay purchased and still treasures. Having done our shopping, we determined the next day's shoot would be over deep, deep water. We had no idea what was available but we were going to try and troll something up. With makeshift trolling gear, we showed up at Goo's boat in the morning. Lindsay excitedly told him about our chance meeting with the artisan on the beach and watched with confusion as Goo pushed the boat back on the sand and declared he would not fish today. "Dominican bad luck," he said. "You should never be with Dominican." We took it that we had made our purchases from a Dominican native and that island superstition made that a bad thing. It was a perfectly clear and windless morning, and without a captain we decided to try our luck fishing from the beach. "You talk to Dominican, bad storm come today," called Goo, as we walked away. "You come back tomorrow."

Since native superstition and voodoo stuff was not our bag, we headed merrily for the beach. In less than a half hour, the sky darkened, the wind came screaming toward the beach followed by thunder, lightening and torrential rain. That weather pattern killed the entire fifth day and taught us a good lesson. Never tell Goo we had talked to a Dominican.

On our sixth and last day, we were headed out to sea for our final adventure. We hadn't gone a mile when Goo abruptly stopped the boat and jumped overboard. We were getting quite used to Goo's antics by now and were more than just a little curious as to what he was up to now. He surfaced about twenty yards from the boat and then disappeared beneath the surface again. He repeated that same thing several times until finally he seemed to have hold of something. He was too far away for us to determine what it was, but it was obviously large since his arms were spread very wide. He seemed to be riding something and looked as if he were propelling himself solely with his feet. He reached the side of the boat in a few minutes, hands tightly gripping a giant sea turtle. The turtle looked almost as big as Goo, but he somehow managed to roll it into the boat, belly up. There was little room in the boat for me and Lindsay and the turtle, certainly no place for Goo. He reached up into the boat and grabbed the wooden box-seats we had been using, and tossed them over the side. He told us to get as far forward as we could and then straddle the gunnels with our feet hanging over the side. Having done that, he crawled over the stern and sat on top of the motor. How he got it started, I'll never know, but start it he did and, steering it with his feet, slowly worked the boat back to shore.

Somehow his message was carried on the wind, for as we approached the otherwise empty beach, we could see several people waiting. Before the bottom touched the sand, eager hands were dragging the turtle out of the boat. The folks, the turtle and Goo disappeared quickly, as did our last day of fishing. Well, we had accomplished what we had come for and had a world of fun while doing it.

Our pilot picked us up on time, and the trip back to the States was uneventful. Goo came to see us off and was embarrassed when we offered him money to pay for his time. He said he had sold all the fish we caught and had made plenty of money. He said the Dominican went home and that was good. He went on to say our luck had brought the turtle and that was good. We insisted, however, on paying him and he shyly accepted but could not seem to understand why we didn't understand him. I asked him if he would like to have any of the fishing tackle we had brought, but he graciously refused, saying he would rather use his kind of tackle.

We had come to a place where people had comparatively little. We never saw a frown or heard a voice raised in anger in all the time we were there. We witnessed good manners, helping hands, happy children and the most giving nature man could possess. And we came away humbled. Uncle Goo was, in fact, a very good teacher.

19

SHUCKIN' CORN

"Stu, I'm in serious trouble," the husky voice boomed over the phone. "I've got a thirty day deadline to meet, and don't know who else to call but you." The fact that the caller never identified himself was of no consequence. I knew from word one exactly who it was.

Jim Bashline and I had been friends for lots of years. We shared many an hour adventuring together; enough to write a book. I wish he had done it, though, he was so much more talented with words.

Jim was born in the wee town of Tioga, Pennsylvania in 1931. After finishing high school, he attended Penn State for a year, moving on the to Albright Art School. He spent a year there before his draft number came up and he left to do his hitch in the Army. It was Korea time. He lucked out, though, and instead of going off to war, was sent to help survey and protect our biggest Achilles Heel at the time, Alaska.

During those hectic years, he married his high school sweetheart, Sylvia. He and Syl remained a dynamic duo for all these years. She stayed pretty much in the background during his career, but undoubtedly was the spirit from which his talent flowed. I remember well the rare times I was able to spend with them both, the gentle way he touched her and the adoring way he looked at her.

It was on one of those "together occasions" that he played his best practical joke on me. We had been one-upsmanshipping each other forever it seems. Visiting his home, he advised me that he had a well. In this well he explained was a hybrid trout he was raising. "The first of its kind," he said enthusiastically, "and I've trained it to eat out of my hand." Being a show-me kind of guy, I demanded to see this wonder of his. As I peered over the side of the well, I could see nothing but gin-clear water. "Okay, what's the joke?" I said, fully expecting him to fess up to his imaginary pet. "Just put your hand on the surface of the water and he'll come right up to it," he said. I did exactly that, I even wiggled my thumb to make a bit of motion on the water. Without warning, my thumb was attacked and raked with sharp teeth and ripped open to cause much bleeding. As I jerked my thumb out of the water, I turned to see Jim rolling on the ground, laughing hysterically. He had gotten me again!

Sylvia was solicitous and kindly supplied me with a healing lotion and a band aid, while Jim asked if I didn't think I needed a tetanus shot. I owed him that one for a long time before I got even for his attack trout gimmick.

That, and several other "Bashline tricks" he had played on me was very much on my mind but, as always, he sounded so serious he had my attention. Without hesitating for a breath he went on to say "I've committed a piece on fresh water stripers on a fly rod to *Field and Stream*, and I've got thirty days to get final copy in." Jim was an Outdoor Editor for that prestigious mag at the time. He convinced me that he had done one more favor for me than I had done for him, and that I owed him. I never kept count (he didn't either) but it sounded like a fun deal to be involved with so I told him I'd gather some information and get back to him the next day.

It was early April and stripers were beginning to get

aggressive on several impoundments in Tennessee. Eight or ten phone calls to various parts of the state verified my feelings. It would not be tough to catch a striper, but one on a fly rod was a horse of another color. No one I spoke to thought it could be done. I called Jim back and relayed the information, but it did nothing to dissuade him. "I'll be in Tennessee in three days," he said, "and I know you'll have it all worked out." Before I could say boo, he went on, "remember those articles I did for you when you were under pressure to produce." He did not need to say any more, he had me...again!

The articles he referred to practically saved my life. Our publication was new and potential advertisers weren't happy with my editorial staff. Hell, I couldn't pay much at the time and was only attracting new and as yet unknown writers. They wrote great stuff and with Lindsay's help (she was associate editor) put out some of the best striper material ever seen in print. Some of those guys are big names in outdoor writing now; they know who they are.

At any rate, over a beer at an outdoor show we were both attending, I slobbered out my tale of woe to Jim. "No problem," said he, raising his glass in a mock toast. "Here's Jim Dandy to the rescue." And the rescue was exactly that. Jim produced a five series article on the classic baits that in itself remains a classic piece of outdoor work. As a result of being able to add his name to our masthead, we were able to interest enough advertisers to make a go of it. He took the meager amount we were able to pay him in stride and over the years never complained. I think, however, I paid him back in spades. Those are stories for other times.

Knowing Jim was coming in from Pennsylvania in a few days, I put the pressure on some of my resources. I knew our best chance of success would be in one of the river systems so I put the emphasis on that. A call from a farmer friend in Estill Springs, Tennessee convinced me of where we had to place our efforts. There's a small river created by the overflow of Woods Reservoir that empties into Tims Ford. Most of that system runs through private farmland with little or no access. There was, however, a stretch of about two hundred yards that could be reached on foot, and that was the place I intended to key in on.

Jim brought along a photographer, both of them setting up residence in a rental cabin on the lake. We had dinner the first night and turned in early so we could make the twelve mile drive and arrive about daylight. When we parked the car, it was obvious we were not going to be alone. When we approached the river we gasped in amazement at the number of people who were there. I would guess some fifty fisherman lined not one side, but both sides of the river. I didn't see how Jim stood a chance of even finding a place to stand.

You have to picture this. Jim was a tall, broad-shouldered man with a face that looked as if it had been chiseled from granite. He had man's man written all over him. And on this day, he was clad in chest high waders and carried a fly rod that looked like a strand of spaghetti in his huge hands. He was followed by a photographer carrying a tripod, three camera cases and various and sundry other equipment. To this bunch of mostly farm folks who probably only fished at this time of year because it was close to home, and the fishing was easy, he must have looked like an alien life-form.

As we strolled along the bank looking for six inches for Jim to place his feet in, we were met with stares (no comments) that would scare the feathers off a duck. Good natured as he was, Jim just kept smiling and nodding hello, but all the time eyeing the river for a potential spot to cast.

The scene was sort of funny. Every single person fishing was using a top water lure, which was absolutely correct under the circumstances. The guys on one side of the river were casting at the feet of the guys on the other side, and vice versa. It was just breaking daylight and no one as yet had caught a fish. Everyone was using a rod that looked like a telephone pole compared to what Jim held in his hand, but he let all that slip off of his back and concentrated solely on what he had come to do.

As we slowly walked up the river, he noticed a snag sticking straight up out of the water. It was a sizable log that was evidently lodged in the bottom and was creating a sizable eddy on the downstream side of it. There was plenty of space here I suppose because no one wanted to get hung up and lose a lure or a fish. Being an ardent trout fisherman, Jim sensed any predator fish would use that spot as an "ambush point" to hunt prey. He said exactly that and proceeded to step into the river at that point to allow himself a maximum distance for a back cast.

I'll say this about Jim's ability with a fly rod. His talent and timing were to be admired. He was not only good, he was great. I've had the opportunity to be with some of the world's great fly-rodders. Guys like Lee Wulff, the father of fly fishing; Joe Brooks, a close second to Lee; Ted Williams, perhaps the strongest of all. I've never seen anyone empty a spool of line like Ted could. Then there was Gadabout Gaddis who, in his kindness, let me beat him in a "dare" contest at an outdoor expo. I never could have beaten him otherwise. And then there's my son, Mitch; I'll put his artistry up against anyone's. At any rate, this is the kind of company Jim's expertise lived with. And as he plied his trade, much of the activity on the bank ceased as almost all eyes watched him with boyish wonder.

He took only two back casts before he shot his streamer-bait into the top of the eddy. "I had a touch," he said to me as I stood on the bank directly behind him. On the next cast, Jim leaned slightly forward as he watched his line drop below the eddy. Like a coiled spring, he reared his body upward and deftly set the hook into the jaw of a hefty striped bass. The oohs and ahhs from the crowd could be heard even over the water sounds. Jim backed out of the river as gracefully as a ballet dancer and proceeded to follow his fish as it made a mad dash down river.

"Am I seein' what I think I'm seein'," said a voice from somewhere.

"Hell yes you're seein it, same's me."

"Well, I ain't believin' it," came a reply from somewhere else.

Every head, every body and every eye was now on the giant of a man with the little stick in his hand. "Betcha five he don't get him in."

"I'll take that and any more any one wants to bet."

I didn't take a tally but I am certain a couple of hundred bucks changed hands that morning.

One thing about Jim, when he was on camera, he sure did know how to milk it and milk it he did. He worked that fish up and down that stretch for at least twenty minutes, grunting and talking to the fish as he did so. The crowd was buzzing but the speak was difficult to understand. One thing was obvious, though; everyone here knew they were being treated to a show.

As Jim walked up and down the bank, there appeared a smallish man who began to follow Jim's footsteps. He never said a word until another onlooker said, "I see it, I see it, it's a twenty pounder all right." The follower who might have been five feet tall and perhaps in his sixties or better finally uttered his first words.

"Wnmetogafm?"

Jim tried to reply but was a little busy and had to get on with what he was doing. Again the little guy said, "Wnmetogafm?" As Jim passed me for about the tenth time he whispered out of the side of his mouth, "What in hell does that fellow want?"

"You big goof," I answered, he wants to know if you

220

want him to gaff the fish for you. Since the bank was high above the water and Jim's photographer had gotten great action shots he replied, "Hell yes, but tell him not to miss."

"I never miss, mister," said the little guy who had obviously overheard.

The little stranger (whose name we never learned) walked over to where he had laid his rod and picked up what was supposed to be his gaff. It consisted of what was left of an old axe handle with a ten penny nail driven through it. It had a rawhide thong that he wrapped around his wrist so he wouldn't lose it. Following Jim closely now, he waited patiently for an opportunity to gaff the fish. When Jim saw the instrument, his eyes came close to glazing over, but gentleman that he was, said nothing. I later told him that was a good thing since most of the guys on the bank had relatives that had fought the First Pennsylvania during the Civil War and might have wreaked revenge. I got my jabs in whenever I could – such is the way of guys enjoying pure fun.

Jim recognized the fish was tiring and gently led it toward the bank where the little guy with the gaff was waiting. Kneeling down to get as close as he could to the fish, he raised the weapon over his head and with a mighty downward swing, drove the nail into the head of the striper. With one motion, he raised his arm, released the gaff and it, hanging onto the fish, flew over our heads to land on the ground about ten feet away. Jim bent down and slid his hand into the fish's gill so a photo could be taken. One of those photos became the cover of our July 1980 issue of *Striper* Magazine.

As Jim was standing, tall as an oak, the little guy approached him, head on. Jim bent his head to thank the man for his help but the look in the guy's eyes made him stop. It was as if the man was in a hypnotic state. A huge crowd had gathered, much murmuring was being heard as well as much money being passed around to pay off bets won. Then for one magic moment all was silent. All motion stopped. Not even the wind was blowing. Perhaps even the river quieted itself.

The little guy faced Jim, having to bend backwards to meet his gaze. He then bent forward to look at the fish. He repeated this action, surrounded by silence, at least four more times. He finally spoke. "Damn, sumbitch, you sure as hell shucked his corn." With that, he picked up his gaff, his rod and his jacket and slowly walked away without another word.

Jim collapsed to the ground. He was laughing so hard I thought his waders would split. The photographer was laughing so hard, his equipment was strewn all over the place. The crowd was laughing so hard, it was difficult to tell who was having more fun. One thing's for sure, that's how legends begin.

Jim is no longer with us; he passed away in 1995. His impact on our great outdoor heritage was important. He left tracks behind for all to follow. His state honored him by naming an outdoor refuge after him. His peers honor him by never forgetting the magic of his written words. I honor him by keeping in touch with Sylvia and keeping alive the memory of the times we shared.

If I could speak to Jim right now, I'd simply say, "Wherever you are, I sure hope you're shuckin' the hell out of someone's corn."

And he'd smile.

20

THE HEART OF 'FRISCO

Tony Bennett wasn't the only one who lost his heart in San Francisco. Thousands, maybe millions of folks have done the same. Must be a fact because when we visited San Francisco we found so much heart we brought some of it back with us to share with others who, unfortunately, have never had an opportunity to visit there.

Going to the west coast to host a Striper tournament was a crazy idea to begin with. Most of our members and tourney anglers were still familiarizing themselves with the fresh water variety, and didn't have a clue as to how to catch them in the salt. But craziness and pure family fun was what we were all about, so I threw the idea at Lindsay, our event coordinator and associate editor, and told her to see what she could come up with.

One of the things I insisted upon with each event we held (and we did thirty-five a year) was that a local, needy group had to benefit by our being there. In the past, our members had agreed to turn over all their catch to the local charity chosen for the event. Cleaned fish were then sold at fish fries to earn money for the group's projects. In Texas, for example, the fish went to a youth church group who used the money they raised on their summer project to rebuild homes of poor folks that were damaged by storms or other disasters. Putting something back was our credo and was simply a "feel good" for everyone involved.

Lindsay's task on this one was the most difficult I could have given her. Not only dealing with a new place, a different fishery, and absolutely no knowledge of how we would be received, she also had to put the logistics of travel, housing, event location, media coverage, and a list of dozens of other details. If anyone asked me how she could handle that, along with every thing else she had on her plate, I wouldn't have the foggiest notion as to how. But she never failed to deliver, and on this one, in a huge way. And it must be noted, we did not have a single contact in the area at the time. We had lots of members in California who traveled to Nevada and Arizona to fish our events but no one in that part of the state who could help us put together an event in the Bay.

The first thing Lindsay found out was that the California Fish and Game people frowned on tournaments and were more than a little curious why we really wanted to do one so far away from our base to begin with. Again, I never asked how, but when we got to 'Frisco, the fish and game folks were more than cooperative, they were downright friendly. Besides, as Lindsay explained to them, they would have an opportunity to weigh, measure and take samples from a larger number of specimens than was usually available to them. We liked to have fisheries biologists on hand to do such studies at every event we promoted. The end result, over the years, was a national database which could be used to improve the fishery. Another "feel good" for us.

After getting those guys on our side, Lindsay contacted the Chamber of Commerce and the office of the Mayor. I was not privy to letters, phone calls, or any of the details of putting this monster together, but here's the way it shook out.

We were to be housed in a downtown hotel, compliments of the San Francisco Police Department. We were to be picked up and delivered to the airport, compliments of the San Francisco Police Department. We would be assigned a special police officer to help us with any questions or problems that arose. In other words, we would be in the hands of the cops from the minute we arrived until the minute we left. How wild is that?

One's first thought of San Francisco cops would have to be a take-off on all the shows we see about them – speeding patrol cars, drawn guns, perps handcuffed and lying on the ground, face down. Other scenes also imbedded in our minds would be riots or the Rodney King thing. Well, I for one am here to tell you, I learned more about heart from the San Francisco cops we dealt with than I have in most places in this country, and that's saying a bunch.

It seems as if the police department had a special, pet project that dealt with inner-city children. I say project, rather than program, since there is an enormous difference. A program is one that is funded, most times jointly by outside entities such as city, county, federal government or a business or business groups. That makes it a bit easier to operate since budgets can be adopted in advance according to the amount of funding. This "project" was put together solely by a bunch of caring cops that had to sweat, beg, cajole and appeal to folk's benevolence on an almost daily basis, in order to have enough money to make it work. And, I promise, it works. I was blessed to be able to see it first-hand.

The Bay Area has a great number of professional fishing boats that are either sport fishermen, commercial fishermen or those that charter out to private parties from one to fifty or sixty folks. The most popular fish to catch in the area, and certainly the most abundant, are salmon, striped bass and at certain times, sturgeon.

This group of cops had put together a means for taking

inner-city children out on one of these boats, at no cost to them, for a day's fishing. And they took them fifty and sixty at a whack. The logistics? Officers who had personal time off, transportation for the kids, meals for the kids, containers for the kids to take their catch home, a willing skipper and crew of at least three that would be OK with earning just expenses. And dollars to pay for all that each week, that didn't just drop from the sky. It was, to say the least, an enormous project that took a lot of dedication and a ton of "heart." Many of those kids lived in the city and had never once seen the water.

The reason we, strangers to the area, were getting such wonderful cooperation from the police department? Simple. Lindsay had committed that our tournament would be held to benefit that children's project. She had proposed that the night before the event, we would hold a "sportsman's auction" and turn over all proceeds to help maintain that project. Talk about enthusiasm. The policemen hung posters, arranged a place to hold the auction and also to store items that were to be sold. They also promised to look after us. They never broke one promise.

On the home front, Lindsay busied herself gathering items to auction off. Calls to all the major fishing tackle companies brought wonderful results. Garcia and Penn sent boxes of reels, Heddon and Shakespeare sent rods and every lure manufacturer we spoke to sent lures by the gross. Hoping we could lure folks that didn't fish, Lindsay then called an old friend in Louisville, Kentucky. Dave Wilkins, a dear friend and currently CEO of the Doe-Anderson advertising agency, thought the whole idea was wonderful and promised to call on favors from some of his ad clients. As a result, we had ten high-speed Schwinn racing bikes, several crates of Louisville Slugger bats, two cartons of Wilson baseball gloves and probably fifty pairs of men's and women's Red Ball Boots.

I guess I should stop being surprised at the goodness

in the air all around us. Mom was right (as usual) when she said, time and time again, "Look for it, and you'll surely find it." And though the looking is tough sometimes, the finding makes it worthwhile.

When we arrived in 'Frisco and were safely in the hands of our hosts, our first request was to get to our rooms, shower, change and then look over the location in which we were to hold the auction. At that point, we had no idea. for all we knew, we could have been holding the auction in a parking lot, an old warehouse, a high school gymnasium or any number of places that might have been made available to us. We only knew the police folks in charge said, "not to worry, we'll take care of it."

Our assigned guy took us on a short tour of the waterfront, in order for us to see what the boats that the kids fished out of, looked like. They were all huge party boats, certainly capable of handling the numbers of children they took at any one time. We were really interested in a good seafood restaurant to have dinner in, so our driver accommodated us by driving past Scoma's, which later turned out to be the finest seafood restaurant I have ever visited. And I mean any place in the world I've ever eaten.

Finally it was time to see where we would be working the next night. The car stopped in front of a magnificent building, where we were asked to get out. Lindsay and I looked questioningly at each other, knowing surely this could not be it. It takes a lot to blow me away, but it does happen infrequently. We were standing in front of the Palace of Fine Arts Building, one of San Francisco's most prestigious landmarks. This was to be our auction location. It suddenly dawned on us that these folks were really serious. We were in awe for the next hour as we checked the stage, auditorium, sound and lighting systems and storage rooms where all our sale merchandise was being held for us. Wow, were we excited.

In order for us to get the full impact of what the

program did, it was arranged for us to accompany a group of kids on a fishing trip the next morning. Having had more excitement for one day than we could stand, we asked to be dropped off at our hotel and be picked up in the morning for the trip. Jet lag caught up to us so we retired to our rooms to catch some much-needed sleep.

It seemed like such a short time later our phones rang and we were instructed to meet in the lobby. Since the officer who picked us up was officially off duty, he picked us up not in a squad car, but rather his own personal vehicle. I thought that was one small item significantly worth mentioning. We stopped for a quick breakfast and then on to the pier and the boat. There were children standing everywhere. Big ones, small ones, boys and girls of every national distinction imaginable. And loud. And smiling. And excited. It didn't take us long to be swept up into the fantasy they were living, it was so "catching."

We were introduced to the other officers who were along as chaperones and helpers. We then met the captain and the two mates. Everyone we met was so enthusiastic and positive about the morning, it was absolutely impossible not to immediately feel connected. And off we went on a memory-building journey that taught us much about human kindness. There were so many individual incidents to warm our hearts, so many remarks by the children that were the gems of youth and so many helping hands. It was almost as if we had stepped off the planet and, for a short while, were in a perfect world, full of happiness, little-kid giggles and perfect human harmony.

Everyone, including us, was excited to watch a number of harbor seals frolicking around the boat as it left the dock. Passing Alcatraz Island gave us a moment of reflection and some of the comments by the kids had us rolling the deck. After all, these were street-wise youths and knew much about the prison's history. The cops and the mates busied themselves with the mechanics of the trip. Every kid had to have a rod and reel, bait, an assigned place and instructions. To a child, they all listened attentively, taking in information like young sponges. For this instant in their young and troubled lives, they knew nothing other than the joy of the experience. They felt, and were, special.

The rigging of the terminal tackle for this particular kind of fishing was, to say the least, the strangest I had ever seen. At the very bottom of the line was attached a ten-pound lead weight. (Not a typo, really ten pounds.) It was tied on with a breakaway knot. Then a simple hook and leader to keep the bait floating away from the weight. The idea was so that fifty lines, dropped down to a pre-determined depth, could be slowly trolled in the fast bay current, without tangling up with each other. Ingenious! As further proof of the ingenuity, when a fish was hooked, the sinker was released to drop to the bottom. That allowed the fish to swim up and away from all the other lines. With all the excitement of the day, we saw only one major tangle of about ten or twelve lines that the mates and policemen worked through in about ten minutes.

The entire morning was a buzz of excitement. If energy like that could be released in a stuffy board room, miracles would happen. Who was baiting a hook, who was netting a fish, who was screeching, "I got one," or "I lost one." The adults worked hard, the kids were having a ball. It didn't take Lindsay long to get involved, and before long we all smelled like fish. And then, too soon, it was time to stop fishing and go back to shore. The kids were exhausted, as were we. It was time for a little R and R. Rest and reflection. The children were so worn out, barely a word passed between them, and the adults wisely allowed their silence. They had time to think and to realize that someone cared deeply about them and that there was much good in life to be found and enjoyed.

I sat in the wheelhouse with the Captain and visited

for a while. I noticed several other party boats fishing in the same way we had, and immediately began to total up the number of ten-pound sinkers that dropped to the bottom of the Bay. It looked like two hundred fishermen on about six boats were dragging and losing ten pound lead weights. I figured if everyone had at least one hit, that would be a ton of lead on the bottom. In a week, or a month, the total would be staggering. I could not help but ask, "How do they salvage all those sinkers?" The Captain was a man of few words but he managed to say around the pipe clenched tightly in his teeth, "They don't." I was way too curious to let it go at that, so I talked about the dollar value that was being lost. I offered that some enterprising individual could feed his family pretty well on the proceeds of that work if he could figure some way to salvage those sinkers. The Captain put my mind and my curiosity to rest. "Every now and then, a new arrival to the area figures like you are. They come up with great ideas, try 'em out and no one ever sees 'em again." He let that sink in for a moment and with that special eye twinkle that only sea captains have, said, "Guess the sharks get 'em." That was in the mid-eighties and after twenty years one side of my brain tells me "you were had" while the other continues to wonder "could it really be."

The boat pulled up to the dock, mooring lines were secured and the kids and their catch were helped ashore. There were photo ops galore and lots of folks with cameras. We stood in the parking lot for an hour or so taking pictures with the children. All the little girls wanted Lindsay in the picture with them as did the boys with me. Some of the older boys insisted on Lindsay getting in their photos. They had already made the leap to recognizing girls were different. What fun. And then they boarded the bus headed back to who knows where, or under what conditions. It was a moment we hoped that somehow the program and adult mentoring might make some difference in their lives.

It was time to go back to the hotel, clean up, rest, and prepare for the auction that very night. Earlier, I had noticed a strange looking vehicle in the parking lot; it was still there. I asked our driver to hang on a bit so that I could satisfy my curiosity. Walking over to the vehicle and recognizing what it was had me gasping in disbelief. It was really a pick-up truck. Not your ordinary run-of-the-mill truck, mind you, it was a Rolls-Royce pick-up truck. The roof of the Rolls had been cut off and a truck body made of the rear section. The truck body was made out of exotic woods that made you feel like just rubbing your hands on it. And I did. The color of the driver's section was snow white. The glass window in the rear was etched in gold with an Arabian horse. The driver's side of the cab had a gold signature indicating the name of some Arabian horse ranch. I have never in my life seen such opulence. Needless to say, we photographed it from every angle.

The rest of this adventure is almost anti-climactic, though we'll have lots of other individual tales to tell, another time. The auction went well, folks bid on every single item. We were able to raise several thousand dollars for "the cause." The tournament went better than we could have hoped for with lots of fish being caught and much information made available to the fish and game folks who put in a bunch of time and effort. The whole deal turned out to be win-win for everyone, but the most satisfying part of it all was the "kid thing."

And you want to know something neat? The program still exists, so someone is definitely doing something right. If our tale has touched your heart and you want to be part of the same "feel good" that we were, drop a check in the mail to: The San Francisco Police Youth Fishing Program, 850 Bryant Street, San Francisco CA, 94103, Attn: Captain Sandy Tong.

And you know, the thing about that Rolls. At the

time the thoughts that went through my mind were, beautiful machine. And on and on about the wonders of what money can do. As I reach the calmer years of my life I begin to think of the great distances between wealth and poverty. I wonder how many children could have fished on the money it cost to convert that auto into something really silly. I wonder how many young eyes could have been opened up to a new and happy world, even for a day, simply by being touched by the heart of 'Frisco.

21

LES, DON AND PHIL

Les Rose, Don Everly and Phil Everly. That's the sequence in which I met these three wonderful guys. Only thing is, enough time elapsed between those meetings for almost two lifetimes to have been lived. Les and I met in 1971. He introduced me to Don two years later, in the spring of 1973. Thirty years later, a chance meeting with brother Phil has offered the possibilities of a new friendship, or at least some fun and uproarious times. How strange is life, and how never-ending its circle has always baffled me. One thing I've learned for sure, as Frank Sinatra used to say, "You might as well live it while you got it."

In the early seventies, I operated a corporate fishing guide service on J. Percy Priest Lake, just a few miles outside of Nashville. Since Nashville is considered the Country Music Capital of the world, it was not at all unusual for my company to be called upon to supply a few hours of outdoor entertainment to recording industry folks.

For my part, it was all fun and glamour. I got to spend quality time with recording artists who had nothing on their minds save to relax and share a bit of outdoor excitement, in the early morning hours of a newly breaking day. Many of those same folks repeated that experience, sharing it with their children. Kids like those of Mel Tillis, Bobby Bare and Bobby Goldsboro thought that being out with their dads was like magic. Few experiences in life offer opportunities to see uninhibited love between parent and child. I've been fortunate to have shared enough of those moments to fill another book; perhaps I'll do that someday!

But for the people in the record business who shared a moment in their busy lives with me, it was not all the glitz you might want to believe. Recording stars had to continue to produce records that would sell. That meant a tremendous amount of pressure on writers to create quality songs, producers to dream up acceptable compositions, session musicians to strive to "get it right." Then there were endless numbers of folks in art, production, promotion and sales, all of whom had to coordinate efforts to bring in a profit on the sale of a product with an enormous initial outlay of expense, and a very small percentage of hope for a hit. Add to that, radio station managers and disc jockeys who have to agree to play any given record, and a more than finicky public that has to hear, relate to, and finally buy the record.

On top of all of that, recording artists have to travel endless miles to perform, so that they can be personally in touch with their fans, the folks who buy their records. The travel schedules are hectic, time is of the essence, and mistakes are not acceptable. And that goes for the lowest to the highest. To say the least, these folks are keyed up and running on high octane most of their working hours. I've known session musicians who have worked twenty-four straight hours. I've fished with performers who have had five gigs in five nights, and traveled almost two thousand miles to accomplish same.

Record company executives, though leading a slightly calmer life, still have the enormous pressure of "bringing in a winner." There can be only one top hit at a time, and hundreds upon hundreds of records are vying for that attention. So it really didn't matter who I got the chance to fish with, they were all super-charged, and needing to get as far away from their workaday life as was possible, and still be close enough to home or office to take care of an emergency if it arose. My service was the perfect answer. It was one of those magical times when I was in the right place at the right time.

When I got the call from Les Rose to arrange a fishing trip, it was hardly different from any other call I would expect to get. We arranged a time and place to meet, and he let me know he would be alone. The name Rose was more than just a little famous in song-town. Roy Acuff and Wesley Rose owned a monstrously huge music publishing company that, if anything, was getting even bigger and more successful. Les, as I learned, was the brother of Wes, and worked at that music mill. He admitted he wasn't much of a fisherman, but he'd heard from lots of folks that an early morning trip on the lake with me would afford tons of fun and excitement. He said he'd heard it was a "hell of a lot better than taking tranquilizers." That remark got a smile from me, and as usual, I looked forward to having him as a new client.

I knew he was going to be different than my usual customer the minute he showed up at the dock. Rather than being dressed in jeans and a knock-around shirt, he was dressed at least to the eights. Dress pants, a dress shirt open at the collar, a cashmere slip-over vee neck sweater, and shiny dress shoes that had that GI spit shine look to them. Not the kind of garb you'd expect someone to be wearing with the prospect of soon handling messy, smelly fish. When I asked if he had brought a change of clothing, he simply remarked that he had to get right to work as soon as our trip was over. His movements and his speech were almost spastic, and I knew instantly I had a very nervous-type dude this morning. He definitely needed a bit of coaching in relax 101.

It turned out to be one of those dream mornings a

professional guide hopes for, but seldom gets. A slight breeze made drifting a snap, the morning was cool, and a slightly overcast sky created a sort of dreamy mist that hovered just over the surface. Every now and then the silence was punctuated with the sharp sound of a fish feeding on the surface, close enough to hear, but mysteriously invisible in the mist. An occasional seagull screech or a noise from a woods creature was all we heard. Les was not much of a conversationalist on this trip, so I concentrated on being the instructor, and went about the business of showing him the things that were necessary in order for him to catch fish. He listened intently, and obviously caught on quickly, for he made no mistakes at all throughout the entire morning.

My records show that on the first trip with Les, we boated and released seventeen striped bass, ranging from twelve to twenty-nine pounds. In my book, a heckuva rousing morning. Normally my clients wanted to take home whatever was legally allowable, but in this case, Les informed me he had to get right to work and didn't have time to fool with that. When we got back to the dock at around nine a.m. he shook my hand, said, "Thanks," and headed for his car at a rather quick pace.

My after thoughts were, "Strange guy, but nice. Good fisherman potential, learns quickly. Doesn't respond well to guy talk or idle chatter...seems inwardly intent and a little fearful of new relationships." It was impossible for me to determine whether he had a good time or not. I did not expect that he would call again. I chalked him off as a "one-timer" who could say, "Been there, done that."

I was wrong. Two weeks later, another trip was scheduled. Les showed up in what was to become his usual "got to get right to work" attire. I decided right then and there to let that alone. I'd just go with the thought that he's won the Best Dressed Fisherman award, and try to loosen him up a bit personally.

My attempts at finding and catching fish that day, on a scale of one-to-ten, rated me a perfect ten. My try at getting Les involved in personal conversation was, if there was under a one, that's where I'd be scored. It didn't make me think Les was weird, or a snob. If anything, it made me feel sorry for the guy. I had not much to base that feeling on – after all, he was part of a monster company, drove a fine car, wore very expensive clothes and, most of all, could afford my services. It was just a gut feeling that left me a bit uncomfortable. I vowed to myself to continue to try to reach the guy. My failure at that left me with a punk feeling. This had been the way it was, sometimes twice a month, for the best part of two years. Something was missing, and I just couldn't put my finger on it.

The missing ingredient showed up, quite unexpectedly, on our next scheduled trip. I wasn't informed that there would be two people fishing that morning, but it certainly was okay. Les's guest was young, full of that wonderful exuberance one learns to expect from young people. Big smile, firm handhake, look you right in the eye kind of kid. And most importantly, dressed properly for a fishing trip in jeans, sneakers and a ratty t-shirt. As Les introduced me to his young friend he said only, "This is Don, I didn't know he could come until the last minute. It's all right, isn't it?"

After assuring them that all was well, I loaded the two in the boat and headed out on the lake. That morning ranks as one of the fondest memories among an enormous collection of fond memories. It wasn't the fish we caught, and we did catch lots of fish. What it truly was, was the interaction between my two clients. Les had turned into a fun-loving, joke-telling, boisterous kid. The two included me in their fun-loving antics, and in between catching fish, we played "have you heard this one," over and over until we were sagging at the seams with gut-wrenching laughter.

Of course, and for the first time, Les wanted to take the biggest fish home with him. Bragging rights had always been a big part of my trips. When you are able to show your friends, "Look what I caught," in most circles, for that moment, you become, if nothing else, the center of attraction. Especially because the critter we were fishing for oft times tipped the scales at well over thirty pounds. That's huge for a fresh water game fish. There weren't many coolers that could hold one without bending it in two.

The next trip blew my socks off. It, of course, included the pair I began to lovingly think of as "the deadly duo." For the first time ever, Les showed up in a pair of jeans, a pair of Nikes, and a tee shirt that had imprinted on it, "Kiss My Bass." Don wore his usual relaxed garb, but this time, brought along a snack. I supplied iced water or coffee, but no snacks. Normally, most of my clients wanted to prolong their morning experience over breakfast at the dock. It allowed for much re-living the trip's highlights, and sharing it with other breakfast eaters. Like I said, bragging rights are mighty important in a fisherman's life.

After catching a few fish, Don decided to partake of his snack, which was packed in a sizeable plastic container. When he opened the lid, even being at the other end of a twenty-one foot boat, it smelled to me like dead bait. Of course, it wasn't. What it was, was sushi.

You have to remember, this was the early 1970s. Sushi was not as big a thing as it is nowadays. Don offered me some, but the thought of eating raw fish not only was repulsive in my mind, but made my stomach almost as queasy as if I were seasick. When Spencer Tracy ate raw tuna in a scene from *The Old Man and the Sea*, it seemed an okay way to survive. But short of being close to starving to death, I vowed never to touch the stuff.

Seizing on my apparent revulsion, the two instantly ganged up on me. They had a lot of good-natured fun at my expense, and even as good as I consider myself at one-upsmanhip, I couldn't get past their jibes, no matter how hard I tried. There were several more trips with the two that included sushi jokes and "lets get over on Stu" moments whose memories still create a warm fuzzy for me.

During that time I learned some things simply by listening to the two interacting with each other. I learned that the Everly Brothers truly enjoyed what they were doing, and never tired of the work or the travel. I learned that they relied heavily on the friendship and business advice they got from Les. I got the feelng that without Les, the pair might easily be persuaded to fly the coop, so to speak. The loyalty so apparent to see was like a breath of fresh air, in a business that was so volatile.

I learned some other things that were not so happy. Things I know I was not supposed to be a part of. It seemed like Les was destined to be the invisible brother. His ideas were useless and not worth exploring. He had a job, only because he was "family." He spent a lifetime dealing with being put down by what I heard was a domineering brother. And so much more, hardly worth repeating. All that I heard made crystal clear the reasons I could never get close to Les. He had withdrawn internally to avoid any potential hurt. He was, however, open to Don Everly, and the kinship between the two was overpowering in the feelings it emitted. What a joy for me to be a small part of that moment in time. Don obviously thought Les was a genius, and he hung on to every word the man uttered. And, at least for that period in his life, Les Rose was somebody's hero. And who knows, if it hadn't been for Les, the magic of the Everly Brothers might not have been so great.

For a while, Les continued to fish with me by himself. The brothers were constantly on tour, so Don wasn't available much to be his fishing partner. Les never invited anyone else to join him. We enjoyed some nice mornings together, and even though Les remained somewhat reserved with me personally, he did show up in proper fisherman attire, and always took the two biggest fish home with him. I remember the last words Les ever spoke to me. As I was helping him load the biggest fish he had ever caught in my boat into his cooler, he said, "Think I'll make sushi out of this one, would you like me to save you some?" The twinkle in his eyes, and the smile on his face said volumes.

Had I finally reached the guy? I'll never know, since that was the last I ever heard from him.

Normally, this is where a story would end. Life is wonderfully peculiar, however, and stories have a way of rejuvenating themselves and living on. Particularly if there are story tellers.

I now live in a small, quaint country town, full of history and "southern charm." I chose to retire here so I could finally know my neighbors and be involved in a community. Lindsay and I own a farm where we raise horses and miniature donkeys. It has a lake full of fish, and we enjoy entertaining, especially children of all ages. Lots of celebrities have moved to areas fairly close to us. Breathing space (sizeable acreage) is still available at reasonable prices, and the proximity of a large city makes it a bargain. Peter Jenkins, the author, lives in our neighboring village of Spring Hill. Not too far away from there is the magical village of Leiper's Fork. No telling how many recording artists and other entertainers live there. The number is quite staggering.

Not too long ago, perhaps two years, it was rumored that Phil Everly was looking to purchase and refurbish an old historic home in our little town of Columbia. The rumor turned into a reality, and Mr. Everly did, in fact, do exactly that. There was no fanfare, no newspaper article, no brass band to welcome him. That's the way it is in a small town; folks are not easily impressed, and more than likely tend to mind their own business.

Charlie Mann, a local entrepeneur, recently began to purchase and upgrade some properties in our town square. In one of these stores he built a restaurant and dubbed it "Square Market Cafe." He immediately turned it over to his wife, Deborah, to operate as she saw fit. Since liquor by the drink is only a recent addition to modernizing our town, she was able to get a license to sell wine and beer.

Deb is particularly interested in entertaining, having done some herself. She put together an upscale menu, added fine wine and beer, and decorated the place to look like a street cafe one might find in Paris. Pretty upbeat for our little town, but it became hugely successful. On the third Thursday night of each month, she holds a "writer's night." With so many great songwriters and even terrific wannabes available, the night's entertainment is always great. Since the place holds only fifty or sixty people, Lindsay and I have a standing reservation held for us. There's a waiting list a mile long.

On one of those Thursday nights, about a year ago, Lindsay recognized Phil Everly, who was seated with a group of people at the table next to us. I wouldn't have known him or recognized him if we had fallen over each other. There were several wine bottles on their table, and they seemed like they were having a fun time. The entertainment that night was especially good, featuring the writer that had penned the number one country hit, "Sum Beach."

During the first band break, I elected to barge in on our neighbor's party and introduce myself to Phil. "Hi," I said, "I'm Stu Tinney. Years ago I fished several times with your brother and Les Rose."

I had no earthly idea what that comment would bring, but something was compelling me to move into the guy's space. Phil instantly stood up, grabbed my hand in an enormously strong grip and began pumping it as if he were trying to draw water out of my well.

"I remember a lot about you," he said, as I stood there with mouth agape. "Les talked about you all the time, you meant a lot to him. Boy, am I glad to finally meet you."

That remark alone was enough to throw me off balance. All of my attempts at trying and seemingly failing to reach Les flooded back into my memory. Phil assured me that I had, indeed, gotten to the man, and had been, for a short time, a major part of his existance. All these years, and I never had a clue.

Though the room was full and noisy, it was as if we two were alone. We stood there, oblivious to anything or anyone else, relating Les Rose stories to each other. When the musicians again took the stage, we shook hands and promised to get together again sometime. A bit later, with much cajoling and minor begging, Phil was coerced into getting on stage to do a number or two. The results were indescribable. To say the least, the man still has a rich and strong voice, and certainly retains that magic over fans that a ton of years ago had so much impact on audiences.

Over the past year, Phil and I have been thrown together at mostly fun events. A block party in his neighborhood, a dinner thrown by mutual friends, where we were introduced to Patty, Phil's wife. Lindsay and she instantly connected.

There's lots going on in our town. Dress-up benefit balls, fundraisers of all kinds as well as special events held for any number of reasons. Lindsay and I are really active in the community, and try to attend all that we can. It seems like we run into Phil and Patty everywhere we go. We kind of gravitate together and spend a little fun time. Recently our local newspaper had a "breakfast of champions" fundraiser, and for some reason they included Phil and me as part of the autograph-signing delegation. We sat next to each other, and in between autographing pictures and Wheaties boxes, we relived Les Rose stories, some of which I'd never heard.

Well, Phil and I have gotten past needing always to talk about Les and Don, and have entered into a new phase of kind of getting to know each other. Phil and Patty, and

Phil's best buddy, recently-retired detective Ray Messick and wife Dianne, have accepted our invitation to spend a day at our place, Southwind Farms.

We have a new baby miniature donkey that's cuter than any Disney character you've ever seen. Phil roared when he heard Lindsay tell Patty that Stu owned the cutest ass in the world, and that if Phil behaved properly, she might convince it to get in his lap. We're all looking forward to that.

And as for Les, my mind is finally at peace over that issue. I have Phil to thank for that.

22

THE CROWN JEWEL

No matter where I travel, nor how many seminars and symposiums I may be involved in, at some point I will always be asked the one question that is both easiest and also most difficult to answer in complete honesty. That question being, "Where is your absolute most favorite place to fish?"

The question is always asked by one eager to know the location of fishing's Valhalla. I've been asked by men and women of all ages, as well as boys and girls from five-year-olds to teenagers. Doctors, lawyers, presidents of huge corporations, regular working stiffs, politicians, and even morticians seem to want to know the "perfect place" to dream about visiting. And the question is certainly not "Americanized," since I am asked the same question in languages I do not understand. The eagerness in the eyes gives away the meaning. Everyone wants to know where "fishing heaven" is.

The question seems simple, but sometimes the simplest things are the most complex. For example, will my response hurt the feelings of my host or hosts at the time? Will it deny a local economy of the advantage of touring fishermen's dollars, because that was not the location I responded with? Will it cause great disagreement and controversy among people who are not like-minded? How can you possibly compare any one place with any other? There are as many questions as there are answers.

For years I have satisfied the question with a simplistic answer, one that always seems to satisfy. "Why, of course, wherever I find myself with fishing rod in hand, at that moment, is my most favorite place in the entire world."

And I have gotten away with that response for years and years. It's time now, however, that I come clean and tell it like it is. You must know how much remembering of countless locations I have fished over the last sixty years, and what a tremendously difficult task it is to sift through those memories in order to choose the best of the best.

There is much truth to the fact that the newest experience is quickest to be remembered. In all fairness, many factors other than just excellent fishing must be considered. With state-of-the-art technology in fishing tackle, boats, electronic gear, and modern day fisheries management programs, it is not difficult to find great fishing spots anywhere in the country. And, if the truth be known, it is not necessary for very many folks to have to travel very far from where they live to get in a great day of fishing. Even huge cities like Detroit, San Francisco and New York offer nearby locations. With so many available places, what's the realistic equation that solves the question of what is the very best?

For the sake of sound reasoning, lets eliminate all the salt water mega spots, and concentrate on an area that deals with fresh water. In truth, I could never honestly say where my favorite salt water fishing hole might be. Or what my favorite species to chase was, or my favorite angling method.

Having been fortunate enough to have been at the beginning of salt water fly rodding, and learned from the greatest masters of the art, one might think that would be preference number one; not so. When the owner of the famed Penn Tackle Company put a "squidder" in the hands of a thirteen-year-old kid, and said, "Learn how to use this, it's yours," you might think that single incident would tend to make surf casting the favorite way; not so. Catching a tuna or a billfish on trolling tackle off a well-equipped boat would be an easy choice, but not so. Handlining, the most primitive form of angling, and one that puts you in closest contact with your prey, would be easy to choose, but not so. After all these years, the verdict on which is the best method is yet to be answered.

And how about the best place? That's even more impossible. The jetties along the east coast, from Maine to North Carolina, offer a combination of danger and great fishing that is hard to beat. That is until you fish the hundreds of flats along the southern coast. And let's not leave out the Keys. I would also offer literally thousands of miles of beaches that surround our entire country, that offer spectacular fishing. Of course, timing is a factor, but not the most important.

And if you have had the opportunity, as I have, to fish in other countries, around tons of islands, over sunken ships, around oil rigs and reefs, and bottomless depths, the problem of "where" becomes impossible to solve. So let's leave salt water fishing out of this problem-solving, and make it easier on this old man.

I'm going to put this thing together like a many-pieced jigsaw puzzle. The best fishing location must have all the pieces fit snugly, so that the entire picture, when completed, is not only recognizable, but acceptable as well.

First, lets take visual beauty. True, beauty is definitely in the eye of the beholder, but personal quirks aside, let's face it, beautiful is still beautiful.

What could be lovelier than a clear-as-gin mountain stream meandering through wooded glens, unaffected by developers encroachment? I would guess nothing, that is until you put it next to a placid lake, either natural or man-made, that shares the same benefit of lack of human development.

It is simple to remove one scab from the sore. My favorite place could never be one that has been raped by a bulldozer, backhoe or logging crew, except perhaps to aid in its creation. It's taken a long, long time for great management to be put in place, as far as our pristine fishing spots are concerned, but better late than never. We have come to a place in our history where the naturalness of our surroundings can be preserved. It's up to us, collectively and individually, to see that it is done. In order to be in the center of beautiful, a fisherman needs to be able to look north, east, west and south, and be consumed by wonder.

The first parts of the puzzle are now in place. Our "spot" has got to make us feel as if this is the way God meant it to look. It must take our breath away, no matter how many times we visit.

A small piece of our puzzle, of course, would be accessibility. Can the average Joe get there without mortgaging the ranch? There are wonderful places in the world to fish that we must eliminate, because they are available only at great personal cost. Of course, a houseboat stay on the Amazon, fishing for peacock bass, offers beauty, excitement, and superb fishing. As do the trips that advertise snook and tarpon adventures. Flying into Alaska affords a marvelous experience. It is still pristine, fishing is top notch, guides and fish camps range from average to top drawer. Let's face it, though, it's getting a bit pricey. Not that I'm against skimping on some stuff in order to save up enough to make one of these trips, I've done it more times than I care to confess. And, I won't deny every one of those places was a worthwhile destination. I've never regretted paying for any fishing experience I have ever had. By the same token, I've never regretted taking advantage of the hundreds of "freebies" made available to me in this lifetime. In a word, our "place" has got to be one that is available to anyone, at a cost reasonable enough to allow a dreaming kid with a piggy bank full of coins, to be able to get there. Trust me on that one, and re-read the Holy Cow story in this book. Been there, and done that.

So now we have a place that's beautiful and accessible. Now, we're going to eliminate tons of confusion. In every outdoor magazine I subscribe to, the last pages are almost always dedicated to advertisements from wonderful fish camps. It's even made easy for us to decipher, because they are listed in categories that include states or countries. They advertise either complete packages, rustic accommodations, meals, guides, and on and on.

They are all probably great places, and I'm not saying not to take advantage of the offers. What I'm saying is, our spot would not require advertising to promote it. Hell, I've got a quality lake on my own property that answers all we've talked about thus far, and then some, but still I daydream often about my true favorite. And you can bet, I didn't discover it by reading a magazine; my finding it was pure luck. Think about how much luck has been involved in the world's greatest discoveries. It doesn't take a rocket scientist to figure out that discovering the best of the best requires less skill than a kiss from lady luck. Before this is done, I'll (grudgingly) share it with you. That piece of the puzzle will be my personal gift, and a thank you for being nutty enough to buy this book.

The key piece of our puzzle, of course, is will it still be the same twenty-five or fifty years from now? I can only answer to the twenty-five year part, and hope for the rest. For twenty-five years now, I have been revisiting this place at least once a year. Every time I top the final hill, and catch sight of this diamond, my lungs demand that I fill them to capacity. It never changes, and after this amount of time, I guess it never will. But, in a lifetime of traveling to places near and far, I have learned a somber lesson – that lesson being that man seems determined to wreak change to suit his own special needs and interests. Instant gratification, growth, expansion, ownership, and most of all greed, play so heavily on the loss of our natural treasures. It takes people, a virtual army of people, to protect against those attacks that inevitably will always occur. Our puzzle would crumble without those many tiny pieces that are represented by the stewards of our "place."

During the time that *Striper* Magazine was hosting tournaments all over the country, I was a strong advocate of creating chapters around each body of water that we used for our events. The purpose of these chapters was to promote safe and intelligent use of their waterway, and to protect it from harm. That required getting in bed with local fisheries managers, working hand in hand with them, and offering eyes and effort that could otherwise not be budgeted. It's a tough task for just plain folks to try and offer help to bureaucracies, long established and historically close-eared to any suggestions or criticisms from outside. Even though at every event we made scientific studies available to fisheries biologists, and even though at the end of each year our chapters donated sums of money to fisheries and other projects, for the most part, our chapters were politely ignored. They sure as hell took the money, though. I take my hat off to the few state fish and game agencies that recognize the importance of input from outside.

With that in mind, I'll introduce you to a few of the folks that guard our crown jewel, with no thought in mind of failure to communicate. I'll also add that the bureaucracy they deal with is one of the best organized in the country, and like most others, turns a deaf ear to outsiders. The stewards in this particular case, however, have done their homework, and for every negative they get, they have a positive, scientifically accurate response. They sometimes make it embarrassing, if not impossible, to go along with their suggestions. After twenty-five years, it's still a tug of war, but the end result is that our place remains even better for the effort. They know they will forever have to deal with folks that look down on them but still, they go about the business of stewarding, showing skin so thick that a well set hook would not penetrate. I'll not use last names, they'd all be embarrassed at being recognized as special. And, sadly, I'll not be able to introduce them all, as there are so many, space just won't allow. I have not a doubt that those not mentioned will not only forgive, but be happy they were not singled out. Such is the way with real heroes.

First there's Dwight, who virtually runs the whole show. Talk about a bureaucracy; he is a civilian project manager who answers directly to the U.S. Corps of Engineers. Through the years, he has learned the necessary diplomacy needed to get done the things he knows to be important. He oft-times shares a room with almost violent adversaries, and yet, with patient understanding of all factors to be considered, is able to render decisions in a fair and realistic manner. His decisions are not always acceptable to everyone, but he is the man, and what he says goes. His sense of fairness and love of "the place" are obvious at all times. In olden times, his name might have been Solomon.

Then there is the family of three. Dad Jim is a retired school teacher who first saw the importance of maintaining the beauty of our place, and thus submitted plans to build its first waterfront marina facility. The plans were lovingly drawn up with both commerce and area protection being strong factors. The plans were adopted, and though there have been other facilities approved over the years, his original plans still play heavily on most decisions made regarding other facilities. Most importantly, impact on the impoundment must always be the deciding factor. Jim's a short little guy, who hides his business brilliance behind a mask of nutty antics. The one that always gets to me is, when the weather is so cold that everyone is bundled up in parkas and gloves, Jim can be seen running around his marina in shorts and no socks. Looks can be deceiving, however, even though he looks like a nut case at the time, he's as sly as a fox, and much admired.

Jim's son B.J. is only a chip off the old block in that he is a brilliant and successful businessman. As a youth, he was rough as a cob. As an adult, he is a loving husband and father, and is absolutely unswerving when it comes to giving back to the place that nurtured him. His teenage son is beginning to show signs of being capable of picking up the standard whenever it might be offered.

Pam, the daughter, is something else again. Slight of build, and a single mom, she is unknown to herself, to be the toughest of them all. Pam is head of the area visitor's bureau, and has an office in a most magnificent building overlooking a wide expanse of water and its surrounding mountains. Every day, she is able to look at what she is sworn to protect. She lives in constant fear that the ideas that are brought to her on a daily basis could somehow impact the delicate balance. Her job is to create more opportunities for visitors to enjoy, and yet not disturb the balance. Talk about pressure! And so biking and hiking trails have been gently and lovingly introduced, as well as special places to view birds. After all, a place this wonderful should have the capacity to allow for more than just fishing.

Even with Dwight's gentle kindness, and our three family members' numerical advantage, the four oft times disagree on issues. Love of the place is always the deciding factor. That enormously important piece of the puzzle. As for the rest of the folks I'll give you a slight insight into— some of them actually don't even like each other personally. They are, however, all in agreement about one thing, and that is the protection of the thing they love most. Would that world leaders could take note of how truly simple that concept is.

Jim was the toughest cop I have ever known, and believe me, I've known tough cops. Jim was a waterways cop.

His reputation was that he would arrest his wife, his mother, his dad, and his best friend over the smallest infraction. And he did some of the above. He was hated and loved, but never questioned about his motives. His job was to protect his place at any cost, and he did just that. He was hated, feared, and admired. He is now retired, but having set the standard for all future water cops to reach for, has turned the job over to Cory. Cory is young, not quite as seasoned, attempts to be a bit more reasonable, but will not deviate from the law under any circumstance. Everyone feels the safety of being protected.

The rest of the folks I'll mention are the troops that do whatever is necessary to get the job done. They are all mountain people, not any different than folks you know. They wear beards, spit tobacco, look disheveled, have strong opinions, argue over the darndest silliness, mostly for the sake of argument. They are strong-willed and argumentative. Putting them all in one room would be cause for a serious fight. However, when it comes to "the place," it is not hard to get their attention. They have single-handedly, for the past twenty-five years, been able to maintain a fishery whose quality is almost indescribable in its excellence. Some of these folks never finished high school, but that has never been an issue. To a man, they have taken it upon themselves to study all the details necessary to make them experts in their particular fishery. Their knowledge is so accurate that it can not be ignored. That's where they have their antagonists pinned to the wall. How in the hell can you argue with the facts?

There's Vic, who never went to college but wound up a crew chief responsible for installing ATT's coaxial and fiber optic cables from Maine to North Carolina. Vic would argue with the devil over something as stupid as what is red. Then there's Vince, a retired pharmaceutical factory worker who, as treasurer, cares for the huge amounts of money raised by the group, its sole purpose to pour back into projects to improve or protect "the place." You can be certain not a penny will ever be misplaced.

John. John is an enigma. Once impossible to live with, he has emerged as the absolute soul of generosity. Once so dour and down, he was no fun to be around. He works in a factory that makes, of all things, the grass that goes in Easter baskets. I know that in itself wouldn't make me a happy camper. Perhaps it's the new wife he recently acquired. If so, Liz has wrought a miracle. They fish together, make wine together, dye thousands of deer tails together, and hold hands a lot. Their combined energy directed at protecting the "place" is inspirational, to say the least. And their personal generosity is way beyond what could be called normal. They give, as they explain, as small payment for what they get.

Then there's Sparky. Sparky is loud, Sparky is a braggart, Sparky does and says things that make people talk about him. Sparky is a full-time guide, and a part-time preacher. Helluva combination! Most folks believe whatever Sparky says – many don't. I take him with a grain of salt. But none of that is important, trust me on that one. When the chips are down, Sparky will be the first in line to help. Whatever he is hiding inside that forces the personality he shows to come forward, takes a back seat when it becomes necessary to help someone in need. And as far as our place is concerned, I think no one in the group cares more than he. In choosing sides, Sparky would be on my top three draft list.

Don is a retired teacher, and brings that quiet, self-assuredness to the table. He must have been a great educator, since he seems to have the power to calm the savage beasts long enough for some sense to be made.

Then there's Pap. Pap is a farmer who lives a good distance from our place, but has a love for it like no other. He has shared that love with his children, and they with theirs. He has created an almost dynasty of people who will always be watchful. What a legacy that is, and how far-reaching.

In a word, the few folks I've mentioned are just folks. There are no rocket scientists here, no corporate CEO's, no politicians, no Ph.D.s, and certainly no one who is looking for personal gain. These are just people who truly love and care about something, and are quietly dedicated to maintaining its beauty and its safety. And that's what it takes to cement every other puzzle piece together. Without them, it would all collapse. So in choosing my best of the best, it would be quite impossible to leave them out.

Lest I forget, there are two folks worthy of special mention. The written word can calm or it can incite. There are those writers who love to stir up the muck, just to create a reaction, not caring a hoot about how far-reaching that reaction might be. Then there are those who diligently research, calmly and accurately report, and bask in the sunlight of their truths. Sadly, they are outnumbered.

My dear friend, Wes, is one of the latter. A retired Game Commission employee, he turned his talents to outdoor writing. I published several of his submitted pieces in *Striper* Magazine. Through all these years, Wes has resisted the temptation of embellishing, and opted to tell it exactly as it was. That's disagreeable to some folks, as you might imagine. His honest reporting and his diligent research of what is factual and what is not has helped immensely to maintain the spot in which he shares our love affair. Though he would be the first to disagree, I hereby place him into our puzzle, as a necessary piece.

And finally, there is Marc. If a place can be best, so can a man. Regardless of what differences of opinion all our pieces may have, to a person they will all agree on the very special place Marc holds in our hearts. Twenty-five years ago Marc accepted a laughable part-time job with the largest manufacturer of electronic fishing gear in the world. He was young and inexperienced. His love, however, of his surroundings gave him special insight as to how things could and should be. His part-time gig soon became his full-time vocation. He left the place he loved to follow the career path he chose. His reward for his labors was his elevation to executive vice president of the corporation. His duties carry him to every state and virtually every country in the world. He rubs shoulders with the wealthy and connected. He is, without a doubt, the most respected man in his industry. He, with all his success, has never forgotten his roots, and frequently returns to visit his boyhood friend "Duck," for periods of R and R. He gives greatly of his time, energy and resources to make him a major player in the preservation of our place. There is no question that his piece of the puzzle is easily recognizable. To give a tiny hint of how he is regarded, when he announced he had purchased property on which to build his retirement home, he was confronted with a bunch of men who offered to help to build it. And they have.

And now, finally, to the chewy caramel center of the puzzle, the fishery itself. Everything described thus far is wonderful for the weary or even adventurous traveler. We can even add that there is nearby shopping, good restaurants, and welcoming inhabitants of the town closest to our place. Perhaps thirty minutes away, at most. There is theater and movies and the hope of growth that has even attracted a WalMart Superstore. All that makes it not only a nice place to live, but a really nice place to visit. It's not fancy, but it's downright homey. But, how about the fishing?

Our very special place must have spectacular fishing opportunities. Not just good, not even just great, but truly spectacular. To have spectacular fishing, a place must offer a wide variety of species to seek. It must offer a fishing opportunity regardless of time of day, month of year, or condition of weather. In other words, a place that allows for no excuses. It must offer trophy-size fish in every species available, and allow for every legal angling method that one can dream up. When captured, the fish must be healthy and free of any sign of disease. In other words, the water quality must be constantly maintained at its highest level. A proper balance of predator and prey must be maintained. It must be a place so pure that it invites both eagles and ospreys to permanently nest and raise young. And solely because of the diligence of human hands, this is where we have come. An added thrill for me, always, is to stop fishing long enough to watch the eagles show me how it's done, without rod and reel.

Largemouth and smallmouth bass abound, and it is not uncommon for fish of five pounds or more of either species to be caught. Muskellunge of twenty-five pounds hardly get any one's attention, they're common occurrences. And there are more walleye of seven and eight pounds caught accidentally than is imaginable. On my last visit I caught six, while fishing for something else entirely.

Then there is the lake's premier attraction, the striped bass. The lake record is over fifty pounds with fish in the thirties being taken every week of the year. A recent experiment, based on the multi-depth possibilities, has seen an introduction of lake trout in large numbers. The fish are currently topping out a bit under ten pounds, but promise to reach weights equaling that of the stripers. The fantastic thing about all of this is that there is no shortage of forage, since both predator and prey seek their most comfortable zones in which to live. There is food enough for all.

Take away the game species, and you have a viable fishery for quality-size edibles like yellow perch, crappie and bluegill. And let's not overlook the occasional ten-pound brown or rainbow trout that succumbs to a lure and surprises the hell out of an unsuspecting fisher person.

That's what I mean when I talk about spectacular fishing.

You might think, and in most cases be correct in your thinking, that the local folks would want to keep this place a secret. Not so. They are proud of what has been accomplished here, and to a person, want to share it with others. I would caution, however, that if you so much as drop a candy wrapper on the ground, you will appear before the hanging judge. These folks are serious about obeying all the rules that apply to keeping perfection perfect.

And now, with the appropriate roll of drums, clash of cymbals, and waving flags, I present you with my personal best of the best, my crown jewel, Raystown Lake, nestled in the arms of friendly hills, on the outskirts of Huntingdon, Pennsylvania.

For travel information, call Pam at the Raystown Visitor's Center. The number is 1-888-RAYSTOWN.

And please, treat our place with the love and dignity she deserves. If you do so, you can claim to be one more piece of this amazing puzzle.

23

The Best Laid Plans of Mice And Men
by Mitch Tinney

Some of the greatest fishing stories I possess have absolutely nothing to do with fishing, but with all the events that surround a trip. You see, there is so much more to fishing than just the act itself. It's the accoutrements, if you will. I don't necessarily mean the gear. It might be the odd duck you meet at the store where you get coffee before you hit the road to go fishing. It might be the night before, when you meticulously thumb through your tackle boxes, selecting the morning's fare. Or, it might be picking out just the right color shirt to blend with the background of a trout stream, making you less visible to the wary fish. It might even be your lucky breakfast.

Not always does the angler meet with what a non-angler would calculate as success. True anglers' success is measured in their personal growth as a human being, gleaned from hours of patience and hard work. Everything wild lives in a symbiotic relationship with the other life forms around it. A real angler tries to find room for himself in such a place. Sometimes we prove ourselves unworthy of this challenge. This is the story about such a day.

It was about eleven at night, and I could not sleep. My season had just ended, and I had plans to get off the lake that I had been married to for the past seven months, and do a little trout fishing. The season had been a great one, and I finally bit the bullet and invested in my first of many highly crafted and oh-so-expensive fly rods. I was so damned excited that you wouldn't think that I fished for a living. I went about the routine of getting the gear together. I checked the list: waders, boots, fly vest, fly boxes, leaders, lanyard of tools, net, polarized glasses, and a trusty flop hat. I looked lovingly at my new fly rod and reel. I visualized trout leaping on my fly with reckless abandon. The sheer honor of being caught on such a handsome piece of equipment must be obvious, even for a trout.

Well before sunrise my wall clock started clanging. It is a wind-up type with two bells and a hammer. I call it a wall clock because it is so loud that my wife will fling it against the nearest wall. Lest I digress, the clock did its job, and I did mine. I got dressed and loaded the car. At that time I was driving a little Mazda Miata, a two seater much more suitable for a school teacher than a fisherman. Nonetheless, I loaded my fishing buggy to the gills with all my paraphernalia and headed to the Smoky Mountains. I was on the road.

Three-and-a-half hours later I pulled into the dusty little turn-off to the stream. I found a spot to park, but there wasn't quite enough light to see, so I opted to do a little scouting until it got lighter. Leaving everything in the car, I scuttled down to the water for a quick look-see. I smoked a cigarette and finished my coffee. Light started breaking, so I headed back to the car to gear up. While fumbling in my pocket for the keys to unlock the car, I looked through the window. What do you think I saw? Yeah, my keys.

Right next to my keys was my cell phone. Sitting in the front seat was about two thousand dollars worth of fishing gear. Here I was, in the middle of God-knows-where, in a place that a house would price out at less than what my rod cost. The newest vehicle I saw was a 1951 Ford pickup. I was in trouble. A sports-car-driving fly fisherman in *Deliverance* country didn't sound like what I signed up for. I figured my only chance was to find a telephone fast. A simple solution, or so I thought.

The first house I came to didn't look habitable, but there was a dog on the front porch and a truck in the drive, so I thought I would try. One foot on the porch, and the door cracked open. A pair of barrels from a shotgun greeted me with that tell-tale click, click. Behind the hammer glared a pair of eyes belonging to a small-framed, white-haired woman with no teeth. Her meaning was plain, so I backed off the porch without an argument.

It took about two miles of walking before the shakes stopped, but I still found myself looking over my shoulder for the woman with the gun and no teeth. I saw the next house, but before I could approach the drive I was chased by a dozen hound dogs for almost a mile. At that point I had covered five miles, and was getting no closer to getting into my car. I tried to hitch a ride, but the first fellow who went by looked like Ned Beatty's squeal-like-a-pig friend. I thought better of it.

I walked eleven miles that morning before finding a country store. I know because the owner of the store told me how far it was. He said that the walk back would take less time since it was mostly downhill. Since my wallet was in the car, and the store owner did not like the way I looked, he did not offer to give me a ride back. Perhaps it was the color of my shirt. However, he was kind enough to allow me to make a collect call to my wife.

I told her to find the nearest locksmith to my location, and to offer him furs and gold to come and save me. She said that she would, and she told me to be careful. I pulled a Forrest Gump. I *ran*. Eleven miles this set of two-pack-a-day lungs flew. I am unwilling to spend much time thinking about the true motivation for running so hard. The ego is a fragile thing. So I am sticking with the whole I-didn't-want-to-miss-the-locksmith excuse.

When I finally dragged my spent carcass to the place my car was parked, I noticed a lot of activity. Lots of guys in lots of new cars from all over the state were stowing their waders and other gear back in their vehicles. They all had a great day of fishing. When they asked how had I done, I told them I was scouting some water further upstream, and that I didn't want to be encumbered by any gear. They nodded their understanding, and one by one they left.

Two hours later the locksmith showed up. I think he was married to the lady with the shotgun and no teeth. I say that because when I saw his bill I felt like I was being held up. I even said as much. To that he suggested that he could put the keys back in my car. I paid the man, folded my weary body into my too-small car, and left without hesitation.

My new fly rod, as yet unused, sat in a tube with all the tools of the trade piled up on my front seat. I was out of cigarettes and out of patience by the time I rounded the shotgun lady's curve. It was about then that my gas light blinked on. If I'd have had a pistol, I probably would have shot myself. Fortunately for me the most dangerous weapon available was a rod tube, and I just couldn't see beating myself to death with a perfectly good rod tube.

As I said before, a true angler must appreciate all of the little things about fishing. Some of those things we appreciate more than others. Going fishing can be a great adventure, but if you want a little less adventure in your life, remember these incredibly important words. Stick a damn hide-a-key under your bumper!

24

KARMIC DEBT
by Mitch Tinney

This story comes with an "R" rating on the current Tinney grossness scale. If you tend to be a bit squeamish, you just might prefer to skip this story and move on to something less graphic. If you can stand a bit of the yucky, then I think you will find this as comical as I do.

Have you ever had one of those days that held the promise of being almost perfect, only to have it disintegrate in the flash of a second? This is a tale of a guide's worst nightmare coming to fruition. All names have been changed to protect the embarrassed. You will not need an artist's rendering to appreciate fully the impact of the moment.

I got a call that went like this. "Are you Tinney, the striper guide?" I replied that I was.

"I want to buy a boat."

To this I responded, "My boat is not for sale."

"I don't want to buy your boat, I just want to buy a boat."

"Sir," I said, "I am a fishing guide, not a boat salesman, but I would be happy to refer you to a boat dealer."

"No," he said, "my wife won't let me buy one. I want

you to convince her that it would be good purchase for us."

I understand that as a fishing guide I am often required to wear several different hats, but this fellow was trying to make me wear one that would not fit my skull.

"Mister," I said, "I have been married three times, and I just don't think I am qualified to act as a marriage counselor for you." This guy was not going to be put off, despite my attempts to dissuade him. This was his rationale.

If his wife caught a big fish, and had a good time on the trip, it might better grease the skids for the purchase of their new boat. I started to get a better picture of his backdoor plan. Now that he had me on the same page, I booked the trip. I received regular calls from him as their date approached, reminding me of the purpose and importance of the "mission."

Finally the big day dawned. It was an early spring morning, with unusually warm temperatures. They came walking down the dock in the predawn half-light, and I never saw two people who looked more unalike. Sara looked as if she had just finished a photo shoot featuring picnic clothes for Sunday School teachers. Spike looked as if he had just been dragged out of a biker bar after losing a nasty fight.

Now I have a tattoo, one that is invisible unless I am sleeveless. And yes, before you ask, it is a fish. Spike, on the other hand, had more than eighty percent of his body covered in art. In addition to the ink, he sported a steel spike through his tongue. He had steel rings in his eyebrows, his lips, and surely a few others in places I am pleased to report I did not see. He also had disks like those in *National Geographic* in his ears. I could have just about chipped a golf ball through the holes. The guy looked like a freak of nature.

Mom always told me not to judge a book by its cover, but this fellow was pushing the edge of the judgment envelope. As it turned out, I didn't, and it was well that I didn't because Sara was absolutely charming, and Spike, despite all his visible dysfunction, turned out to be a very nice guy.

I can't speak for everyone, but I rarely have a good day of fishing when there is no wind and the lake is like a sheet of glass. The day was shaping up to be a tough one. I explained to Sara and Spike that we were on top of a school of fish that we could catch if we could get a little wind. While he looked at me with genuine hope, Sara gave me a quizzical look like, "I'll bet that's what you tell everybody, if you're not catching fish."

When the fishing really gets bad, what do the great guides do? I don't know about everyone else, but I tell stories to amuse my guests until the fish start to feed. After three hours of story telling, I started to get a little nervous. Most of the time anglers understand that it is called "fishing" not "catching," and the occasional bad day can be expected. This was going to be a one-time shot, and I had to produce or poor Spike would never see a boat in his garage.

Sara looked keenly into her husband's eyes. "This is why we will never own a boat. I will be trapped on this wasteland and have to pay twenty-five thousand dollars for the privilege."

Spike looked at me as if he were dying of thirst, and I owned the only well around. He leaned over the console and whispered a plaintive plea in my ear. "Captain, is there anything else you can do to make them hit?"

I suggested that shy of electricity or explosives we needed a breeze. I couldn't tell by his look if he was a religious man, but an appeal to the god of winds wouldn't hurt. Just as I was about to regale them with another story, I detected a slight movement on the water's surface. Could it be...maybe... the slightest breath of wind kissed the surface into gentle ripples. It came out of nowhere, and only lasted about thirty minutes, but it was just what we needed, or so I thought.

We drifted about ten feet when the rod in the holder she was sitting behind began to peel. I told her to hit the fish, and she set the hook like an old pro. As the fish ripped off a quick hundred yards of line, I strapped the fighting belt around her waist. This belt allows an angler to fight a big fish with less risk of getting a bruised belly from the rod butt.

Five minutes into the battle, I had Sara on the bow of the boat for easier maneuvering. Ten minutes into the fight had her panting and out of breath, but grinning. Fifteen minutes after hooking up, she was already arguing with Spike as to the color boat they were going to get. When we saw the fish for the first time, it became clear that Spike wasn't ever going to get a boat, but that Sara was heading to a dealership that afternoon to buy hers.

Spike didn't care. He had visions of grandeur, catching monster fish in his wife's new boat. He looked at me with a Cheshire cat grin. Leaning over, he whispered the magical words to a guide's ear. "When we get in, breakfast is on me, anywhere you want to go. Your tip will be whatever you can grab out of my wallet, and I will need about five hundred of your brochures. When I show off the pictures of her fish and our new boat, I'll get you more business than you can handle."

I was in tall cotton as they say in the South, or so I thought. Ten minutes later we landed her fish. It was a huge male, close to thirty pounds. Knowing it was going to be the only fish of the morning, I intended to milk it for all it was worth. I had a roll of film with twenty-four shots, and I planned to shoot it all on her one fish. I treated her as if she were modeling for *Vogue*. She held the fish this way, then that. I had Spike join her for the proud husband shot. With the camera shutter snapping like that of a paparazzi chasing a film star, I was oblivious to the wind that had gotten brisker.

With about four shots left, I realized that the fish she was holding was beginning to leak sperm. This happens often if you hold a pre-spawned male out of the water. Holding the fish by its lip at chest level had its tail hanging between her knees and ankles. Sara had on shorts, and as her fish struggled in her hands, it began to sling sperm on her bare legs.

266

Normally I would take a damp towel and wipe off my clients before they realized what was happening. I should have recognized that nothing about this day could possibly be constituted as normal, and that caution is the better part of valor.

As I approached her with a towel, I heard a loud SQUAAWK over my right shoulder. The only bird capable of making such a racket is the great blue heron. I didn't give it a moment's thought. Wiping her legs, I quickly went back to being Ansel Adams, camera in hands. The next squawk was considerably closer and with one shot remaining, I looked up in horror.

Let's be realistic. Big birds are capable of making big messes. A mature blue heron has a wingspan of almost eight feet. These guys eat nothing but fish, and the messes they create are of enormous proportion. They have a rapid digestive system, and sometimes you can tell what they have been eating by the mess they leave behind.

When I looked up, I saw what happened to be a two-foot long rope of fish heads and guts wafting through our new-found breeze. Being a firm believer in karmic debt, I was pretty sure the mess would fall short, or overshoot the boat. I failed to take into account any debt my passengers might owe. Neither Spike nor Sara had seen or heard the bird.

There simply wasn't enough time. Before I could yell run, duck, jump, or anything else, Spike saw for the first time what the fish was dripping on Sara's legs. Thinking all would be fine, he took the opportunity to explore his witty nature. Laughingly, he pointed out what the fish had done. No, this is not a good time for a direct quote. Please remember that all of this happened in less than ten seconds.

Sara looked down at her legs in disgust, threw her head back and screamed, "AWWGH."

Maybe the wind gods had smiled on us for a few brief

moments that morning, but they surely had plans to abandon us before all was said and done. As the poor woman looked to the sky with mouth agape, she caught the full brunt of heron mess squarely in the kisser. She had fish eyes in her hair, and semi-digested fish guts sliding down her cheeks. She became an instant projectile vomiter.

The boat's bow was covered in fish sperm, bird pooh, and volumes of upchuck. Adding insult to her injury, Sara slipped on the slimy wildlife soup and landed with a resounding SPLAT on her fanny, right in the middle of it all. Unable to find anything not slick with goo in which to find purchase, she was covered in a complete head-to-toe cocoon of the stuff.

To make matters worse...I know what you're thinking ...it could get worse? Yes, it can, and yes it does. Spike was laughing so uncontrollably that he bit down on the steel bar in his tongue and shattered two teeth. Even with broken teeth, his laughter went unabated. He was spitting broken teeth and blood all over the boat's stern, while his lovely wife was writhing on the bow, in all her dripping glory.

When bad things occur, the foremost thing in my mind is damage control. I looked forward and realized that despite any effort I might muster, the cause was lost. I turned around, in hopes of finding some way to salvage the day. I took one look at Spike and decided the best course of action was a direct beeline for the marina. This day was one of those I'd just have to write off as a "who'd have thunk it day." That's just what I did.

Needless to say, I didn't get the breakfast Spike promised. For some reason I wasn't permitted to reach into his wallet for that gratuity. There were no requests for that stack of brochures. To this day there have been no requests for the trip's photos. I think it's safe to say that Spike is still boatless and probably still sleeping on the sofa.

If you're thinking that perhaps a moral might be salvaged from this, you're absolutely correct. You're on your own to think up yours, but for me, if I ever try some lame-brained scheme to get one over on my wife, this incident will be a subtle reminder for me to forget about it. Also if I hear a big squawk and I am stupid enough to look up, for once in my life I should keep my big mouth shut.

WANT A SPEAKER?

Stu and Mitch Tinney are available to speak to crowds from five to five hundred.

Mitch is an expert fly-rodder, both salt and fresh water. His special fly patterns are used by many notables. He is well known as a teacher, a lecturer and a conservationist. His seminars are extremely well-attended. Mitch can and does draw crowds. He can be reached by calling 615-355-1799.

Stu has been named the "father of fresh water striper fishing." His tackle innovations are legendary. His seminars range from the history of the striper, to how to catch and even cook fish. He also has dedicated much time to speaking to auditoriums full of anxious high-schoolers who are interested in how to make a living in the out-of-doors. These seminars focus on continuing education, and have been deemed quite successful. He can be reached at 931-381-8653 or saletinn@charter.net.